THE LONG MARCH OF ISRAEL

by Jacques Soustelle

Translated from the French by Shirley Tomkievicz

American Heritage Press · New York

Published in 1969 by American Heritage Publishing Co., Inc.
Copyright © 1968 Librairie Arthème Sayard.
All rights reserved.
Library of Congress Catalog Card Number: 77-83807
SBN: 8281-0018-7
Endsheets: Photograph of Israel and the Middle East, taken from outer space by Gemini
astronauts in 1966: NASA
Book design by Barbara Asch

CONTENTS

1
A
PEOPLE
IN
EXILE

Six thousand years ago the first known civilization, Sumer, sprang to life in the southern part of Mesopotamia. Two thousand years later, Abraham led a small group southward out of this same region. Another thousand years of wandering, slavery, and struggle would pass before these Hebrews, led by Moses, escaped from Egyptian domination, conquered the land of Canaan under Joshua, and at last created the monarchial state whose first king was crowned by the prophet Samuel. The golden age of this kingdom, in the reigns of David and Solomon, was brief—some eighty years. But during this time the society established around Jerusalem, small though it was when compared with the enormous empires of Mesopotamia and Egypt, bloomed into an original civilization quite distinct from its neighbors.

The word civilization implies structures: social, political, and, above all, mental—a certain attitude toward life, a certain vision of the world. When Solomon opened the first Temple of Jerusalem in the tenth century B.C., the fundamentals of Jewish civilization had already been laid down. The monuments would fall, but the ideas would endure.

Alone among the peoples of antiquity, the Jews passionately clung to the idea of one God. "Hear, O Israel: The Lord our God is one Lord" (Deut. 6:4). Doubtless they were often subjected to the influence of the religions practiced by other Semitic peoples. We know that they occasionally adopted fertility cults, or worshiped bulls (the "golden calf"), Baal, sacred pillars. But they always went back to monotheism, while in Egypt, for example, Pharaoh Akhenaten's revolutionary attempt at monotheism came to nothing.

Hebrew cosmology, theology, morality, law, and literature all gravitated around this unique God. He was not identified with any force of nature nor with any star. He was conceived as a moral being who enacted commandments and prohibitions, forbade murder and theft, condemned oppression and injustice, asked each man to love his neighbor as himself (Lev. 19:18), and was solicitous even toward animals (Deut. 15, Ex. 23:4). He was not only the master of the universe but also the source of all good and every virtue. Jewish monotheism was a system of ethics as well as a religion.

The Jews believed that a covenant had been made in the time of Abraham between God and themselves, and that this covenant had been renewed and confirmed by Moses in the Sinai desert. Israel was meant to be "a kingdom of priests and a holy nation" (Ex. 19:6) — an inspiring alliance, but a heavy obligation. From this idea of a privileged agreement between God and His people there sprang a peculiar strength and an unshakable and sacred confidence. In this strength the Maccabees found the force to revolt; the Zealot defenders of Masada, their heroism; the Zionist pioneers, their enthusiasm. And yet this God did not belong exclusively to them in the way that each city between the Tigris and the Euphrates had its own private divinity. He was a universal God who loved the stranger (Deut. 10:18). The reign of divine justice, the Kingdom of God, would embrace the entire world when the Messiah appeared at the end of historical time.

Of course the Hebrews were not the only ancient people with lofty moral and religious preoccupations, but they expressed them more systematically. They made them the basis of personal and national existence, and wrote them down in a book, the Torah. Equally characteristic was the often decisive role played by the spiritual leaders who guided Israel through the ages and through all its troubles.

Like all others, the Hebrew civilization of the tenth century B.C. had its roots in a specific tract of land: the Promised Land, including Jerusalem, the capital and the site of the Temple. But a series of catastrophes were to strain to the breaking point the bond between the Jewish people and their homeland. They had the ill luck to be at the crossroads of the great trade routes between Africa, Asia, and Europe, and for a thousand years they were at the mercy of the great empires. In the eighth century B.C., Sargon II of Assyria conquered the nothern half of the country and deported its inhabitants, the "lost tribes" who vanished forever. In the sixth century B.C., Nebuchadnezzar destroyed the Temple and carried off the people of Judea to Babylonia. This was the first Diaspora, which lasted only fifty years. When Cyrus of Persia conquered Babylonia, over forty thousand Jews returned to Jerusalem, where, in 516 B.C., they inaugurated the second Temple. Others chose to stay on in Babylonia.

Beginning in the fourth century B.C., the European empires came to the fore as Persia and Egypt fell into decay. Under Alexander the

Great and the Ptolemies, Jerusalem managed without much difficulty to keep at least its cultural independence. But as power shifted in the Hellenistic world and Judea came into the orbit of Seleucid Syria, an ideological conflict burst out between the Jews, who wanted to retain their religion and way of life, and the Greek monarchy, which tried to Hellenize them by force. Twenty-four years of warfare finally ended in the victory of the Maccabees.

Then the Hellenistic kingdoms crumbled in their turn before the might of Rome. Pompey marched into Jerusalem in A.D. 63. Judea became sometimes a Roman province (or more exactly, an administrative district ruled by such second-rate functionaries as Pontius Pilate), and sometimes a protectorate administered by a Herod or an Agrippa. Judea vegetated for another century. In A.D. 70 the emperor Titus responded to the Zealot rebellion that had begun four years previously by destroying the Temple. In 135, Hadrian crushed the revolt of Bar Kochba and ordered that Jerusalem henceforth be called Aelia Capitolina and that Jews be forbidden access to the city. Thus began the second—the great—Diaspora. The Jewish state would not be reborn for 1,813 years.

There are some constant themes in Jewish history. In the second century B.C., after the Maccabees had succeeded in restoring the Jewish cult at Jerusalem, they tried to establish an independent state, where- the Roman era, the Sadducees were mainly concerned with the defense upon the Hasidim, the "pious men," withdrew their support. During of the state, to which the Pharisees responded with "First the Torah." The Pharisees refused to support the Zealot uprising of A.D. 66 to 70. Instead, after the triumph of Titus, they even abandoned the notion of a territorial state and preached submission to the will of God, the strict observance of the Torah, the universality of religion, and the direct bond between every individual and God.

Such examples reappear throughout the history of the Diaspora and of Zionism. The Jews have always had their Pharisees and Sadducees, their Hasidim who think only of the invisible kingdom, and their Maccabees determined to defend or restore the earthly one on a certain soil.

Another constant is the appearance, in the midst of adversity and catastrophe, of wise men who rescue the essentials—the Book and the Law—the spiritual and moral framework of Hebrew civilization. Vespasian was still encamped outside the walls of Jerusalem when Rabbi Johanan ben Zakkai obtained permission to create a school for the study of the Torah at Jamnia, on the coast. Thus with the Temple destroyed and Jerusalem occupied, Judaism prepared itself to survive with nothing but a Book and its teaching. Similarly, just before Rabbi Akiva (Bar Kochba) perished in Hadrian's repression of 135, he gave a decisive impetus to the Mishnah, a systematization of the oral traditions and one of the origins of the Talmud.

During the eighteen centuries since the destruction of the second Temple, Jewish history presents the cultural historian with the unique spectacle of a landless, stateless civilization, supported only by a scattered population that is persecuted and even exterminated, and endlessly battered by expulsions and pogroms, yet that survives with an invincible obstinacy. "Civilization" is indeed the right word, for the Jews are not a definite race, if only because of the sometimes massive conversions (like that of the Khazars of the Volga in the eighth century), which have introduced widely divergent elements into the ethnic make-up of the Jews. One has only to look at the Jews of Yemen, the Ashkenazim of Central Europe, and the Sephardim of the Mediterranean to realize that their physical differences preclude any serious reference to a so-called Jewish "race." Nor does Judaism possess any characteristic political institutions. One can scarcely mention even a common language; although Hebrew has certainly survived as the ceremonial language, it has been supplanted in changing times and places by Aramaic, Arabic, Yiddish, Judeo-Spanish, and the modern European languages.

Jewish civilization, thus conceived as distinct from any physical, political, or even linguistic phenomenon, must surely owe its survival to the special character of its spiritual structure. With the possible exception of religious architecture, the arts were of little importance even at the height of the Jewish civilization. After the first Diaspora, Jewish civilization no longer tried to be the incarnation of state power. From the beginning, and increasingly as time went on, it was a religious and ethical civilization, just as that of the Greeks was based on human reason and that of the Romans on law and the state. Thus every rabbi, even every Jew, could say *omnia mecum porto*, as long as he possessed the sacred scrolls of the Torah. A universal, omnipresent God, a Book that translates His word, and men determined, wherever they live, to know and respect this word—this bald simplicity has carried Judaism through every trial and disaster.

Oddly enough, the great theoreticians of cultural history, such as Oswald Spengler and Arnold Toynbee, have neglected to mention

Jewish civilization among all those humanity has known from Sumer to our own. Perhaps they are under the illusion that after the disasters of A.D. 70 and 135, dismembered Judaism ceased to exist as a definite civilization, and that the remnants that survived in scattered communities became fossilized. In actual fact the Diaspora did not put an end to the history of Judaism. From that time on it simply developed on two distinct levels, of which the more important is the less easy to discern.

From the point of view of events, the history of the Diaspora indeed appears as a monotonous series of calamities interspersed with a few periods of relative peace and prosperity: persecution by the Byzantine Christians, the Sassanid Persians, the Arabs; expulsion of the Spanish and French Jews in the seventh century; the imposition of the infamous yellow band in Europe in the thirteenth century; new expulsions from France and Spain in the fourteenth and fifteenth centuries; massacres everywhere from England to Central Europe during the Crusades; extermination of the Ukrainian Jews in the seventeenth century; pogroms in Russia in the nineteenth and twentieth centuries; and finally Hitler's scientific genocide in our own time. Faced with this admittedly incomplete list of atrocity and suffering, one can find only a few rare periods of calm: the Golden Age of the Spanish Moslem civilization of Córdoba and Granada; Cromwell's authorization for the Jews to return to England in 1656; the legal equality granted to the Jews by the French legislature in 1791; and similar decisions made in Germany, England, Hungary, and Italy during the last century. From this standpoint, the history of the Diaspora seems merely a ragged fabric of events in which the Jewish communities are the tragic and bloody playthings of alien powers.

But if we look for Jewish civilization where its heart and treasure are kept, we see something entirely different. In spite of, and in the midst of, these terrible material setbacks, this civilization has kept its spiritual adventure going, and has grown on this level as any civilization does: evolving, influencing, and being influenced by neighboring contemporary civilizations. A soul without a body, perhaps, but a living soul that never has stopped changing.

After the loss of a political and territorial base in 135, the essential had to be saved. From the schools of Mesopotamia and Palestine came the two versions of the Talmud, that of Jerusalem and of Babylonia. These were interpretations of Biblical texts, as well as the "judgments of the Fathers," the collected traditions, precepts, laws, and rituals. The

Talmud is in one sense the spiritual equivalent of what would be a law code for a people with a country and a government. Each Jewish community (indeed, each individual Jew), isolated though it might be, knew from then on where to find its rules of conduct. But significantly, while it crystallizes the cultural personality of Judaism and provides it with a kind of shield against hostile forces, the Talmud remains open to all humanity. Far from excluding nonbelievers from the ranks of the just, it expressly admits any man of whatever origin who will abide by the seven precepts of the sons of Noah (a sort of minimum code of morality forbidding idolatry, blasphemy, murder, and so forth, and requiring one to live a just life).

It is impossible to trace here the evolution of Jewish thought during the Diaspora; many conflicting currents run through it. Hebraic mysticism more than once combined with Greek philosophy, particularly that of Plato and above all the Neoplatonists. From Philo of Alexandria in the first century A.D., to the Spanish Solomon ibn Gabirol in the eleventh, the trace is apparent. The latter's *Source of Life*, written in Arabic and translated into Latin (*Fons Vitae*), profoundly influenced the Christian world of the time. Through its wide diffusion in the eastern Roman Empire, Neoplatonism appealed to many men, Semitic as well as Greek, for the Mediterranean world was then searching confusedly for new paths of thought. The imprint of Neoplatonism is apparent on Gnosticism and on Christianity itself. There is a natural affinity between the Platonic doctrine of Ideas, the transcendent models dimly reflected here below, and the Hebraic theory of the *sefirot*, which are spiritual entities from which all created things proceed. Written in Babylonia in the seventh or eighth century, the *Sefir Yetzirah*, or *Book of Creation*, combines with Neoplatonism the idea (already present in the Talmud and probably widespread in Mesopotamia), of the creative role of the letters of the Hebrew alphabet, which are expressions of the divine word. This is the source of the mysticism of the Kabbalah, which was transplanted from Babylonia and Palestine to Italy, Germany, and Provence between the ninth and thirteenth centuries. The Kabbalah, which is at once a speculation on the nature of God and the world, and a moral doctrine attempting to "restore" the unity of God and man, was elaborated in Provence by a series of thinkers, one of whom—Jacob ha-Nazir—foresaw four successive worlds—a curious overlapping with the cosmologies of ancient Mexico.

But the crown of this mystical effort is surely the *Book of Splendor*, the *Zohar*. Written about 1300 at Granada in Hebrew and Aramaic by Moses de León, but attributed to the Rabbi Shimon ben Yochai,[1] the *Zohar* is a complete interpretation of God, man and the world, a mystical vision, a moral doctrine, an explanation of human destiny in general and Jewish destiny in particular. Spread after 1492 by the Jews exiled from Spain, it was quickly adopted by Jews in all nations, notably in Palestine, where it inspired the mystical school of Safed. Like a seed on the wind, the Zoharist doctrine of Rabbi Isaac Luria moved from Safed to the Ukraine, where in the eighteenth century it gave rise to Hasidism. At that time the Jewish communities of the Ukraine were painfully rebuilding after the massacres of 1648, in which two hundred fifty thousand people were killed, and a spiritual revival occurred among the people. It centered upon a sect of mystics, the Zaddikim. One of them, Mendel of Vitebsk, with three hundred disciples, migrated to Safed and Tiberias in 1777.

Mysticism is only one aspect of the civilization of the Diaspora. Like the Moslems and Christians among whom they lived, the Jews took part in the renaissance of rationalism inspired by the works of Aristotle, which were rediscovered in the tenth century. Maimonides, expelled from Córdoba in the twelfth century by the Almohades, Moslem fanatics, took refuge in Egypt, where he wrote his *Guide for the Perplexed,* a key work that tried to reconcile faith and reason, revealed religion and science, tradition and intelligence. His book, which became widely known among cultivated Jews, was particularly influential in Provence. Translated into Latin, it contributed to the evolution of contemporary Christian thought, particularly through the works of St. Thomas Aquinas.

A third aspect of the intellectual and spiritual evolution of Judaism is of evident historical importance—the work of the "Doctors of the Law." These rabbis and sages, even more than the mystics and philosophers, helped maintain the mental framework and unity of Hebrew civilization despite the Diaspora, migrations, and persecutions. By interpreting the Torah and the Talmud, by enacting laws and recording traditions for a landless, stateless people, the sages played the roles that in a government are taken by legislators and judges. Throughout the ages, it was to the *geonim* of the Jewish academies in Babylonia, to the rabbis in France (Rashi of Troyes, 1040–1105), in Germany (Gershom of Mayence, 960–1040), and in Spain (Ben Yechiel of Toledo, thirteenth century) that the Jews turned with the moral problems that tormented them. Hence there exists a whole literature of questions and answers, a veritable jurisprudence expounded case by case across the centuries. Among the important decisions, one can cite that by Gershom of Mayence forbidding polygamy, although it is authorized in the Bible.

At the same time, the Jewish communities felt the need to make coherent collections of the scattered precepts and judgments. This is the origin of the "codes," such as those compiled by Maimonides in the twelfth century and by Rabbi Joseph Karo, who fled from Spain to Safed late in the fifteenth century. Karo's, completed in the next century by the rabbis of Central Europe to make allowance for the tradition of the Ashkenazim, must be considered the definitive expression of Orthodox Jewish law.

And so communities scattered from the snows of the Baltic to the Arabian desert, living among peoples as different as the Poles and the Turks, and speaking diverse languages, still found themselves united, not only by theology and philosophy, but also by law. Another powerfully unifying force, despite certain variations in the liturgy, was the ritual common to all Jews — prayers, attendance at the synagogue, circumcision, the Bar Mitzvah, holidays, dietary laws, respect for the Sabbath. At Vilna as in Yemen, in Holland as in North Africa, every Jew knew that on Friday evening candles would be lighted even on the most humble family table, and that every year at the beginning of Passover, children's voices would ask the traditional question: "What makes this night different from all other nights?" Men and ideas, poems, tales, and myths traveled from one community to another, across continents. Thus, a "magic" nationality survived, to use Spengler's word, a nationality made up of shared beliefs, suffering, hope, and a jealously guarded psychic identity.

It is perhaps understandable that anti-Semitism has accompanied Judaism like a shadow. Every civilization instinctively mistrusts those who are different, especially when they are different because they want to be, and are too numerous to escape notice but too few in number to escape arousing the lowest instincts of the majority and the desire to torture the helpless. Anti-Semitism found a metaphysical justification when the Christian or Moslem persecutor saw in the Jew an enemy of his religion, a deicide, an infidel. But the atheistic anti-Semitism of the twentieth century, thinly varnished with a few absurd racial theories, amounts to a pure outburst of hate against those who are different, and whom one can torture at will.

It is also surely true that anti-Semitism, by building walls around the Jews, closing most professions to them, and shutting them up in ghettos, has powerfully aided in maintaining Judaism's identity. The proof is that in Western countries where anti-Semitism has faded in the twentieth century, a notable proportion of the Jewish communities have gone from emancipation to assimilation. Judaism and anti-Semitism react indefinitely against one another. However, one of the most lucid of the Zionists, Vladimir Jabotinsky, was right in speaking of an "anti-Semitism of things" (as opposed to personal anti-Semitism), by which he meant the spontaneous and inevitable hostility of a majority toward a strong minority whose customs, religion, and language are different and who compete in the economic domain — as in pre-1940 Poland, for example. The almost physical tension between the majority and the minority bursts forth in the form of discrimination, persecution, and pogroms, especially if the government — as was the case in czarist Russia — more or less openly encourages the violence as a welcome diversion from its own political difficulties.

One of the fundamental objects of Zionism was to ease this tension by leading some, if not all, of the endangered Jewish communities toward a national home. Where were they to build this home if not in Palestine?

The bond between the Jews and their land, Eretz Israel (renamed Palestine during the Roman era in reference to the ancient Philistines), had never been completely broken despite the fall of Jerusalem, the destruction of the Temple, and the Diaspora. The spiritual and intellectual life of Jewish communities all over the world, the ritual, the formula of the prayers had ceaselessly turned the thoughts of the faithful to the Promised Land and its capital. During the first Babylonian exile the Psalmist said, "If I forget thee, O Jerusalem, let my right hand forget her cunning" (Ps. 137). This lost none of its passionate force in the ghettos of Hungary and the *yeshivot* of Lithuania. The annual celebrations at Vitebsk and Amsterdam, at Algiers and Baghdad, for the most part commemorated events associated with the history of Israel. The Passover Seder marks the deliverance of the Jewish people from Egyptian bondage and the migration to Palestine. The feast of Purim recalls the salvation of the Jews in the Persian Empire under the reign of Ahasuerus, thanks to the intercession of Esther. Hanukkah commemorates the victory of the Maccabees and the rededication of the Temple, which the Hellenistic Syrians had profaned. Other feasts are connected with the seasons and farming according to the Palestinian calendar — Shabuoth, to mark the grain harvest; Sukkoth, for the gathering of grapes. Under the skies of northern Europe and in the southern hemisphere, the rhythm of the Palestinian seasons still determined life's great phases.

Moreover, the physical bond between the Jews and Israel had never totally disappeared. Palestine was successively occupied by the Romans, the Byzantines, the Persians, the Arabs, the Crusaders, and the Turks, and it decayed economically, culturally, and demographically. The land of milk and honey, which at the beginning of the Christian era supported a population of about three million people, was gradually abandoned to desert and swamp, and by the nineteenth century was inhabited by two hundred thousand starving *fellahin* and Bedouin nomads.

But in spite of all manner of persecution, and the impoverishment caused by the Arab and Turkish administrations, a Jewish presence was maintained throughout the centuries.

The Roman emperors after Hadrian did not continue to enforce his harsh policies toward the Palestinian Jews. Antoninus Pius recognized Shimon ben Gamliel as the spiritual representative of the Israelites who had remained on their own soil, and there is a tradition that Marcus Aurelius cordially received Judah the Patriarch, Shimon's son. A Sanhedrin with essentially religious and ritual responsibilities, and a Jewish patriarchate subsisted in Palestine until 425, at which time Theodosius II, a Christian emperor, suppressed the patriarchate. Nevertheless, the schools, particularly at Tiberias, continued as living centers of thought and tradition after the Islamic conquest of Palestine and until the tenth century. Jewish intellectual, theological, and literary life was maintained and developed, as is shown by the poetry of the *paitanim* in the seventh century, and the influence of the Palestinian *geonim* in the ninth century throughout the East and even in Italy.

Moreover, as persecutions in various parts of the world shook the Jewish communities, immigrants came back to Palestine to reinforce the small core of Jews who had never left. The massive expulsion of the Jews from Spain in 1492 resulted in the growth of the Safed school in Galilee. Doctrines and poems spread from this center to Tiberias, Hebron, and Jerusalem during the succeeding centuries. Even during Ottoman domination there was no lack of pious Jews, often elderly people wanting to live out their days in the Holy Land, who emigrated to Palestine, and especially to Jerusalem, where they could pray at the Wailing Wall and await the coming of the Messiah. Often in dire straits, these isolated little communities living in their dreams nonetheless imprinted upon the land the historical right of the Jewish people to be there.

At the end of the eighteenth century and the beginning of the nineteenth, a liberal ideology spread quickly in Europe with the armies of the First Republic and Napoleon. For the Jews of Western Europe, this meant emancipation, which was confirmed by the French imperial decree of 1806 and, a bit later, by the convocation of a Grand Sanhedrin. In Germany, a sect called the Maskilim rebelled against Yiddish as the language of the ghetto and began to write and publish in Biblical Hebrew. A cultural rebirth resulted from this political emancipation. The movement reflected two contradictory tendencies: sometimes the Jews, freed at last from old constraints and discriminations, assimilated with those among whom they lived; sometimes emancipation caused them to steep themselves in their own culture, to renew it, and in so doing, to seek and to emphasize their own originality.

Eastern Europe was something else again. There the ghetto walls, instead of falling, separated Polish and Russian Jews more implacably than ever from the rest of the population. Western ideas did cross these barriers, but their seed fell upon ground long dried out by despair and misery, by tradition, and indeed by mysticism. The Eastern Jew met nothing but discrimination, hatred, and injustice, and he saw no hope of breaking through the wall. The national conscience of Judaism was aroused by the bitter contrast between the new freedom of the West and the harsh reality of segregation and poverty in the East. Faced with scorn and violence, Eastern Judaism was no longer content with Hasidic pietism. It had to find in the very sources of its civilization a new reason for living. The renaissance of the Hebrew language gave rise to an intense intellectual ferment. By the end of the nineteenth century, the poetry of Chaim Nachman Bialik, the many-sided work of Ahad Ha'am,[2] and of Eliezer ben Yehuda, who adapted Hebrew to the needs of modern life, bore witness to the richness of this renaissance.

With an upsurge of nationalism similar to that of all European peoples, the question of a Jewish homeland naturally arose. It was no longer a matter of waiting for the Messiah while chanting, "Next year at Jerusalem," but of actually realizing the return of the Jewish people to Eretz Israel.

The Zionist idea (the word "Zionist" was only coined in 1886 by an Austrian journalist named Nathan Birnbaum) took almost a century to ripen, and was nurtured by almost as many non-Jews as Jews.

Among the former, the most famous was undoubtedly Napoleon Bonaparte. In his proclamation of March, 1799, he called upon the Jews to "rally under their flag and restore Jerusalem of old," and to end the "ignominy inflicted upon the legitimate heirs of Palestine." Shortly before the siege of Acre, he tried to recruit a Jewish contingent. His plan was to rebuild the Temple and create a Jewish state.[3]

Napoleon failed at Acre and had to renounce his grand design for the East, but Napoleon III's secretary, Ernest Laharanne, revived the idea in 1860 in a small book about "the new Eastern question — reconstitution of the Jewish nation." In this pamphlet one finds such statements as, "You [he spoke to the Jews] can rebuild the gates of Jerusalem. . . . A high endeavor can be yours. . . . You will be the intermediaries between Europe and the Far East, and you will open the great routes leading to India and China. In your work of renewal our hearts will follow you, and our arms will aid you. . . . Your ancient homeland calls."

Jean Henri Dunant, the famous Genevan who founded the Red Cross and won the first Nobel Prize in 1901, formulated in 1866 the practical principle that, as we shall see, Zionism later tried to apply. He stated the problem simply: How were the Jews to colonize Palestine, then Turkish territory? His solution was to create under the Sultan's nominal authority an International Eastern Society, which would undertake to improve agriculture in Palestine, introduce industry, construct a port at Jaffa and a railroad from there to Jerusalem, to organize Jewish immigration from Morocco, Poland, Moldavia, and so on. "The colonies which will develop," he added, "can be diplomatically neutralized, like Switzerland."[4] Another Swiss, A. F. Pétavel, a Protestant from Neuchâtel, proposed in his booklet *Israel, People of the Future*, written in 1861, that the Jews return to Palestine.

There were numerous Jewish writers and thinkers who in the last half of the nineteenth century cleared the way for what soon would be called Zionism. In France, Joseph Salvador from Montpellier wrote in 1853 that "a new state will be founded on the shores of Galilee and in ancient Canaan. The Jews will return through the combined forces of historical memory, persecution in various countries, and the puritan sympathy of Biblical England."

In 1862 the Talmudist Zvi Hirsch Kalischer of Thorn asserted in his *The Search for Zion*, written in Hebrew, that the return of the Jews to Palestine could come about only through agricultural colonization. He created a Jewish agricultural society at Frankfurt, the first of its kind. It was in 1862, too, that Moses Hess, who had fought at Karl Marx's side but had broken with him in 1848, expounded in *Rome and Jerusalem* what might be called the first Zionist doctrine. He affirmed that the Jews ought to be able to realize their national aspirations in the same way as the Italians, or any other people.

In 1871 a Jewish doctor of Odessa, Leon Pinsker, witnessed a pogrom in his city. Ten years later, after the assassination of Alexander II, a wave of repression and pogroms swept Russia. The ghettos were raped, murdered, pillaged. Russian authorities did nothing to protect the Jews, if indeed they themselves had not covertly organized the atrocities. Before long anti-Semitism actually had legal support. "Temporary Legislation Concerning the Jews" decreed a whole series of discriminatory measures, such as a ban on living outside certain areas, and the *numerus clausus* in secondary schools and universities. Leon Pinsker was convinced that nothing better could be expected from Russian society or the government, and in 1882 he launched his incendiary *Auto-Emancipation*. Anti-Semitism, he wrote, is an incurable disease. It comes about because the Jew has no country of his own. "To the living he is dead, to the native an alien, to the sedentary a vagabond, to the rich a beggar, to the poor an exploiting millionaire, to the citizen a man without a country, to all classes a detested competitor." He concluded: "The Jews must become a nation once more, a people with its own land."

In a conference at Katowice two years later, these embryonic movements from Central and Eastern Europe resulted in the creation of the *Hoveve Zion* — the Lovers of Zion — of which Pinsker became president. In Russia, Poland, Rumania, Germany, even England, groups were formed with one very precise purpose: the agricultural colonization of Palestine. At Kharkov a group of young students founded the *Bilu* movement with the same purpose.

And so it was that in the midst of unspeakable misery, continual danger, injustice, and oppression, Eastern Jewry gave birth to what can be called practical Zionism, a movement to return to the land and to the labors of the country, begun by a people who had not pushed a plow in centuries. To escape from anti-Semitism, to build a homeland, to improve the land, and to create a new society were the objectives that fired the hearts of these pioneers, who fled Russia and Poland in little groups to settle in Ottoman Palestine. For the time being they intended only to establish farming colonies. The idea of a Jewish state was latent, at least for some of them, but it was neither clearly conceived, nor openly expressed.

From the beginning, this scattered but enthusiastic migration had to overcome terrible material and intellectual obstacles. The most Orthodox Jews could not encourage this almost sacrilegious action that sought to hasten the work of the Messiah, rather than to wait until he chose his time to come. Modernist Jews, on the other hand, had often been converted to socialist ideas and denounced what they thought was the reactionary character of Hebrew nationalism. Finally, the disciples of the cultural renaissance objected to the colonization of Palestine, saying that the important thing was to renew culture and language, not to plant trees. Ahad Ha'am, the most famous of the "cultural Zionists," was a member of the Odessa committee that directed the activities of the Lovers of Zion, but he was always most reticent about Palestinian colonization. "That is not the way," he said.

The colonists who finally finished their voyage found a land ravaged by centuries of neglect. Malaria decimated them. The indolent and corrupt Turkish government and marauding Bedouins soon deprived them of their small resources. Disillusion and discouragement were the lot of many a pioneer who had left the ghetto with so much hope in his heart.

It is fortunate that this emigration from Eastern Europe coincided with the philanthropy of certain Western Jews. As early as 1870, Charles Netter, founder of the *Alliance Israélite Universelle*, created Mikveh Israel, a school of agronomy near Jaffa, which furnished the new colonies with the technical staff they lacked. The first villages — Zikhron Yaakov, Rishon Le-Zion, Petach Tikvah, Rosh Pinah, Rehovot — were in grave financial difficulty when, in 1883, Baron Edmond de Rothschild decided to help them. His tomb in the hillside gardens beside Zikhron Yaakov bears witness to his attachment to this land and the gratitude his constant generosity earned for him.

Thus little by little, outside the ancient Hebrew centers at Jerusalem, Safed, Tiberias, and Hebron, a new people took root in the land and worked it with their hands for the first time in nearly two thousand years. This was the *yishuv*, the Jewish community in Palestine. Thinkers, pioneers, and philanthropists had all given this renaissance its impetus. But as a matter of cold fact, all that had been accomplished so far was a few vineyards and orange groves and a few scattered villages existing under foreign laws in natural and human surroundings that were both hostile and indifferent. Certainly these were positive results, acquired at the price of immense labor and heavy sacrifices, but the results were precarious. They were not part of a larger plan, nor was there any guarantee for their future.

It remained for Theodor Herzl, with the vision of a genius, to take up the entire problem and thus to found Zionism and the state of Israel in one stroke.

FOOTNOTES FOR CHAPTER 1

1. Shimon ben Yochai, according to tradition, lived for thirteen years hidden in a cavern in Upper Galilee to escape from the Romans after the fall of Jerusalem in the second century. His tomb is the center of annual rites.

2. "One of the people," the Hebrew pseudonym of Asher Ginsburg.

3. F. Piétri. *Napoléon et les Israélites*. Paris, Berger-Levrault, 1965.

4. Jean-Henri Dunant. *Une Société Universelle pour l'Orient*, Paris, 1866.

2
"HAMELEKH HERZL"

"King Herzl!" Thus was he greeted in Hebrew by a young Jewish worker at Betko, near Vilna, in 1903. Who was this uncrowned, landless king whose granite tomb, set atop the hillside that bears his name, dominates Jerusalem today?

Nothing could be more paradoxical than the course of his brief life. Theodor Herzl died at the age of forty-four, having devoted the last eight years of his life to founding Zionism. Born in Hungary but brought up in Vienna, he became a "boulevard" dramatist, a successful newspaperman, and the permanent Paris correspondent of the great Austrian daily, *Neue Freie Presse*. Herzl spoke no Hebrew, knew nothing whatever of the pre-Zionist movements, and had never heard of the *Hoveve Zion* or the work of Pinsker. He had nothing of the rabbi about him, even less of the Zaddik. To see him leave his elegant apartment near the Parc Monceau each morning and drive in his carriage to the Bois de Boulogne, or to some Parisian literary salon, or perhaps to the press gallery of the Palais Bourbon, who could ever have imagined that this man would soon become the adored and controversial leader of world Judaism and the virtual head of a state that as yet did not even exist?

In the 1880's Herzl was a cosmopolitan young man of essentially Germanic background but attracted by the language and civilization of France. He was twenty when his first play was published at Vienna, twenty-four when he earned his doctorate of law (his career as a lawyer lasted but a year), twenty-five when one of his plays had a successful run in New York. He traveled in Germany and Holland, and then discovered Paris. The Viennese press was happy to print his articles, and before long the *Neue Freie Presse*, the most important German language paper of the day, opened its columns to him. He married in 1889[1] and two years later settled in Paris as correspondent for the Viennese daily.

Theodor Herzl apparently fell instantly in love with the Paris of the nineties. Under the spell of the brilliant life of the capital, he wrote of "a new era [in France], more brilliant and glorious than any in the past." He was seen often at the theater and the Palais Bourbon; he knew Zola, Flaubert, the Goncourts, Anatole France, Huysmans, Proust. Alphonse Daudet and Clemenceau were his friends. All doors opened to this tall, elegant, cultivated young man with his thick black beard.

No one could have been more different from Herzl than the Jew of the Polish or Ukrainian ghettos. However, he had already been forced to face up to the Jewish problem. In his youth he had come across an anti-Semitic pamphlet by Eugen Dühring. In 1883, he was forced to break with his friend Hermann Bahr after a demonstration for Wagner during which Bahr had made a violently anti-Semitic speech. He was twenty-one when he read newspaper reports of pogroms in Kirovograd, Dnepropetrovsk, and Poltava; twenty-two when twenty thousand Jews were deported from Kiev; thirty-one when fourteen thousand Moscow Jews were deported like convicts. In the Russia of Pobedonostsev, a populace drunk with alcohol and blood had year after year raped, murdered, destroyed, and sacked the ghettos. To judge from a few notes that Herzl left in his private journal, the solution that he foresaw was total assimilation, de-Judaization. He imagined a massive conversion of the Jews to Christianity, a grandiose "Judeo-Christian reconciliation"[2] blessed by the Pope. But anti-Semitism was making terrifying progress in the West as well. France was close on Germany's heels: *La France Juive* by Edouard Drumont appeared in 1885, and *La Libre Parole* was founded in 1892. Herzl wrote a study of French anti-Semitism that appeared on August 31, 1892, in the *Neue Freie Presse*. It was calm, objective, faintly ironic. The talented journalist had not yet become a prophet.

The Dreyfus affair broke in November, 1894. It would dominate the entire political life of France until 1906. Herzl covered the trial for his Viennese newspaper. On January 5, 1895, he witnessed the disgrace of Captain Dreyfus in the courtyard of the École Militaire and wrote: "From the extreme right to the extreme left, the cry was the same across the land: 'Down with the Jews.' " Herzl was deeply shocked — the more so because he had believed in France as the home of liberty and the rights of man. He had reacted to the rising anti-Semitism in France as a playwright and wrote *The New Ghetto*. But he realized that this was not enough.

An assimilated Jew, successful author, worldly journalist, and man of letters, a free and generous spirit detached from the problems of Judaism and at best lukewarm in matters of religion, Herzl had carved his place in a universe as distant from the ghettos and *yeshivot* of Eastern Europe as the earth from Mars. This very detachment enabled him to see that the Jewish question must be solved and could only be solved in the *political* arena.

In a few weeks during the summer of 1895, almost beside himself with horror, compassion, and a prophetic vision of the future, he composed his booklet, *Der Judenstaat*, "The Jewish State." Without mentioning cultural and literary pre-Zionism, of which he knew nothing, nor the first attempts at colonization in Palestine, he went straight to the heart of the Jewish condition: since Jews are everywhere a minority, without a homeland of their own, they are condemned to provoke anti-Semitism. Are they weak? Then they are made the scapegoat in every crisis. Are they powerful? Then they are the object of jealousy and hatred. And if they leave their persecutors and emigrate to a country where conditions seem better? They carry the causes of anti-Semitism with them like a virus. The Jewish problem is neither social nor religious but national, and must be put before the conscience of the world as a political matter to be settled by civilized nations. An international charter should guarantee the Jews a territory; then it would be up to *them* to organize and prosper in their territory. He already envisioned the creation of an association and a company, the former charged with political negotiations, the latter to finance and develop the new country. But what country? Herzl left the choice to the association, but not without mentioning two possibilities: Palestine, in spite of the probable opposition of the Turks; and Argentina, where a Jewish philanthropist, Baron Maurice de Hirsch, was already making important funds available to Jewish immigrants.

"The Jewish state is essential to the world, and that is why it will be created." This is the essence of Herzl's idea.

How Herzl had broken away from all his predecessors, how radical his plan was is immediately evident. No longer was it a question of praying, making pious vows, awaiting a decision from On High, as the Orthodox Jews advocated. Nor was it only a matter of renewing Judaism as a culture, as Ahad Ha'am had wished; nor was the solution merely to return to Eretz Israel and plant wheat and vineyards, sprig by sprig. Herzl was a statesman by instinct. He realized immediately that this was a political question to be resolved at the highest level of international politics. His vision was prophetic, for his charter would later materialize in the Balfour Declaration, the San Remo Treaty, and finally the decision of the United Nations. His "association" would be the Zionist organization, and his "company" the *Keren Kayemet Le-Israel* and the *Keren Ha-Yesod*, the two funds that have made possible the colonization and economic development of Palestine.

However, when he recovered from his shock over Dreyfus and emerged from the trancelike state in which he had written his manifesto, he considered the situation more objectively and was scarcely encouraged by what he saw. His friend Friedrich Schiff, to whom he had shown his manuscript before publication, pityingly urged him to see a psychiatrist. He followed this advice, and his doctor, Max Nordau, became a convert and threw his prestige and influence behind Zionism. But for each disciple like Nordau, how many objections, arguments, angry criticisms! For prominent Jews of the West, Herzl's appeal was dangerous because it risked exacerbating anti-Semitism and working against the tendency to assimilation. In the eyes of traditionalist rabbis, Herzl was actually committing a sin by wishing to use worldly methods to anticipate the Messiah's coming. The "practical" Zionists, the *Hoveve Zion*, feared that Herzl's plan would anger the Turks, who ruled Palestine. The socialist Jews saw his national doctrine as a return to the past, a bourgeois tendency. Others, more attached to historical Judaism, scorned his modern, Westernized views — was not this merely the influence of the "assimilationism" that they despised?

At the end of *The Jewish State*, Herzl let it be known that he would stop at that, and that his role would be limited to launching an idea. In fact, and this was characteristic of him, he was already laying a thousand plans for transforming the idea into reality. Since the solution was to be an international one — an accord with Turkey guaranteed by the great powers — he had to negotiate. But how was he to approach the great men of the world? Could a journalist, granted a distinguished one but lacking any political weight, hope to gain the ear of the sultan or the German emperor? It was a Christian who would help him find the way.

He returned to Vienna in 1896, keeping only a minor position at the *Neue Freie Presse* in order to devote himself to the Zionist movement. There he met Pastor William Hechler, chaplain of the British embassy. A devotee of Biblical scholarship, Hechler had published a tract called, "The Restoration of the Jews to Palestine According to the Prophets." He believed that this restoration would begin in 1897. He swore his friendship to Herzl, and a limitless devotion that was to last a lifetime. Having been tutor to the children of the Grand Duke of Baden, uncle of Kaiser Wilhelm II, he arranged a meeting, in April, 1896, between Herzl and the grand duke. After three hours of conversation at Karlsruhe, the emperor's uncle announced that he was a believer. And so he made it possible for Herzl to meet Wilhelm II.

But the most pressing matter was to submit to the sultan a plan for the restoration of Palestine to the Jews. Herzl had already worked out the main line of his diplomatic approach: Since the Ottoman Empire was deep in debt, why not refinance the Turkish treasury in exchange for Palestine? Even so baldly expressed, the idea was fraught with difficulty. How was he to persuade a skittish despot, debt-ridden though he was, to give up sovereignty over even the poorest and most deserted part of his domain? Through the intervention of a Polish nobleman, Nevlinski, who led a needy life in Constantinople on embassy doorsteps and on the fringes of the imperial court, Herzl made his first contact with the palace in June, 1896. He met the Grand Vizir Khalif Rifat Pasha; Daud Effendi, a Jewish confidant of the foreign minister; Munir Pasha, the master of ceremonies. But he could not get an audience with Abdul Hamid. The sultan was suspicious: his empire was not for sale, and he did not intend to see it dismembered. After much palaver, Herzl had to resign himself to going away empty-handed. His only consolation was that one day passing through Sofia he was surrounded by a great Jewish crowd, enthusiastic, uplifted by hope.

Paris, London. Herzl now spent the best part of his time in boats and trains. Everywhere, some of the important men he needed to see avoided him. In England, where the talented writer Israel Zangwill supported him, other eminent Jews were more reserved, among them Sir Samuel Montagu, Claude Montefiore, and even Colonel Goldsmid, who represented the Lovers of Zion in London. Not that men such as Goldsmid or Edmond de Rothschild were less devoted than Herzl to the idea of Palestinian colonization, but they would not look beyond "practical" Zionism. They thought Herzl's political edifice was superfluous, dangerous, and impracticable, but he himself knew that all else depended upon it.

Bitterness and fatigue sometimes almost overcame Herzl's conviction that he was right. His failures in Turkey and among the eminent convinced him that he must seek support from the poor, threatened Jewish masses, like those he had seen at Sofia. In Vienna he organized the Zionist Congress, with branches in every country, and used what money he still possessed to create the magazine, *Die Welt*. Above all he wanted to convoke a great Zionist congress with delegates from all over the world — a parliament of the Jewish nation.

The first Congress was to meet at Munich, but the local Jewish community and the Union of German Rabbis protested violently. On

August 29, 1897, two hundred four delegates from all over the world at last convened in Basel for three days. They spoke German, Russian, Yiddish, French, and English, and represented every political nuance from socialism to religious orthodoxy. Herzl was determined that this Congress should establish organizational rules for itself like those of any parliamentary body. His long experience at the Palais Bourbon helped him. He insisted that all delegates wear dress coats and top hats to the first meeting. When Herzl appeared before the gallery to make the inaugural address, an extraordinary enthusiasm swept the hall. "It's no longer the elegant Dr. Herzl of Vienna," wrote one witness, "but the royal offspring of the line of David. . . . I was overcome by the desire to cry out, in the midst of this storm of joy, 'Long live the King! Yehi Hamelekh!' "[3]

The striking thing about the speech that Herzl made was the lucidity of his intelligence, the burning conviction that animated him, and his total lack of self-interest. Already he had become part of the great work that he originated but that he felt was greater than himself.

Back in Vienna Herzl wrote in his diary, "If I had to sum up what happened at the Congress of Basel, I would say that I founded the Jewish state. This would provoke universal laughter today. But perhaps in twenty years and certainly in fifty, it will be there for all the world to see." And fifty years later, on November 29, 1947, the United Nations decided to create the Jewish state in Palestine. No one, not even Herzl, could have foreseen what rivers of blood, what mountains of dead would have to be crossed before his prophecy would be realized.

The Congress at Basel made Zionism a worldwide movement and Herzl appeared to be its head. He could now get at the many tasks that the assembly had agreed upon. He concentrated on three problems: the creation of a bank to finance the colonization of Palestine, obtaining a charter from Turkey and the Great Powers that would serve as the legal base for the future state (the program of Basel called for "the establishment in Palestine, for the Jewish people, of a homeland guaranteed by public law"), and finally reinforcement of the Zionist organization.

The idea of a bank was skeptically received by the business world. "For the first time doubt is being cast on the ability of Jews to create banks," wrote Herzl ironically. It took five years to form the Jewish Colonial Trust, chartered in London under British law with a capital of two hundred fifty thousand pounds from about one hundred forty thousand subscribers. This capital did not come from the coffers of the rich but from the worn change purses of the poor. Until the day he died, Herzl was to be hounded and paralyzed by the lack of money for his family as well as for the Zionist movement.

Ahad Ha'am had said that "Israel will be saved by prophets, not by diplomats," but Herzl, diplomat *and* prophet, nevertheless renewed his efforts with Turkey and Germany. A German protectorate seemed to him a promising possibility. Wilhelm II was interested in the East, and Turko-German relations were close. Thanks to the grand duke of Baden, Herzl met Count Philipp Eulenburg, who was Germany's ambassador to Vienna; then he met the German foreign minister, Bernhard von Bülow, and the chancellor, Prince von Hohenlohe. Von Bülow let it be known that the kaiser could "advise" the sultan. According to Eulenburg, the emperor was "enthusiastic" about the return of the Jews to the Holy Land. Moreover, the emperor was himself going to Constantinople and then to Palestine, and he would see Herzl.

On October 17, 1898, Herzl for the first time found himself in the presence of Wilhelm II at Constantinople. During the long conversation, in which von Bülow took part, Herzl presented his plan for a "Chartered Company" guaranteed by a German protectorate. The kaiser expressed interest and promised to speak to the sultan.

Then, for the first time in his life, Herzl went to Palestine, landing at Jaffa. With Pastor Hechler and David Wolffsohn he visited the village colonies at Rishon Le-Zion and Rehovot. With his own eyes he saw the weariness and sickness of the settlers, who everywhere greeted him with cheers. On the appointed morning, at the agricultural school of Mikveh Israel, Herzl awaited the arrival of the kaiser. He came on horseback, in full uniform, wearing a pointed helmet with a wide neckpiece. He shook Herzl's hand cordially, uttered two or three sentences about the "great future" of this country and the necessity for irrigation . . . and the interview was over.

A few days later the emperor received Herzl and a delegation at Jerusalem. Herzl handed him a prepared memorandum. This time the reception was chilly. "We shall consider it." Following the audience von Bülow issued a deceptive communiqué that failed to mention Herzl's name. It emphasized that in answer to a Jewish delegation, the kaiser had expressed his interest in "agricultural progress in Palestine," if the rights of the Ottoman Empire were respected.

Clearly, Wilhelm II learned at Constantinople that the sultan had no intention of giving up Palestine. Accordingly, the emperor's "enthusiasm" had evaporated. Germany did not intend to turn its Eastern policies upside down and alienate the Ottoman Empire for the sake of a problematical protectorate in the Holy Land. Herzl was profoundly disappointed, not for the first time, nor indeed for the last.

He had to shore up the crumbling foundations of his idea. In the spring of 1899, at the peace conference called by the czar in The Hague, he met Nouri Bey, secretary general to the Turkish foreign ministry. Nouri promised him an audience with the sultan — after Herzl had delivered a fee of forty thousand gold francs. But time passed, the twentieth century began, and there was still no word from Constantinople.

Pastor Hechler intervened again. He arranged for Herzl to meet Arminius Vámbéry, a strange Hungarian adventurer of Jewish origin who had become a Moslem and then a Protestant. He had been a professor of Oriental languages, then tutor to one of the Ottoman princesses, and he was well connected at the sultan's court. In May, 1901, thanks to Vámbéry, Herzl at last met Abdul Hamid. The sultan seemed interested in Herzl's plan for consolidating the national debt that was crushing the Ottoman Empire, but the subject of Palestine did not come up. At the end of the audience, Herzl and the sultan agreed to keep in touch.

Scarcely had he left the imperial apartments than Herzl became entangled in the unbelieveable intrigues of the court. Abdul Hamid's entourage buzzed ceaselessly, sometimes plotting in favor of his projects and sometimes against them, forming clans and claques that had only one common aim — getting money. Herzl had to go to Europe to try to raise the enormous sum of five million pounds necessary to refinance the Sublime Porte. By letter and cable he tried to keep in touch with Abdul Hamid, who did deign from time to time to acknowledge receipt of his messages.

In February, 1902, and again in July, Herzl returned to Constantinople and was received by the sultan. He had succeeded in collecting three million francs, but it was no use. Each time he met the obstinate distrust of Abdul Hamid. The sultan did not wish to grant a "charter" for Palestinian colonization. He would have allowed a company to colonize certain regions of Mesopotamia or Anatolia, but absolutely nothing in Palestine. Herzl found the alternatives unacceptable. And so the Turkish negotiation, like the German negotiation, failed.

While he pursued this diplomatic task, interrupted by negotiations in England and Austria, Herzl also had to think of the problems of the Zionist organization. Despite the objections of some delegates, he had provided that the Congress should meet every year, and this rule was strictly observed. The Committee of Zionist Action, elected by the Congress, directed the movement between sessions. The first three Congresses met at Basel. The fourth, held at London in 1900, put Herzl in touch with Lord Landsdowne, then secretary of the foreign office. In spite of Herzl's prestige, his repeated failures on the political front had weakened his position at the heart of the movement. Chaim Weizmann, a young Russian Zionist and a not unreserved admirer of Herzl, found him both "powerful and naïve" and was among those who sensed a fundamental "conflict of temperaments" between the Westernized Herzl and the Jews of Russia, who were both passionately Hebraic and passionately Slavic, and who were steeped in their traditional culture. They chided Herzl for neglecting this national culture, for seeking only the support of the rich and powerful, for entering endless and fruitless negotiations instead of concentrating on the practical problem of Palestinian immigration. A feeling of helpless frustration was spreading, as, for example, when the fourth Congress had to sit by powerless while the Jews were brutally expelled from Rumania.

Ironically, from the beginning Herzl had caught the imagination and gained the confidence of the Jewish communities in Eastern Europe while he had received a very cool reception from the rich and powerful men he had sought out in the West. At the same time, he had attracted the bitter opposition of such leaders of Russian Judaism as Menahem Ussischkin, particularly by his attempts to reach agreement with the Turks.

At the fifth Congress, held in Basel in 1901, there was a demonstration by a "Democratic Faction," led in part by Weizmann. Influenced by Ahad Ha'am's ideas, they demanded that more attention be given to the historic Hebrew heritage. A stormy debate on "Zionist culture" almost split the Congress. Since the Congress represented the entire Hebrew people of the Diaspora, it was natural that divergent political tendencies should arise, as they do in any parliamentary body. As the years passed, a definite "left" took shape, the Poalei Zion group with socialist leanings; a religious "right," the Mizrachi; and at the center the general Zionists.

Despite the give and take of this often violent debate, the congresses continued the slow structuring of the future state. The fifth Congress created the *Keren Kayemet Le-Israel*, the Jewish National

Fund, which was to acquire property in Palestine that would belong inalienably to the Jews. This was a decision of capital importance for the future: its consequences still dominate the economic life of Israel.

As one might imagine, Herzl's life during these years consisted of continual journeys, unending discussions, difficult negotiations, dashed hopes, and a precarious personal life. He was obliged to write his articles for the *Neue Freie Presse* hastily between trains and congresses, usually on subjects that had nothing to do with Zionism. His home life was sad because his wife neither understood nor approved of what he was doing. It is incredible that during this period he found the time and strength to write a novel. But in 1902 he published *Altneuland*—"Old New Country"—a work of "political fiction" describing the regenerated Palestine of the future. Alphonse Daudet may have given him the idea. In 1895 Herzl had explained the basis of the Jewish state to Daudet, and he had suggested, "Why not write a novel? You could say even more in a novel."

Like any work of prophecy, *Altneuland* contains naïvetés and mistaken predictions. Yet, how many passages are proof of an extraordinary foresight! How accurate he was in describing Haifa, for example, or the new city of Jerusalem, or the "new society" founded on co-operation. But on the central point, Herzl's vision would differ tragically from reality. In *Altneuland*, Israel is restored without warfare or the shedding of a drop of blood, all because of the cheerfulness of the Jews, the satisfaction of the Arabs, and the benevolent tolerance of the world. Herzl's innate generosity deceived him. He had too much confidence in men and nations.

Herzl, perhaps like all visionaries of his type, had scarcely any idea of how long it would take to achieve what he thought of as obvious. After the first Congress at Basel, he estimated that the establishment of a Jewish state would take twenty to fifty years. In *Altneuland*, the task required only two decades. As time passed, Herzl was increasingly dominated by a desperate sense of urgency. Pogroms were multiplying in Eastern Europe. Every humiliation, every murder of the people whom he now considered his own touched him to the heart. Before anything else, these poor people must be saved—these women destined to be raped, these men who would die in jail or in the burning ruins of their hovels, these children whose heads the Cossacks would laughingly bash against a wall. In the most literal sense it was a question of life and death. Herzl wrung his hands at his own helplessness.

He was indignant at the sheepish or frightened indifference of too many middle-class Jews. He invented his own epitaph: "Here lies the man who thought too highly of the Jews."

As a thinker as well as a man of action, he was sometimes tempted to retreat into dreams. "Let us flee into the clouds," he wrote to Bernard Lazare. But then he added, "yet what would become of the poor beggars whom we would like to have rescued from the mud?" This was the worry that tormented him. What could he do to save these poor, beaten people? He felt responsible for their suffering and death. How could he end it? If Palestine was out of reach for the moment, must he not find a temporary haven for the unfortunates swept from their homes by the winds of hatred? Instead of the Holy Land, Herzl was willing to accept any other country: Cyprus, for example, which belonged to England, or a zone in the Sinai peninsula.

In 1902, he was summoned to London by Lord Hereford, president of the Royal Commission that was preparing a report on alien immigration into Britain. As the condition of the Jews in Russia and Rumania worsened, a growing number of them came knocking on England's door. Herzl was called in as an expert to testify before the commission, of which Lord Rothschild was a member.

In London he lunched at Rothschild's home. The conversation began badly. The elderly lord feared that Herzl would say something in his testimony that might damage the reputation of the Jews in the eyes of the British Parliamentarians. Was not it already being rumored that the Jews had influenced the European press to side with the Boers? By the time coffee was served, however, the tension had lessened. Where could a Jewish colony be founded? Herzl mentioned Cyprus, Sinai, and the south of Palestine, which was then under Egyptian domination. Lord Rothschild spoke of Uganda. A few days later, Herzl's testimony was well received by the commission. Lord Rothschild, definitely interested, had promised to submit to Joseph Chamberlain, the colonial minister, Herzl's memorandum outlining a plan for admitting Jewish emigrés to Cyprus or Egyptian territory.

As he had tried to dazzle the sultan with the prospect of a finanical renewal of Turkey, and the kaiser with a German protectorate in Palestine, Herzl launched an idea of historic importance in his conversations first with Rothschild and then with Chamberlain, whom he met in October, 1902. The idea was to reinforce Great Britain's position in the Near East through Jewish colonization. If a strong, dynamic, hardworking—and grateful—Israelite people could be installed under

British aegis at the crossroads of three continents and on the road to India, would this not be the ace of trump for the British Empire?

Herzl explained this idea to Chamberlain, and then to the prime minister. The Cypriot solution was discarded, because it was already apparent that the Greek and Turkish populations, embroiled as they were, could hardly be expected to welcome the intrusion of a third element. The Egyptian territories remained. The El Arish region in the Sinai peninsula was certainly a desert but it could be irrigated, and the viceroy of Egypt, Lord Cromer, was not at first opposed to the project. But after long wrangling, a committee of experts decided that this land could be made habitable only by an enormous and expensive irrigation system; the project was abandoned. As a matter of fact, technical problems were merely a mask for political ones: the Egyptian government had no wish to see a Jewish colony on its lands, even if these lands were only desert.

Another failure! It was 1903, a terrible year for Russian Jews. A fearful pogrom erupted in Kishinev on the eve of Passover. Forty-five were killed, more than one thousand wounded, fifteen hundred houses leveled, and there was widespread looting. The czar's minister of the interior, von Plehve, waited two days before putting a stop to this massacre. The Kishinev Jews had offered no resistance. In Odessa, however, where a pogrom was being openly prepared, a youth of twenty-three named Vladimir Jabotinsky organized a self-defense corps with the help of one Meier Dizengoff. Jabotinsky was to become Zionism's most powerful and lucid thinker after Herzl. As for Dizengoff, who would have imagined in 1903 that he would become the founder and first mayor of Tel Aviv?

Herzl, overcome by the bloody events in Kishinev, made a decision for which he would later be bitterly reproached. He went to see von Plehve, not so much to plead the cause of Russian Jews as to obtain from this implacable anti-Semite some help for Jewish emigration from Russia. He wanted to enlist anti-Semitism in the service of Zionism. Jabotinsky would try to do the same in Poland on the eve of World War II.

Von Plehve, once chief of police and now minister of the interior, had been either the accomplice or the instigator of every anti-Jewish atrocity since 1880. Groups of vagrants such as the "Black Hundreds" pillaged freely under police protection. Only after a long struggle with his conscience did Herzl approach this man, as Moses had once appeared before Pharaoh to demand the liberation of his people.

He proposed to von Plehve and to Witte, the minister of finance, that the Russian government should first authorize the development of the Zionist movement in Russia, and secondly should encourage Jewish emigration. ("But naturally we encourage it," joked Witte, "with kicks.") Herzl also asked that the czar intervene with the Sublime Porte to obtain a charter for the colonization of Palestine. Strange conversations, in which the czarist hierarchy could unblinkingly listen to such proposals as this: "If it were possible to drown six or seven million Jews in the Black Sea, that would be the perfect solution," and at the same time recognize that the pogroms were giving Russia a bad name in Europe, and that therefore a massive Jewish emigration could have favorable results.

But nothing concrete came out of these meetings. Von Plehve's chief aim, doubtless his only aim, had been to neutralize Herzl and the Zionist Congress. If their attacks against Russia could be stopped, then perhaps one could look into the matter. . . . But the sixth Congress, meeting at Basel in August, 1903, was characterized by an outburst of opposition to Herzl, and his opponents were essentially the delegates of Russian Jewry.

Between times, an event of great importance occurred. The British government officially offered Herzl and the Zionists a territory to colonize in Uganda. Herzl knew that such a proposal would be badly received by the Congress. He also knew that his visit to von Plehve had given rise to bitter criticism. Weizmann condemned this step as "humiliating and utterly senseless." The Democratic Faction was angered by the vain pursuit of a "phantasmagorical diplomatic victory." Ahad Ha'am returned to the lists to denounce Herzl's Westernism, and to point out that the Palestinian utopia of *Altneuland* appeared to be a Jewish state without Jewish culture.

Herzl was expecting a rough time when he arrived in Basel. Exhausted and ill with serious heart trouble, he had resolved to fight for the acceptance of Uganda as an interim solution. The Committee of Zionist Action allowed itself to be convinced, as did a number of important delegates whom Herzl assembled before the opening of the Congress. Among these Yehiel Tchlenov, who was a leader of Russian Judaism and of *Hoveve Zion*, hailed the offer of Uganda as the first historic event since the destruction of the Temple.

The debate opened in the plenary session of the Congress with a speech by Herzl. In horrifying terms he painted the fate of Eastern European Jews, the bloodshed, the hopeless flight of the survivors, the Turkish refusal to help, the failure of the Egyptian and Cypriot projects. But now that all doors were closed, Great Britain in one generous gesture had just opened the way. Could they possibly refuse? A great cheer was the answer.

So it seemed that the matter was settled. Max Nordau, taking the floor in Herzl's support, made some remarks that were perhaps ill-advised. Uganda, he declared, would be a *Nachtasyl*, a "night's lodging," for refugees from persecution who could wait there until they could find their final home in Palestine. There were some contrary opinions. The Russian delegates rose and attacked the proposal obstinately, vehemently. Palestine or nothing! The survivors of Kishinev were more determined than all the rest. And as is usual in such debates, grievance was added to grievance in increasingly harsh language: to accept the British offer would be to betray the program of 1897, to abandon the Zionist ideal. Besides, as the Mizrachi, the religious right, announced itself in favor of Uganda, the essentially Russian left grew all the more stubborn in its opposition.

The motion submitted to a vote at the Congress did not even ask that Uganda be definitely accepted as a place to settle. It was limited to sending a commission to study the matter. The motion passed with a vote of 295 in favor, 178 opposed, and a hundred abstentions. And then followed a pathetic scene. The Russian delegates solemnly rose and left the room. In a chamber nearby they wept for "lost Palestine," and some intoned the prayers for the dead. When Herzl came in, wishing to speak to them, a voice cried, "Traitor!"

It was a terrible moment for Herzl. He had to make the wrenching effort to regain these hearts that had closed to him. Hour after hour he repeated that there was no question of abandoning or betraying the Zionist program. The objective was still a Jewish state in Palestine. He begged his comrades to keep faith in him. At last the protesters agreed to return. Herzl made the adjournment speech, which was to be his last.

The study commission created by the resolution went to Uganda. It was composed of two Jews and an Englishman, Commander Gibbons. Their report was cloudy and rather discouraging. They concluded that at most twenty thousand pioneers could be accommodated by the territory in question at the foot of the Mau-Mau mountains, and only after considerable effort and heavy expense. The seventh Zionist Congress, meeting at Basel in 1905, definitely rejected the proposal.[4] But Herzl was not there to hear the vote.

Physically broken and profoundly discouraged, he gave himself another year to achieve his aims or abandon them. He went to see the grand duke of Baden and took up the thread of his correspondence with von Plehve, but Germany and Russia turned their backs. From the Jews there was only opposition, contradictory at that. The English Jew Lucien Wolf conducted a campaign against Zionism in *The Times*, while the Russian Zionist leader, Menahem Ussischkin, threatened to provoke a schism in the movement by convoking a congress in Palestine. A Russian student, named Louban, fired on Nordau, fortunately without hitting him, during a Paris meeting. In January, 1904, Herzl was received in Rome by the king of Italy and the Pope. Victor Emmanuel gave him a sympathetic welcome and promised to intercede with the sultan. Pius X gave him a friendly but firm *non possumus*. In April, Herzl brought the Committee of Zionist Action to Vienna again, only to have to battle the opposition step by step for two days. But his heart ailment had grown worse, and on the evidence of those who saw him at this period, he knew that death was near.

He spent his last weeks in Vienna and at a little country resort, Edlach, writing, making new assignments to his colleagues, guiding the steps of Zionism. On July 2, he received a visit from Pastor Hechler, whose devotion had never faltered.

On July 3, 1904, Herzl died.

And what did he leave behind after eight years of combat that cost him his life? Not much, truly, if a legacy is limited to tangibles. There was the annual Congress, a permanent committee, a worldwide Zionist federation, a bank, and the *Keren Kayemet*. His attempts to find a quick solution to the Jewish problem had failed. Zionism itself seemed deeply split. The obstacles in the path of a return to Palestine seemed more insurmountable than ever.

What Herzl left not only to Judaism but also to the world was an impalpable thing capable of working miracles — an idea. The idea of embodying a civilization that had been disembodied for eighteen centuries; of giving a country back to a suffering and persecuted people. The greatness of the idea lay in its simplicity, and the greatness of the man who had conceived it and sacrificed everything for it was now part of the idea for which he had been the powerful but humble spokesman. Statesman without a state, king without a kingdom, Herzl nevertheless made a deeper mark on history than many a general. He had never sought prestige, so he obtained something better — the veneration of his people. In addition, the name of Theodor Herzl deserves the respect and gratitude of all people for whom the words "justice" and "humanity" have a meaning. In a world where brute force, hate, and falsehood so often play the decisive role, the nobility of his message and the unselfishness of his action shine out like a ray of light.

FOOTNOTES FOR CHAPTER 2

1. The three children born of this marriage were to die tragically. Two of them committed suicide, and the youngest daughter died in a concentration camp during World War II.
2. André Chouraqui. *Théodor Herzl.* Paris (Seuil), 1960, p. 93.
3. Cited by André Chouraqui, *op. cit.,* p. 160.
4. After this decision Israel Zangwill left the Zionist movement to found the Jewish Territorial Organization, which was supposed to look for land for Jewish colonization. The organization rejoined the Zionists after the Balfour Declaration was made.

3
THE
NEW
PROMISE

The years that followed Herzl's death were full of division, frustration, and impasse for Zionism. For the Jews of Eastern Europe, they were an endless voyage through a dark nightmare. In Palestine during this time the Jewish community did indeed continue to grow and it even began to transform the country, but very slowly, hampered by the arbitrary whim and corruption of the Ottoman administration.

Max Nordau refused to succeed Herzl. An executive committee of seven members was elected in 1905, presided over by an early Zionist, David Wolffsohn, who had also accompanied Herzl to Turkey and Palestine. Wolffsohn moved the Zionist headquarters from Vienna to Cologne, where he was director of a wood company. It was he who in 1900 had taken charge of the Jewish Colonial Trust. As president of the Zionist executive committee he tried to continue Herzl's policies. He seemed to be making some progress in his negotiations with the sultan when, in 1908, the Young Turks seized power in Constantinople.

Herzl's death had freed the Zionist left, right, and center to go their own ways, but the organization found itself principally torn between the "political" and the "practical" Zionists. The former, faithful to the line laid down by Herzl and to the Basel program, still believed that their essential objective was the Charter, that is, the international guarantee without which all colonization in Palestine would remain in jeopardy. Not that they were any more hostile to colonization than Herzl had been, but they quite rightly insisted that this necessary and salutary undertaking would be severely limited as long as the fate of Palestine depended on the nod or frown of the Ottoman ruler. They refused to "sneak into Palestine by the back door." They thought that the Jews should not migrate to Palestine until they were assured of finding a homeland where they could settle en masse by lawful right.[1]

The "practical" opposition stated that on the contrary the Charter, desirable as it might seem, would be only a "scrap of paper," as Chaim Weizmann described it to the Congress of 1907. What he thought most important was first to settle in Palestine, cultivate the land, and create villages. In fact, these "practical" Zionists were essentially mystics. They dreamed of creating by the sweat of their brows "a model society founded on social, political, and economic equality."[2] It was no accident that most advocates of this idea were of Russian origin. Tolstoy's theory about regeneration through work, the revolutionary socialism stirring the czarist empire, and Biblical messianism were the three sources of their inspiration.

With the perspective of time, it is clear that both tendencies were right in important respects: the political tendency because, as Herzl saw so clearly and as events have so strikingly confirmed, the ultimate aim of Zionism had to be a legally constituted state; the practical tendency because the colonization of Palestine, the slow crystallization of a new society on the ancient soil, was indeed a necessary step in the long march of the Jewish people. But as usually happens, doctrinal and personal differences between the two parties degenerated into a violent quarrel. At the Congress of 1909 Wolffsohn had to agree to the formation of a presidium of which he was the nominal head, but which actually held him prisoner. In 1911, although the majority of the delegates wished to re-elect him, he refused and ceded the presidency to the candidate of the "practical" Zionists, Otto Warburg. Warburg, a famous botanist,[3] moved the Zionist headquarters to Berlin.

The influence of Ussischkin and above all of Weizmann was then preponderant, but the Zionist movement found itself in a state of permanent crisis, attacked from all sides.

At the beginning of the twentieth century there were about six million Jews in the Russian empire, including Poland. Russia's defeat by the ascendant imperialism of Japan, and the abortive revolution of 1905, shook the czarist regime profoundly. Russian authorities, as always, sought a diversionary action in anti-Semitism. A wave of pogroms engulfed the land, leaving a fearful train of ruin and death. All Zionist activity was outlawed and severely punished. The organization had only thirty thousand to forty thousand members in Russia. As Herzl had once done, Wolffsohn decided to plead the Jewish cause before P. A. Stolypin, the Russian chief of state. The Russians listened and promised to end the repression and the extortionary taxes, but they kept their promises no better than von Plehve had kept his.

Moreover, opposition to Zionism had hardened even in Jewish quarters. Orthodox rabbis continued to condemn even the idea of a state in Palestine. Certain "liberals" blamed Zionism for diverting toward a utopia in Palestine the very energies that should have been devoted to reforming the Russian state. This was, for example, the position of the lawyer Maxim Vinaver, one of the leaders of the Constitutional Democratic party, the Cadets. The Bund, proudly called in Yiddish the General Union of Jewish Workers of Russia and Poland, bitterly opposed Zionism in the name of a socialist ideal that many Zionists themselves shared. "What is the use of dreaming of a new society in Palestine," asked the Bundists, "when one ought to be created here in Europe?" Although Lenin and his group bitterly attacked the Bund as a bourgeois deviation, it nevertheless maintained itself at the heart of the Social Democratic party as a distinct organization with a program for Jewish cultural autonomy founded upon Yiddish, rather than Hebrew. The Bund rained its harshest blows on the Zionists, accusing them of betraying the proletariat and deserting the class struggle. The Polish and Russian Jews who emigrated to the United States and Great Britain at the start of the twentieth century were largely members of the Bund. They brought their anti-Zionism with them and transmitted it to English and American labor movements.

Against this backdrop of fierce internal disputes and pogroms, with their cortege of fire, theft, and death, the Pan-Russian Zionist convention opened in Helsinki in November, 1906. It was the proving ground for the mastery, personal magnetism, and eloquence of the twenty-six-year-old Vladimir Jabotinsky.[4] It was he who drew up the Helsinki Program that the convention adopted. It stated two principles: first, that the Jews of Russia must put an end to the Diaspora, for there was no salvation for them except in a state they created, in Palestine, where they would be masters of their fate; second, that they must organize in the heart of the czarist empire to fight for their rights as men and citizens, win recognition for their cultural originality, and obtain the legal status of a national minority, while waiting and working for the return. This was a synthesis of Herzl's doctrine and the practical necessities of a desperate situation. Jabotinsky gave a divided Zionism the means of overcoming its contradictions by attacking immediate and long-range problems at the same time.

Who was this young tribune? His name would henceforth be interwoven with the history of Zionism. "The Conquistador of the Promised Land"[5] was born at Odessa and conformed as little as Herzl to the prototype of the traditional Eastern European Jew. He had an essentially Russian education, loved poetry and literature, and had been brought up on the works of Pushkin, Lermontov, Turgenev, and

Tolstoy. He had an extraordinary talent for languages, and had found it child's play to learn German, Italian, French, Spanish, English, and Polish; then he learned Yiddish and Hebrew. At the age of eighteen he left Russia; on his way west he experienced a profound shock when he saw the ghettos of Galicia and Hungary for the first time. He discovered Western Europe with complete delight, particularly Italy, where he spent three years. He studied Roman law, philosophy, and sociology, the works of Labriola and Benedetto Croce, and became passionately interested in the history of the *risorgimento*, Mazzini, and Garibaldi. But most of all, he plunged happily into Italian life, wandering tirelessly through the old streets of Rome and making friends with those instinctively wise people. He spoke not only Italian but the dialect of Rome as well. He wrote poetry in Italian and translated some of Chekhov and Gorky into Italian. The Odessa newspapers published his chronicles of Italian life under the by-line "Egal," or "Altalena."

A career as a writer and Russian journalist opened up for him when he returned to Odessa in 1901. The next year, Gorky expressed his admiration for one of Jabotinsky's poems. But in 1902 the Russian police arrested him on the grounds that while in Italy he had written articles in the socialist organ *Avanti*. Thus he discovered the virulence of anti-Semitism. He reacted by becoming interested in Hebrew culture and Zionism. He translated a poem by Bialik from Hebrew into Russian. And when the pogroms threatened to reach Odessa, he naturally found himself with Dizengoff at the head of a self-defense movement. He now became a militant Zionist, a delegate to the sixth and seventh congresses, and a member of the Helsinki convention. He traveled far and wide between Saint Petersburg and Odessa and spoke at innumerable meetings. He was opposed by the Bund, by anti-Zionist Jews, and by Russian anti-Semites — a coalition that twice (in 1906 and 1907) barred his election to the Duma after energetic campaigns.

In the following years Jabotinsky aroused contradictory passions. But everyone who knew him, even his fiercest adversaries, were susceptible to his extraordinary charm and to the irresistible attraction of this man whose plain face was transfigured the moment he began to speak.[6] His speeches, his articles, and his books demonstrated his innate gift for clarifying the most complex problems and reducing them to memorable formulas. He had a sure eye and an intellectual honesty that were sometimes shocking, the ability to reason precisely, and a profoundly human liberalism supported by a vast knowledge of history, philosophy, and literature. Jewish patriot, European writer, polished representative of the Russian intelligentsia at the turn of the century—Jabotinsky was all of these. His powerful personality synthesized the East and the West, Biblical tradition and modern thought. And another synthesis: this mystic had his feet on the ground; he could pick out the essential and stick to it tenaciously.

A spirit so vigorous had to try to surmount the divisive quarrels of Zionism. The proof is the Helsinki convention, and the fact that from 1905 onward—unlike most of the Russian militants—Jabotinsky energetically supported the "political" Zionists, while taking an equally firm stand in favor of the pioneer movement that urged the immediate colonization of Palestine.

Although the Russian revolution of 1905 had been abortive, the 1908 revolution in Turkey raised the hopes of the Zionists, particularly because the Young Turk movement had been born in Salonika, an Ottoman city with a large Jewish population. A certain number of Ottoman Jews had played a role in the beginning of the movement. The Zionist organization immediately established an office in Constantinople, directed by Victor Jacobson. Having spent a year in Vienna studying the question of national minorities in the Austro-Hungarian empire, Jabotinsky went to Turkey and Palestine in 1908, and the next year settled in Constantinople at the request of David Wolffsohn. In the Turkish capital he assumed the direction of a Zionist propaganda network that included newspapers in French, the *Jeune Turc* and *Aurore;* in Judeo-Spanish, *El Judio;* and in Hebrew, *Ha-Mevasser.*

Unhappily, the Young Turks soon disappointed the Zionists. Once masters of a state in which seven million Turks dominated fourteen million Arabs, Armenians, Greeks, Kurds, Druses, Jews, and so forth, they proved no less conservative and obstinate than Abdul Hamid in their views on national minorities. They were no more receptive than the sultan they had deposed to the idea of a largely autonomous Jewish Palestine.

As the chief of propaganda, Jabotinsky found himself in a tight spot. For tactical reasons, as a matter of prudence, and because it was the official policy of the Zionist organization, he should only advocate free immigration to Palestine and the cultural independence of the Jewish community there. But he was firmly devoted to Herzl's doctrine and this seemed far too little to ask, while for the Young Turks it was far too much. An unfortunate incident compromised everything. A member of the Zionist directorate, J. H. Kann, published a brochure in which he said flatly that a Jewish state should be created under a vague Ottoman suzerainty. Jabotinsky could only approve of this thesis, yet he was obliged to oppose it because it affronted the already hostile Young Turks. He resigned in May, 1909. Wolffsohn, paralyzed by the internal contradictions of the movement, could not help him. Jabotinsky left Turkey with a rich fund of knowledge about what he would later describe as "the historical absurdum called the Ottoman Empire,"[7] and a conviction that only the breakup of that worn-out empire would permit a solution to the problem of Palestine.

Victor Jacobson, who was born in Russia and educated in Germany, still hoped that in spite of Herzl's failures in German diplomacy, the kaiser's influence with the Turks might be turned to Zionist advantage. Jewish propaganda in Turkey quite often had a Germanophile tone that did not go unnoticed in the West. The correspondent of *The Times* at Constantinople published a number of articles in 1911 and 1912 accusing the Zionists in Turkey of conducting a pro-German, anti-Russian, anti-British campaign. Sir Gerald Lowther, the British ambassador, called the attention of the foreign office to certain articles that appeared in the *Jeune Turc* (after Jabotinsky's departure), expressing a marked hostility to Russia and England.

Russian Jews understandably hated the country and the regime that made their lives hell on earth, and this hatred was matched by that of the Young Turks for the czarist empire. As for the Jews at Salonika who had taken part in the Young Turks's rebellion, they were also violently anti-Russian, and though they were not Zionists, they nonetheless compromised Zionism in the eyes of Western observers.

All this finally gained Zionism the reputation of being a pro-German movement. Wolffsohn and Nordau were aware of the danger and tried to combat it by publishing letters in *The Times* and by making public declarations at the Congress, but much harm had been done. And in certain circles in England it was said that any support for Zionism "would probably cost us the confidence of the best elements of the Arab World."[8] This was not the last time the Arab argument would be heard.

Although in certain countries, notably in England, Zionism was thought of as a more or less conscious instrument of German policy, the movement was in the gravest difficulties in Germany itself. The imperial government had not shown the slightest interest in Zionism since Herzl's last meeting with Wilhelm II. The kaiser had renounced all interest in Palestine lest he arouse the chauvinism of the Young

Turks and weaken Turko-German relations. The Union of German Rabbis fought Zionism tooth and nail. Many German Jews, particularly the influential leaders of the community, the *Kaiserjuden*, rivaled the Prussians in German patriotism. The *Hilfsverein der deutschen Juden*, an official organization supported by the German authorities, was willing to see something done in Palestine, but much more for the glory of Germany than for the Hebraic renaissance. This became quite clear when the creation of the Technical Institute at Haifa aired the following conflict.

Ahad Ha'am and the Russian Zionist Shmarya Levin had, in 1913, obtained the then enormous sum of one hundred thousand rubles from the Russian multimillionaire Vissotzky, "the tea king," to establish a *technicum* in Palestine. Money in hand, they set out to buy the land and to obtain the necessary authorization from the Sublime Porte. At the request of the *Hilfsverein*, the undersecretary of the German foreign office, Arthur Zimmermann, intervened with the government at Constantinople. When the founding committee met at Berlin in June, 1914, a violent argument broke out between the *Kaiserjuden* and the Zionists over whether classes at the Technical Institute should be given in German or Hebrew. The committee finally chose German, but the teachers in Palestine rebelled and went on strike. Thereupon, the *Hilfsverein* withdrew its financial support. The Zionist organization was still able to establish the Institute, thanks to funds provided by American Jews. The incident marked the rupture between traditional German Judaism and Zionism, and the latter found itself in the uncomfortable position of being regarded as pro-German in London and anti-German in Berlin.

In France, where the trouble stirred up by the Dreyfus affair was only slowly dying down, Zionism remained weak. The *Alliance Israélite Universelle* contributed positively to the improvement of Palestine, but the leaders of French Judaism were still for the most part hostile to the idea of the Jewish state. They were willing to sympathize with, and even actively support the undertakings of "practical" Zionism, but they did not intend to compromise themselves with "political" Zionism.

This was also the attitude of Jewish leaders in England such as Claude Montefiore and Lucien Wolff. Their opposition to Zionism stiffened in 1905 when the Balfour government voted the Aliens Act to restrict immigration to Great Britain. Its principal aim, as the Parliamentary debates show, was to stop the influx of Eastern European

Jews who were seeking refuge in England from the horror of the pogroms. Between 1881 and 1905 an estimated one hundred thousand Jewish immigrants had been admitted. The solidly established, assimilated Jewish community of England viewed this massive immigration with alarm, particularly because of the xenophobic, anti-Semitic reactions that it was provoking. Having missed the point that Herzl's brand of Zionism would have offered a solution to this unhappy problem by opening Palestine to Russian, Polish, and Rumanian refugees, the Jewish leaders in England reproached Zionism for aggravating the problem. According to them, to insist on Jewishness, to speak of a nation and a state, was to endanger not only the latecomers, but the Jewish community already established in England. In 1909, twenty-five Jewish notables, among them Leopold de Rothschild, Claude Montefiore, Sir Robert Waley Cohen, and Sir Osmond d'Avigdor Goldsmid, published a strong protest against the creation of Zionist societies by students at certain universities. The Zionist doctrine, they declared specifically, could only "tend to separate Jews from other Englishmen," and "arouse suspicions in all social classes, particularly among the workers, as to the patriotism of British Jews." The chief rabbi of London, Hermann Adler, defended this point of view.

Chaim Weizmann was thirty when he settled in Manchester in 1904. A great chemist, he had been born in White Russia but educated in Germany and Switzerland, had received his doctorate at the University of Freiburg, and had taught at Geneva. Among Russian students and revolutionary emigrés he had brushed with Marxists, notably Georgi Plekhanov. A confirmed Zionist, he was opposed to Herzl from the first: he was among those who criticized the founder of Zionism for vainly seeking a Charter guaranteed by the great powers. He was utterly opposed to the idea of colonizing Uganda. Finally, as a mover in the Democratic Faction, he criticized the "rightist tendencies" of the Mizrachi, who supported Herzl.

As a scientist, Weizmann distrusted sudden insights like Herzl's and long-range views like Jabotinsky's. Herzl struck him as "naïve," Jabotinsky as a "quixotic, utterly un-Jewish boy wonder." He held that history, philosophy, and literature were merely "vague and attractive subjects," that "there are never any quick solutions to great historical problems," that things could only be done slowly, gradually, empirically.[9] Still, Weizmann had a deep and burning faith in the future of a renewed Eretz Israel. He knew how to communicate this faith to others, for although he did not have the oratorical talents of

Herzl or Jabotinsky, he could nevertheless assert himself powerfully in a conversation. He was at once positive and impassioned, dignified and persuasive.

When Chaim Weizmann came to Manchester, scarcely able to speak English and in financial straits, neither he nor anyone else could have imagined that thirteen years later he would be the chief architect of a British decision on which the future of Palestine and, to a certain extent, the future of the British Empire would depend. Absorbed in his research on fermentation, he found almost nothing to encourage him outside the laboratory. English Jews, either anti-Zionist or in favor of the colonization of Uganda, had no sympathy for Weizmann. Then, in 1906, Charles Dreyfus, president of the Zionist Society of Manchester and director of an important chemical factory, introduced Weizmann to Lord Balfour. An electoral campaign was in full swing, and Balfour had been accused of anti-Semitism because of the Alien Act that he had submitted to Parliament the previous year. He wanted to explain his position. At the close of the interview Balfour said to the young scientist, "One day, you will be a force." The British statesman would do more than any one else to make this prophecy come true.

Weizmann first visited Palestine in 1907. To anyone who has seen Israel today, it is hard to imagine the desolation of Turko-Arabian Palestine in those days, without trees or greenery, a land where arid sands gave way to rotten marshes, a country abandoned for centuries to dust and malaria, where miserable little villages existed under the drooping eye of an indolent, venal administration.

In a population of about six hundred thousand there were some eighty thousand Jews. Some, the *Halukah*, were concentrated in the holy cities: Jerusalem, where they were in the majority, Safed, Hebron, Tiberias, Haifa, and Jaffa. Cut off from the world and deep in the study of the Torah and the Talmud, they got by on charity and on collections made for them in Europe and America. Weizmann was appalled to find in Jerusalem "a miserable ghetto, neglected and unworthy." Other Jews in the colonized villages had begun to renew the soil. These colonies were strung from one end of the country to the other, from Metulla in the north to Ness Ziona in the south. Laudable though their efforts and successes were, they had a mere ten thousand inhabitants. Worse still, they employed almost nothing but Arab labor, the Jews having confined themselves to directing and supervising the farming. This was not in line with the aims of Zionism, which sought to create a

Jewish economy with Jewish labor, and morally it was remote from the ideal of the regeneration of man — more important even than renewing the earth.

This is why the password, "Conquest through work," *Kibbush Ha-avoda,* launched by the young Russian pioneers who came to Palestine after the abortive revolution of 1905, took on historical significance. Manual labor was not just a necessity for them, it was a moral and social imperative. As their number grew they exerted a greater and greater pressure on the Jewish colonists to hire them to do most or all of the day labor jobs on their farms. "We wanted to work with our hands and build the country ourselves," wrote David Ben Gurion, "not turn ourselves into overseers by letting the Arabs work in our place."[10] Groups of *halutzim,* or pioneers, soon organized to offer their services to individual landowners, or, preferably, to clear land acquired by the National Jewish Fund and the Jewish Colonization Association. They cleared away the underbrush and the rocks, drained and dried marshes; once this acreage was ready to be planted, they turned it over to new immigrants and started again somewhere else, always in the harshest conditions, for little pay, and under the double menace of malaria and marauding Arabs.

Largely owing to the unflagging enthusiasm of these pioneers, Palestinian colonization took an upward turn in the years before World War I, and acquired some of its enduring traits. The first kibbutz was founded in 1909 at Deganiah, at the southern end of Lake Tiberias, and that same year on the sterile dunes by the lake, sixty Jews from Jaffa, led by Meier Dizengoff, founded what would become Tel Aviv. To defend themselves against the inevitable raiders, the colonists recruited guards amongst themselves, *shomrim,* who formed a federation called *Hashomer.* This was the nucleus from which the Jewish militia would arise, and eventually the Israeli army.

In the last months of peace in 1914 (a precarious peace, since the Balkans were in an incessant state of agitation), the Jewish population grew to one hundred thousand. Collective villages sprang up beside the ancient colonies. A secondary school (*gymnazium*) was founded at Jaffa, and as has been noted, the Technical Institute of Haifa was about to begin work. The foundation of the Hebrew University was under way under the initiative of Chaim Weizmann, Ahad Ha'am, the great bacteriologist Paul Ehrlich, James de Rothschild, Martin Buber, and others. A site for it had been bought on the summit of Mount Scopus near Jerusalem.[11]

And so the land that had slept for so many centuries began to stir again in this vigorous development that joined the idealism of youth to the practical sense of organizers such as Arthur Ruppin, delegate of the Zionist organization to Palestine. The work both confirmed Herzl's doctrine, and vindicated the theses of practical Zionism. Ruppin declared at the Congress of Vienna in 1913 that "we must reach our goal, not with a 'charter' but with practical work in Palestine." In fact, however, the threat of Ottoman domination and Arab hostility weighed heavily against this brilliant progress. The Turks watched uneasily as the number and activity of the colonists increased. And the Jews, whether they were actually Ottoman subjects (but still "infidels"), or retained their Russian or German nationalities (and the small protection of their respective consuls), were only tolerated, and owed what security they had to the weakness of the administration and often to the greed of its functionaries who had to be bought with baksheesh. As for the Arabs, they had not put up the least resistance to the early colonies, which either offered them a chance for paid work, or else were fruitful targets for thieves and pillagers. But the wave of *halutzim* and the *Kibbush Ha-avoda* movement began to worry them. Frustrated by the Young Turks, nascent Arab nationalism tended toward anti-Zionism.[12] As early as 1912 Ahad Ha'am, after a trip to Palestine, noted a certain opposition by the Arabs to the acquisition of land by Jews, and in 1914, the Zionist executive committee thought it necessary to send one of its members, Nahum Sokolow, to make contact with Arab officials in Egypt and Syria.

It was obvious that the work of colonization, as energetic and well directed as it might be, was subject to political fluctuations and to the will of whoever ruled Palestine, as well as to the good or evil intentions of a part of Palestine's population. As Herzl so plainly understood, the work of colonization could be fulfilled only if it became legal. There had to be a political solution; the events of 1914–18 would permit one to be sketched out.

When war broke out in August, 1914, an already weakened and divided Zionist movement was split into many branches. The greatest number of Jews lived in Russia. The *yishuv* was in the Ottoman Empire. Headquarters were in Berlin. Zionist financial institutions such as the Jewish Colonial Trust and the *Keren Kayemet* were based in London. Of the six members of the executive committee, two were German (one of them the president, Otto Warburg), three were Russian, one

Austro-Hungarian; the twenty-six members of the permanent council included thirteen Germans and Austro-Hungarians, seven Russians, two Englishmen (one being Weizmann, now a British subject), one Frenchman, one Belgian, one Dutchman, and one Rumanian.

Feelings were no less divided than nationalities. Most of the Russians hated the discriminatory czarist regime and the pogroms so much that they longed for a victory for the Central Powers even more fervently than the Germans did. They maintained, not without cause, that if Zionism supported the Allies, it would seriously endanger the Jewish community of Palestine, which was defenseless against the Turks. The *yishuv*, they said, ran the risk of being massacred by the Ottomans, as the hapless Armenians had been.

Only a minority, in which Chaim Weizmann and Vladimir Jabotinsky found themselves side by side, dared to say that Zionism could triumph only when the Ottoman Empire was liquidated, and that consequently the Jews ought to support the Allies.

Jabotinsky was at Bordeaux as correspondent for the newspaper *Russkiya Vyedomosti* when he learned from an official wall poster that Turkey had entered the war on the side of Germany and Austro-Hungary. From that moment, he later wrote,[13] his mind was made up, knowing what he did about Turkey. He had to contribute to the Allied war effort and put an end to the sovereignty of the Sublime Porte in Palestine. He immediately envisaged the creation of a Jewish legion to fight on the side of the Allies, with its own flag and insignia. It would take an active part in dismantling the Turkish empire and with victory, it would establish the rights of the Jewish people.

At Alexandria he soon met one of the most astonishing characters in Zionist history, Josef Vladimirovitch Trumpeldor, a Jew from the Caucasus, a sort of Scandinavian colossus and the only Palestinian officer in the Russian army. Though not yet twenty-five during the Russo-Japanese War, Trumpeldor had fought in Asia, where he lost an arm. Captured by the Japanese and freed after the Russian defeat, he had made his way to Palestine and joined the kibbutz at Deganiah. Like Jabotinsky he was Russian-educated, and in spite of the *numerus clausus* had studied law and medicine. A generous man, full of the socialist ideals of his country and his era, he immediately got on with Jabotinsky, who was a cosmopolitan intellectual but who was also profoundly Russian.

The first negotiations concerning the creation of a Jewish legion in the East took place in Egypt, where Sir Ronald Graham, adviser to the Egyptian government, at first looked favorably on the idea. But under the influence of Sir John Grenfell Maxwell, commander in chief of British forces in Egypt, the enterprise was quickly sidetracked: English authorities only allowed the formation of a transport unit called the Zion Mule Corps. The six hundred muleteers, under the command of Lt. Col. John Henry Patterson, assisted by Trumpeldor, were transferred to Gallipoli and played a glorious role in the disappointing Dardanelles campaign.

But Jabotinsky could not be satisfied with this partial solution. Realizing that he had to interest the government of some great power in the Palestinian question, and at the political level rather than the military, he thought first of France, a country he knew and loved well (in contrast to Weizmann).

Jabotinsky was aware that certain French political circles attentively followed events in the East in the hope of winning a vast new sphere of influence for France once peace was made. This sphere would include Syria and Lebanon, and possibly Palestine; this was the notion of "Integral Syria," to which Jean Leygues was tenaciously attached.

"The Zionist aspirations tend not so much to full independence — at least not for the present — as to a sort of 'Charter' including guarantees of self-government and privileges for colonization," Jabotinsky later wrote in *Turkey and the War*. "Such a Charter could be granted, theoretically speaking, by any liberal government, be it French or English."

In this state of mind he obtained an interview in 1915 with the French foreign minister, Théophile Delcassé. He had previously conveyed his intentions to Weizmann, who was opening negotiations with the British authorities. Unfortunately Delcassé was unreceptive. He did not think that Palestine could be included in the French sphere of influence in the Near East. The interview had no result.[14]

So, like Weizmann, Jabotinsky had to turn to England. But he wanted to see Russia again, and he went there for three months. He found that the entire Russian Zionist movement had turned against him. "Your son ought to be hanged," said the Jewish leader Ussischkin to Vladimir's mother. Everywhere he was reproached for attempting to mobilize the Jews to serve their worst enemies, the Russian anti-Semites. And in fact, anti-Semitism in Russia was more virulent than ever. So-called Jewish spies were hanged by the dozens; entire villages were deported. And it was to serve this executioner-state, or at least its allies, that Jabotinsky wanted to enlist the Jews, without flinching at what Palestine might suffer! The aberration of a madman!

Without any doubt Jabotinsky must have had singular determination and an extraordinary will to persist in the plan that he deemed necessary. He left Russia brokenhearted, but resolved. He would never return. He went next to London where the French historian Charles Seignobos introduced him to Henry Wickham Steed, the editor of *The Times* and one of the most influential journalists of the time. He began work in close collaboration with Weizmann. The chemist and "Jabo," as he was called familiarly, shared an apartment in Chelsea.

Lord Derby, the minister of war, was greatly attracted by the idea of a regiment of Jewish volunteers incorporated in the British forces, but carrying the insignia of the Star of David. But such important military figures as Lord Kitchener were opposed, and so were the anti-Zionist British Jews. As for the poor Israelites of Whitechapel — struggling shopkeepers, tailors, furriers, most of them refugees from the hellish Russian pogroms, they were violently opposed to Jabotinsky. Ah, as Voltaire remarked, "being a prophet is a sorry profession." Vladimir had much leisure to meditate on this maxim after tumultuous meetings during which the Jewish masses spat upon him while the Judeo-British aristocracy disdainfully condemned his efforts and military officials threw obstacle after obstacle in his path, according to the time-honored technique of officialdom.

"When I try to use the [Jewish] regiment as a means of concentrating Jewish sympathies throughout the world on the idea of a complete victory for the Entente," he wrote to Balfour on November 16, 1917, "I believe I am performing a service, and rather than throwing obstacles in my path, Whitehall ought to support me. But instead of helping me, they do all they can to hinder my work and make a mockery of the Jewish regiment. They suppress even the name, and forbid any publicity."

But the year 1917 would bring two powerful motives for change: on the one hand, the Balfour Declaration, Britain's official blessing for Zionism; and on the other, the Russian Revolution. As soon as the czarist regime fell and Russia left the war, the psychological wall against which Jabotinsky had been throwing himself dissolved. Volunteers began to arrive and the hostility of the war office abated. The first Jewish battalion (the first Jewish military force since A.D. 135) marched from the city to Whitechapel on February 2, 1918, amidst acclamations. On the fourth, the "39th Regiment of the Royal Fusiliers" commanded by Col. Eliezer Margoline,[15] with thirty officers, of whom twenty were Jews, left for Palestine via France, Italy, and Egypt. Jabotinsky served as a noncommissioned officer. The regiment and its creator would arrive in Palestine in time to help conquer the Ottoman Empire.

But the crucial drama was being enacted in London on the political stage, or rather in the wings. Circumstances had divided the Zionist executive committee. The main office was theoretically in Berlin, but obviously it could remain in close touch only with the German and Austro-Hungarian branches. An office was created in Copenhagen, in neutral territory, and a "provisional" commission set up in the United States. This commission was headed by Louis Brandeis, the lawyer and judge whom President Woodrow Wilson named to the Supreme Court in 1916. In London, the executive committee was headed by Nahum Sokolow, but Weizmann soon assumed responsibility for negotiating with the British government.

Endowed with invincible tenacity and great persuasive talents, Weizmann was also served by his scientific achievements. His discoveries in Manchester included a process for making acetone by fermenting substances such as corn, and this process enabled the admiralty and armaments ministry to meet the demand for explosives. Without taking literally Lloyd George's joke that "acetone converted me to Zionism," it was clear that Weizmann's biochemical knowledge had opened many a door for him, notably those leading to Lloyd George and Winston Churchill.

The editor in chief of the *Manchester Guardian*, C. P. Scott, impressed by a conversation with Weizmann and aware as early as November, 1914, of the acuteness of the Jewish problem, introduced Weizmann into political circles.

In 1914, Prime Minister Asquith, a positive and phlegmatic man, was surprised to see Lloyd George — who had once said that he did not "give a damn for Jews" — suddenly become enthusiastic for the Zionist idea. He had underestimated the influence of Biblical tradition on this Presbyterian Welshman with his lively Celtic imagination. Herbert Samuel, later Lord Samuel, the only Jewish member of the government and a member of one of the oldest Jewish families in England, also astonished Weizmann by becoming a convinced Zionist.

As long as Turkey stayed out of the war, the British cabinet clung to its traditional policy, that is, the maintainance of the Ottoman Empire, for better or worse. But the moment Constantinople joined Berlin and Vienna, the dismemberment of that empire became one of the war aims of the Entente. The future of the territories to be taken away from the Sublime Porte had to be decided — a delicate and complex question since France also felt it had a role to play and interests to defend in that part of the world.

In a secret memorandum submitted to the cabinet in March, 1915, Herbert Samuel addressed himself to the issue: "If the war results in the breaking up of the Turkish empire in Asia, what should be Palestine's future?"

Would France annex it? he asked. "The establishment of a great European power so close to the Suez Canal would constitute a permanent and formidable menace to the essential lines of communication of the British Empire. . . . We can hardly believe that our relations with France, today excellent, will always be so."

Would Palestine then be left in Turkish hands? Samuel scarcely needed to remind his readers that the country had been virtually abandoned under Ottoman rule.

Could there be an international regime? Not only would such a regime, composed of representatives of various nations, be naturally impotent, but more to the point, Germany had already been most active in Palestine, which would make one fear that an international regime might lead to a German protectorate.

Should one plan to establish immediately an independent Jewish state in Palestine? Herbert Samuel did not think this solution was yet "ripe." Comprising only one sixth of the total population, the Jews would not be able to establish a viable government. "The dream of a prosperous Jewish state steadily improving, the home of a brilliant civilization, could vanish in a series of sordid conflicts with the Arab population. . . . To wish to fulfill the hope for a Jewish state a century too soon could well delay its realization for a number of centuries more."

The only possible solution was a British protectorate. Herbert Samuel emphasized the strategic importance of the port of Haifa. He spoke of the necessity of a special law for the holy places under the control of France, Russia, and the Vatican. He added: "I have received the assurance of Zionists and non-Zionists that this solution of the Palestinian question would be by far the best received by worldwide Jewish opinion. We hope that under a British regime, Jewish organizations would be furnished facilities for acquiring land, founding colonies, creating schools and religious institutions, and for co-operating in the economic development of the country, and that Jewish immigration, carefully regulated [would allow the Jews, once they became] the established majority in the country, to attain the self-government that the conditions of the time might justify."

Certainly, Samuel went on, "a country the size of Wales, made up largely of bare mountains and often without water" would not alone resolve the Jewish problem. But in time surely some three million people could settle there and thus diminish pressure in Russia. Finally he sketched out a number of arguments that have often been repeated since: Great Britain would have the gratitude of world Jewry. British public opinion would like seeing the Union Jack protecting the Holy Land. It would be wiser to look for compensations in Mesopotamia and Palestine than in Black Africa at the expense of the German colonies, lest Germany be provoked to lasting bitterness and a war of revenge.

Samuel's memorandum seemed to have no effect on Asquith, but Sir Edward Grey, the foreign minister, was more favorable. At the start of the next year, and despite the somewhat hostile indifference of the prime minister, he instructed his ambassadors in Paris and Petrograd to consult the French and Russian governments about the possibility of offering the Jews a sort of autonomous establishment in Palestine after the war. The formula was prudently vague (having after all been set down by Lucien Wolff, the British anti-Zionist leader) and it said nothing about whether the country would be in the French or British zone of influence. Nothing came of all this, for France and Russia refused to discuss it.

Lord Balfour came into the Asquith government in the ministerial reshuffle of June, 1915, as first lord of the admiralty. Weizmann was made his technical adviser. There, too, acetone served the Zionist cause: when Lloyd George came to power late in 1916, Weizmann found open doors at 10 Downing Street and at the foreign office. With the aid of Sokolow and the British Committee for Palestine, made up of Jews and non-Jews, he undertook to get the government to take a clear position on Palestine's future.

The need for taking such a stand appeared all the more urgent because during the first two years of the war Germany had skillfully captured the sympathy of Jews all over the world, and particularly those in America. For the three million Jews of America, who in large proportion had known the horrors of the ghetto, Russia was the enemy. German propaganda played up the correctness of the German soldiers toward the Jews, while the Russian armies unleashed their habitual atrocities wherever they went. As Turkey's powerful ally, Germany boasted of intervening—and did in fact intervene at various times—to prevent Constantinople from savagely repressing the *yishuv*. In 1915 the German chargé d'affaires in Constantinople, Konstantin von Neurath (later the "protector" of Bohemia and Moravia), was in constant touch with the Zionist bureau in Constantinople. By this intermediary, Berlin made known its sympathy for Jewish activities in Turkey, and German consuls in Palestine were instructed to give aid and comfort to Jewish immigrants, taking care, at the same time, not to offend the Turks.

One of the stakes in this game, as Berlin knew well, was the mass of American Jews, who could weigh heavily in the balance either to keep the United States neutral, or to bring it into war. Although Brandeis had always leaned toward France and England, opinion was divided, and the general Russophobia of the Jews disposed them toward Germany. A certain Committee for the East, *Komitee für den Osten*, created in Germany ostensibly to defend the interests of Eastern European Jews but in fact to organize pro-German propaganda in Jewish circles everywhere, sent an active agent, Isaac Straus, to the United States in 1915. The next year he founded the *American Jewish Chronicle*, a Germanophile magazine aimed at Jewish communities. The anti-Semitic atrocities committed by Russian troops furnished Straus with an inexhaustible source of material.

The relative success of German propaganda with American Jews was by no means the least factor that brought the British government to make a statement. Most probably it would have acted sooner had not two series of complicated events created obstacles and delays.

The first of these had to do with the rival claims of France and England in the Levant. Not until May, 1916, after secret negotiations carried out by Ambassador Georges Picot and Sir Mark Sykes, was an equally secret treaty concluded by the two governments. The Sykes-Picot Treaty ceded to France the land along the coast north of Haifa, while the port was to become a British enclave. England would also receive the south of Iraq from the Persian Gulf to just north of Baghdad. Palestine (minus Haifa and the north of Galilee) would be split off from the Ottoman Empire and governed separately as fixed in an accord between France, England, and Russia. Finally, the rest of the Levant would form "an Arab state, or a confederation of Arab states," with the understanding that France would dominate in Syria, and England in northern Iraq and east of the Jordan River in all matters of technical assistance and administration of the new states.

Neither the Zionists nor the Arabs were informed of this agreement, which, as is apparent, did not sin in the direction of excessive clarity. The future of Palestine, especially, remained most uncertain. While this was going on, the Russian Revolution of 1917 first brought to power liberal governments that hastened to disavow the anti-Semitism and anti-Zionism of the czarist regime, and next the Bolsheviks, who pulled Russia out of the war. For this reason, the fate of Palestine was to be settled not by the three powers, but by France and England alone.

Having given up the idea of an "integral Syria" and contenting itself with the sphere of influence granted by the secret treaty, France was unopposed to a British protectorate in Palestine. Besides, the government was well aware of the need to counter the German propaganda in American Jewish circles. Victor Basch, sent to the United States in 1916 by Briand and Poincaré, had insisted upon the growing importance of the Zionist movement. Pointing to Jewish hate and mistrust of Russia, he had suggested that the French government issue a declaration assuring French support for the viewpoint of the Palestinian Jews at the forthcoming peace conference.

In addition, when Nahum Sokolow visited Paris in May, 1917, he had no trouble getting into the Quai d'Orsay to explain the Zionist position. On June 4, the secretary general of the Quai, Jules Cambon, wrote him an official letter that, in the name of the government, assured him that France would work for the renaissance of the Jewish nation in the land from which it had been exiled. Carried immediately to Weizmann, this letter, one may suppose, helped overcome the final hesitation of the British Cabinet.

Then the second series of events—the opposition of the anti-Zionist British Jews—caused the cabinet to delay until almost the end of 1917. The opposition was led inside the cabinet itself by Edwin Montagu, secretary of state for India, and outside by the Conjoint Committee of Claude Montefiore and David L. Alexander. Balfour and Lloyd George were disconcerted. In spite of the confidence Weizmann inspired, they wondered if he were not indulging in wishful thinking. Would not it look rather ridiculous for His Majesty's government to be more Jewish than the Jews? On May 24, 1917, the Conjoint Committee published a long anti-Zionist declaration in *The Times*, to which Henry Wickham Steed himself responded. Twice, in September and October, the energetic intervention of Edwin Montagu squelched ideas for a declaration submitted by Lord Rothschild and Weizmann to Lord Balfour. Hairs were split, commas rearranged. On October 16, at the urging of Louis Brandeis, President Wilson's adviser, Colonel Edward

House, wired London that the President of the United States urged the British government at last to take a stand.

Finally, on November 2, 1917, following a private cabinet debate, Lord Balfour published, in the form of a letter addressed to Lord Rothschild, the declaration that still bears his name:

"His Majesty's Government view with favour the establishment[16] in Palestine of a national home for the Jewish people, and will use their best endeavours to facilitate the achievement of this object, it being clearly understood that nothing shall be done which may prejudice the civil and religious rights of existing non-Jewish communities in Palestine, or the rights and political status enjoyed by Jews in any other country."

After so many debates and passionate quarrels, Weizmann reacted with mixed feelings to this ambiguous text that reflected only too well the contradictions that trapped its authors.

The Balfour Declaration has inspired as many commentaries and interpretations as there are grains of sand on the beaches from Tel Aviv to Haifa. What exactly is a "national home?" And whatever it is, did they mean it should be founded *in* Palestine somewhere, or that Palestine *itself* would be the national home? What did the British government mean by "use their best endeavours?" Did it or did it not intend to play the role of protector? What was the significance of mentioning the "civil and religious" rights of the non-Jewish communities, but not their political rights? One could then, and one still can wrangle endlessly about these and many other points. The expressions used "were vague and ambiguous because they were supposed to be vague and ambiguous."[17] The British government meant to win all the moral and political advantage it could from the Declaration without tying its hands. Already it began to fear being torn between its Jewish policy and its Arab policy.

However, above and beyond all interpretations and doubts, it seems likely that the principal architects of the Declaration shared the viewpoint later enunciated by Lloyd George: "A Jewish state would not be organized immediately . . . [but] when the moment would come to grant representative institutions to Palestine, provided that the Jews in the meantime had used the opportunity afforded them by the idea of a national home, and if they had become the absolute majority of the population, Palestine would then become a Jewish State."[18] As early as December 2, 1917, Sir Robert Cecil, undersecretary of state for Balfour, declared, "We desire that Arab countries be left to the

Arabs, Armenia to the Armenians, and Judea to the Jews."

Mrs. Weizmann relates in her memoirs[19] that as soon as Sir Mark Sykes informed her husband of the decision the government had finally made, he "ran to Ahad Ha'am to tell him the news personally. . . . Then he came home with a small group of friends, and forming a circle we all danced in the library in the Hasidic manner." But the joy was not unmixed. Certain Zionist leaders, such as Tchlenov, were reticent. The anti-Zionist British Jews did not let their guard down. Claude Montefiore made it known that as president of the Anglo-Jewish Association he looked upon the Declaration "with grave and serious misgivings." A "League of British Jews" founded by Sir Philip Magnus, undertook to protest against the very idea of a Jewish nation. Its president, Lionel de Rothschild, approached Lord Beaverbrook (then minister of information) and appealed to him insistently "not to do anything that might encourage the idea of a Jewish National Home."[20]

However, the Declaration had a considerable impact among Polish, Russian, and German Jews, as well as those in America. For the first time a great power expressed its interest in the Zionist idea. That was the important thing, in spite of all the obscurities in the text.

The Declaration made Palestine "the twice-promised land," as Herzl had wished, and as the Basel program had proclaimed twenty years earlier. Henceforth the reconstruction of Palestine would be carried out under the guarantee of "public law."

The Balfour Declaration, a sudden reality after twenty years of effort—a time that doubtless seemed desperately long to those men who fought for it, but very short in the perspective of world history— was at once an end and a beginning: the end of what the passionate Herzl had thought of as a first stage to be accomplished in a few years; and the start of a new chain of actions and reactions that would last almost thirty years to the day until the powers of the world would recognize a "Home" no longer, but a State.

FOOTNOTES FOR CHAPTER 3

1. Leonard Stein. *The Balfour Declaration*. London, Valentine-Mitchell, 1961, p. 62.

2. Ben Gurion. *Regards sur le Passé*. Monaco, Éditions du Rocher, 1965, p. 19.

3. After World War I, he became the director of the experimental agricultural station at Rehovot.

4. Cf. Joseph Schechtman. *The Vladimir Jabotinsky Story*. Vol. I, "Rebel and Statesman," New York, 1956. Vol. II, "Fighter and Prophet," New York, 1961.

5. Anatole de Monzie. *Destins hors-série*. Paris, Éditions de France, 1927, pp. 169–87.

6. David Ben Gurion, a determined opponent of Jabotinsky, said to this writer in 1967, "He was the greatest Jewish orator."

7. Vladimir Jabotinsky. *Turkey and the War*. London, T. Fisher Unwin, Ltd. 1917, p. 142.

8. *The Times*, September 28, 1912.

9. This paragraph summarizes or quotes parts of Weizmann's autobiography, *Trial and Error*.

10. *Op. cit.*, p. 23.

11. The first meeting of the Committee for the Hebrew University was set for August 4, 1914. For obvious reasons it did not take place.

12. See George Antonius. *The Arab Awakening*. London, Hamish Hamilton, 1938.

13. Vladimir Jabotinsky. *The Story of the Jewish Legion*. New York, 1945. See also his *Turkey and the War*. London, 1917.

14. After the Balfour Declaration, Delcassé remarked to Paul Cambron, the French ambassador to London, that he was sorry not to have received Jabotinsky's suggestions more warmly.

15. Margoline, of Russian origin, had already served in the Australian army in Egypt and Flanders. A solemn, taciturn man, he was reluctant to accept this command. "I am afraid," he said. "Of what?" he was asked. "I am afraid of the Jews; one has to talk too much."

16. Weizmann suggested the word "re-establishment" in order to underline the historical continuity of the Jewish presence in Palestine.

17. John Marlowe. *Rebellion in Palestine*. London, 1946, p. 41.

18. Quoted by Herbert Sidebotham. *Great Britain and Palestine*. London, McMillan, 1937, p. 238.

19. Vera Weizmann. *The Impossible Takes Longer*. London, Hamish Hamilton, 1967, p. 78.

20. Stein, *op. cit.*, p. 566.

4
PALESTINE UNDER THE UNION JACK

Between 1914 and 1918, the Jewish community in the Ottoman province of Palestine was overwhelmed with physical and spiritual suffering. About half of the *yishuv* were Jews who technically remained Russian citizens, thus enemies. Serious thought was given to deporting them en masse, and no doubt only the intercession of Germany saved them. The touchy chauvinism of the Turks, aggravated by the war, caused them to see spies for the Entente everywhere. Cruel jokes, searches, harassments, and threats rained down on the Jews of Palestine. Economic activity was reduced to a minimum, and there was barely enough food. A few of the recent immigrants, such as Ben Gurion and the future president of Israel, Itzhak Ben Zvi, succeeded in escaping to America. The most dynamic leaders of the community, such as Dizengoff and Arthur Ruppin, were banished from Palestine to Turkey. The *yishuv* was reduced to about sixty thousand people. Only three thousand lived in Tel Aviv.

Aaron Aaronsohn, who had come from Rumania at the age of six with his father (himself one of the founders of Zikhron Yaakov), had become a botanist and agronomist of the first rank, after studying at Montpellier in France, in Germany, and in the United States. He directed experimental stations at Metulla in Galilee, then at Atlit near Haifa. His work on the origin of wheat had won him a certain fame, and the Turks themselves asked him to find a way to rid Palestine of grasshoppers. In 1915, convinced that the defeat of Turkey and the liquidation of its authority over Palestine was the *sine qua non* for the creation of a Hebrew state, Aaronsohn made contact with the intelligence service at Port Said. He set up an information network under the code name *Nili*, with headquarters in the house that he shared with his sisters at Zikhron Yaakov. The military intelligence that this network supplied to the British was apparently highly appreciated. In any case, in 1916 the English authorities brought Aaronsohn to London (by way of Constantinople, Berlin, and Copenhagen) in order to put his knowledge to use in the forthcoming Eastern campaign against Turkey. His contacts in England with influential people such as Sir Mark Sykes, and later with the military authorities in Egypt, doubtless played a part in reinforcing pro-Zionist feelings in political circles. Aaronsohn was certainly among those who made the Balfour Declaration possible. His vast learning, the power and clarity of his arguments, and his unequivocal commitment to the British side in the war lent him an authority that would work in favor of the restoration of the Hebrew state.[1]

Aaronsohn was aware—as Jabotinsky had been when he undertook to form a Jewish legion—that however beneficial his actions might be for Zionism, they could endanger the Jewish community in Palestine. Djemal Pasha, the Turkish commander in Syria and Palestine, was only too ready to use any pretext to deal severely with the *yishuv*. In 1917, during Aaronsohn's absence, the still-functioning *Nili* network was discovered and dismantled by the Ottoman police. Aaronsohn's sister Sara, fearfully tortured for three days, committed suicide rather than talk. Brutal reprisals then added to the sufferings of the Jews in Palestine.[2]

However, at the end of 1917 and the beginning of 1918, the British offensive under the command of General [later Sir] Edmund Allenby, crossed the Palestinian-Egyptian border and moved toward Tel Aviv, Jaffa, and Jerusalem. The Turks fought back obstinately. Jabotinsky's Jewish Legion fought on the Shechem front, in the Jordan valley, and at Jericho with a valor that astonished the British officers, who had been rather skeptical about the military value of these "little Whitechapel tailors." Despite his sympathy for Aaronsohn, Allenby had at first shared this skepticism and would have preferred a Jewish brigade under the command of Colonel Patterson, formerly Trumpeldor's superior officer and friend. At the end of 1918, the Jewish units formed three battalions with a fighting force of some five thousand men, of which one third were from Palestine, one third from Great Britain, and the rest from the United States and Canada.

Jabotinsky, now a lieutenant, believed then and later that these units should never have been dissolved. He thought, reasonably enough, that they should remain as the nucleus of the future army of a Jewish state. The Jewish population welcomed the British troops enthusiastically, and a considerable number of Jews volunteered for service, in marked contrast to the indifference and apathy of the Arabs. Unfortunately, instead of listening to Jabotinsky, the British authorities hastily demobilized the Jewish units. This shortsighted decision must be counted among the causes of the bloody events that were to take place the following year when the Arabs attacked an unarmed Jewish population.

Weizmann left for Palestine in March, 1918, as the head of a Zionist commission (of which Sylvain Lévi, a notorious anti-Zionist, was also a member). An event of some significance had occurred just before his departure. Lord Balfour had been able to arrange an audience for Weizmann with King George V, but at the very moment when the Zionist leader, wearing a top hat that he had purchased for the occasion, was to present himself to the king, the audience was cancelled. The British authorities in Cairo had cabled that there would be hostile Arab reactions if Weizmann were received by the king! Balfour managed to set things straight and the audience later took place, but this incident shed a disturbing light not only on Arab inclinations but also on the state of mind of British authorities in the Levant.

When the commission reached Palestine it found desolation and chaos, and an extremely confused military and political situation. The Turks were camped a few miles from Jerusalem. The Arab population still did not believe that the Allies had won, for they were profoundly influenced by German and Ottoman agents with vast resources. "The British," Weizmann wrote to Balfour on May 30, "look upon us with suspicion, the Arabs with hostility.... The administration is headed by honest and intelligent British officers, but the rest of the administrative machinery has been left intact. The offices are full of Arabs and Syrians.... It's the Arabs who are giving orders to the English."[3]

Allenby received Weizmann courteously but did not hide his doubts about the future of the country. "Do you really believe," he asked with thoroughly military harshness, "that any damn Jew will come to this bloody country?" Most of Allenby's lower-echelon officers, such as General Louis Bols, chief of military administration, and the Maltese colonel Vivian Gabriel were pro-Arab and anti-Zionist. Influenced by T. E. Lawrence, they dreamed of a "Greater Arabia," England's ally, picturesque and medieval, with "camels, caravans, white burnooses, green turbans, veiled women, and harems," according to Jabotinsky's sarcastic description. The Balfour Declaration? They pretended not to know of it. It was not officially published in Palestine until 1920. It was only, they said, a lot of verbiage from "the politicians in London," with no roots in the local realities that they themselves understood so well.

And besides, who exactly were these Zionists, so unpicturesque, so unfeudal, always busy, always building something, farming the land, digging canals, laying out roads? The Bolshevik revolution in Russia—was not that the work of the Jews? And these Russian Jews in Palestine, with their kibbutzim—were not they really Bolsheviks? In the officers' mess they passed around not the Balfour Declaration but the *Protocols of the Elders of Zion,* that crude, anti-Semitic forgery that had just been brought back from Russia by English liaison officers sent to Grand Duke Nicholas.

And so the Jews, regarded with suspicion by the Turks because of their Russian connections, were not similarly treated by the English. Evidently no one realized that the Bolsheviks, even the Jewish ones, were violent enemies of Zionism and that moreover anti-Semitism flourished among the White Russians as well as the Reds.[4]

Finally, like any military administration, the British army in occupied Turkish territory looked upon civilian meddling as insupportable. The extreme desolation of the land and the failure of the economy did not make the transition any easier.

But henceforth the Arab problem exerted its full weight on this new "Eastern question." We must backtrack to understand its origins.

At the start of World War I the Arabs made up one half of the population of the Ottoman Empire. The great majority of them were Moslem, and therefore linked to the Turks by their religion: the Ottoman sultan bore the title of caliph. Thus, it was chiefly among the Christian Arabs that the first timid nationalistic inclinations began to spread. The structure of Arab society had remained medieval. While the desert peninsula was held by a few great rival families, the farm lands of Palestine and Syria, ruined by centuries of neglect, were being feebly cultivated by the poverty-stricken *fellahin,* sharecroppers or tenant farmers, working for the wealthy owners, *effendi,* who generally preferred to go to Damascus or Beirut or Cairo to spend the money these poor people earned for them. In the cities a sometimes prosperous commercial bourgeoisie got along as best it could with an Ottoman administration as inefficient as it was dishonest.

On the whole, Arab nationalism at this period was insignificant. No community feeling united the Bedouin "princes," the country *fellahin,* the *effendi,* and the bourgeoisie. No serious attempt was made, even after the revolution of the Young Turks, to throw off the yoke of Constantinople. It would hardly be an exaggeration to say that Arab nationalism was invented by England more as a political than as a military weapon when war against Turkey became inevitable.

Before the hostilities broke out, Lord Kitchener—at the time high commissioner in Egypt—became interested in the prospect of an Arab revolt, in case of war with the Ottoman Empire. His successor, Sir Henry McMahon, took up the idea.

At Hejaz, the Hashemite family, whose chieftain was Sherif Husein ibn-Ali, was the guardian of the two holy cities, Mecca and Medina. The caliph wished to gain their support for a *djihad*, or holy war, against the Allies. The English wanted to lure Husein into the Allied camp.[5] Husein prudently held out a hand to both belligerents. One of his sons, Abdullah, maintained contact with the English in Cairo while another son, Faisal, negotiated in Constantinople.

In 1915 Husein still had not been able to make up his mind. The Sublime Porte proved to be obtuse, but military operations in Western Europe and the Dardanelles were hardly encouraging for the Entente. The sherif was reluctant to lay down his cards. But when Faisal established relations with nationalistic circles in Damascus, made up principally of students and officers, his father was emboldened to ask Sir Henry McMahon what support the British might eventually give to the independence not only of Arabia but of Syria too—territories that he planned to set up as his own kingdom.

The embarrassment of the British high commissioner and his government can be imagined. A discreet correspondence between McMahon and Husein ensued. The most important document of this exchange was the famous "McMahon Letter" of October, 1915. In this lengthy and often obscure epistle, the high commissioner tried to satisfy Husein without at the same time violating British commitments to France. The coastal zone of Syria, Lebanon, and what was then called Lower Syria, that is, Palestine, were exempted from the territories that would later make up one or more Arab states.

The McMahon Letter has been subjected to almost as many commentaries and interpretations as the Balfour Declaration. It certainly was ambiguous enough, chiefly because the English could not let their correspondent know of the bargaining with France. Clearly, however, Lebanon and Palestine remained outside the framework of the agreement. Lawrence himself recognized this in a letter addressed to *The Times* in September, 1919, and if this was Lawrence's view, Husein and Faisal could hardly have been ignorant of it. McMahon himself declared, "I feel it my duty to state, and do so definitely and emphatically, that it was not intended by me in giving this pledge to King Husein to include Palestine in the area in which Arab independence was promised. I also had every reason to believe at the time that the fact that Palestine was not included in my pledge was well understood by King Husein."[6] Supplied with arms and funds by the British, Husein called the Arab tribes to revolt. Nejd (under ibn-Saud) and Yemen refused to rally to his banner. The Arab uprising, which has since been magnified by an entire literature, was in fact quite small and contributed very little to shaking the Ottoman Empire. It was essentially the work of Colonel Lawrence, who, having chosen Faisal, made him the leader of the revolt and the Arab spokesman with the Allies. Behind the scenes, there were never more than a few thousand Bedouins from Hejaz and Transjordan, and their role in the war was just about nil.

It is hard to decide whether Colonel Lawrence was or was not fundamentally hostile to the Jews. Aaronsohn, after speaking with him in Cairo, called him "a Prussian anti-Semite who speaks English."[7] Weizmann, for his part, thought Lawrence sincerely hoped to see Jews and Arabs co-operate in Palestine. Whatever the truth of the matter, Lawrence did not object to the first meeting of Weizmann with Faisal, which took place in his presence in June, 1918.

After two hours' conversation, the Zionist leader and the emir found themselves agreeing that the interests of the Jews and the Arabs could very well coincide, that the development of Palestine by the Jews would offer the Arabs a splendid chance for progress, and that Arab and Jewish delegations to the peace conference should support each other. These principles were later set forth in a paper drawn up on January 3, 1919, by Lawrence and signed by Weizmann and Faisal. The emir, however, agreed to live up to the accord only if he was granted sovereignty over Syria. This condition was not fulfilled, nor was it Weizmann's job to see that it was executed, nor perhaps should he have allowed it to be included in the statement.

Faisal was, of course, familiar with the letter from McMahon to his father. Besides, the Soviet government, hoping to do a bad turn to the capitalist powers, had published the secret Sykes-Picot Treaty, of which there was a copy in the Petrograd archives. Husein and Faisal, comparing these two texts and the Balfour Declaration, might well have concluded that for the moment at least they had better join forces with the Zionists in order to meet the British and French ambitions. Besides, an arrangement that required an Arab state only to surrender poor little Palestine in exchange for all the rest of the former Ottoman lands could scarcely displease the Hashemite dynasty. The Hashemites were sacrificing a penny (which did not belong to them anyhow), in order to gain a fortune.

At the peace conference, a Zionist delegation led by Weizmann and Sokolow explained the basis of Zionist policies to the council, made up of Balfour, Lord Milner, André Tardieu and Stephen Pichon, Lansing and White, Sonnino and Clemenceau. The session was marred by a painful incident: Sylvain Lévi, a Zionist delegate, made an anti-Zionist speech. When he had finished, Weizmann accused him of treason and refused to shake his hand. But on the whole, the powers welcomed the delegation. A communiqué published by André Tardieu on February 23, 1919, affirmed that France would not stand in the way of a British mandate in Palestine nor of the formation of a Jewish state.

It is worth noting that Faisal reacted unfavorably in an interview published in *Le Matin*. But the next day he published a denial of what he had said, and on March 3, he wrote as follows to Felix Frankfurter, the American Zionist leader:

"We Arabs, especially those who have received an education, look upon the Zionist movement with the deepest sympathy. We shall do our best to wish the Jews a hearty welcome home. The Jewish movement is nationalistic, not imperialistic. Our movement is nationalistic, not imperialistic. There is room in Syria for one and the other." He added that "local disputes" would necessarily arise in Palestine "in the first phase of our movements," but that these would concern only details, not principles.

Had Faisal been able to realize the goal of his ambitions—a goal that Lawrence encouraged him to pursue—he might possibly have kept his promises. But when an Arab congress sitting at Damascus acclaimed him "king of Syria and Palestine,"[8] he was summarily thrown out of Syria by General Henri Gouraud. The English, by way of compensation, gave him the throne of Iraq and created an emirate expressly for his brother Abdullah in Transjordan. And ibn-Saud, emir of Nejd, irritated by the favors that Great Britain rained upon the Hashemites, expelled Husein from Mecca. Lawrence's dream fell apart, but it haunted the Middle East for many years to come, like an unexorcised ghost.

From the end of 1919, seeing the gathering storm, Jabotinsky had begun trying to establish a self-defense force in Jerusalem. He united a certain number of Zionist leaders, among them the engineer Pinchas Rutenberg, pioneer of the electrification of Palestine, and various labor leaders. Most of the labor men envisioned only a clandestine force. Vladimir, on the contrary, wanted it to be as official as possible. In spite of this dispute, they proceeded to found and equip armed groups. Their first weapons were bought from an Armenian smuggler. Jabotinsky trained the troops without the slightest attempt at secrecy, even organizing maneuvers on the slopes of the Mount of Olives, under the very windows of the British high command. "He organized this self-defense corps with the full knowledge of the authorities. . . . His first act as commander was to inform the British authorities," Colonel Patterson later testified. As for the Zionist commission of Dr. Weizmann and Ussischkin, it was kept informed of these activities, and it supplied some of the funds. These first groups, whose "chief of staff" was the young Jeremiah Halperin, were the historical nucleus of the Haganah. As one might expect, the Orthodox Jews of the Old City were categorically opposed to Jabotinsky and even refused to admit his patrols to their quarter.

In December, 1919, the situation became critical in the four Jewish villages of Upper Galilee: Kfar Guiladi, Tel Hai, Metulla, and Hamara. Bedouin attacks were facilitated by the uncertain status of this zone. Neither British nor French authority had been successfully imposed. Joseph Trumpeldor, the "one-armed hero" of Gallipoli, was killed at Tel Hai with a number of pioneers at the end of February, 1920.

A violent pogrom broke out in Jerusalem at Passover. The self-defense units successfully repelled the assaults of the Arab populace except in the Old City. In fact, their entry to it was barred by British units, while at the heart of the Jewish quarter, rape and murder were carried out under the indifferent eye of the Arab police. More than two hundred Jews were wounded or killed.

To top it all off, Jabotinsky was accused of violating Article 58 of the Ottoman code by having "armed the inhabitants of the Ottoman Empire one against the other with the perverse intention of provoking rape, pillage, devastation, and assassinations," and a British military tribunal sentenced him to fifteen years in prison.

Shut up in a cell in the ancient fortress of Saint John of Acre, he read and wrote, notably a beautiful poem in memory of Joseph Trumpeldor. Jabotinsky refused a pardon, the more energetically because it was also extended to the instigators of the pogrom, the agitator Aref and the famous Grand Mufti Haj Amin el Husseini. He appealed the sentence, which had aroused strong emotions everywhere—especially in England—and was acquitted several months later. But when set free, he was exiled from Palestine.

At the San Remo conference of April, 1920, the Zionist movement was represented by Sokolow and Weizmann. Two important decisions were made in concert with the Allies: to confirm the Balfour Declaration and to give Great Britain the Mandate for Palestine. The idea of the Mandate came out of President Wilson's "Fourteen Points," and was said to have been suggested by Jan Smuts. It seemed a perfect solution to the problem of Palestine. Under the protection of the British flag, the Jewish community would be able, as Lord Balfour had promised, to create a national home. This idea was generally agreed upon by all the delegates at San Remo, including, it must be emphasized, the Arabs. In the dining room of the Hotel Royal, Weizmann wrote, "the Jewish and Arab delegations [were] seated together at a really festive board, congratulating each other under the benevolent paternal gaze of the British delegation at a neighboring table."

Unhappily, two years went by before the text of the British Mandate was published, in July, 1922. During this lapse of time, Lawrence's structure began to crumble. Faisal was expelled from Damascus and the Bedouin tribes in Transjordan fell prey to xenophobic agitators. The situation in the Middle East only deteriorated in these two years. The British military administration that remained in Palestine until the summer of 1920 "did some excellent work in the country after the war, but it is doubtful whether the military authorities either approved of or even understood the Balfour promise."[9] The new provisional civil administration was imbued with a similar spirit. The delay in announcing the Mandate only made more precarious a state of affairs that above all demanded clarification and decision.

The Mandate is a long document of which the preamble sanctions the Balfour Declaration not only on behalf of England and its allies but of all members of the League of Nations. It states that "the historical connection of the Jewish people with Palestine" is recognized, as well as "the grounds for reconstituting their national home in that country," and the authority of the Mandate was proclaimed "responsible for putting into effect the declaration originally made on November 2, 1917, by the Government of His Britannic Majesty."

Article 2 imposed on the Mandatory the task of "placing the country under such political, administrative, and economic conditions as will secure the establishment of the Jewish national home." Article 4 officially recognized a "Jewish agency," which was to come from the Zionist organization and whose function would be to advise the administration and co-operate with it in every domain, "economic, social and other matters as may affect the establishment of the Jewish national home and the interests of the Jewish population. . . ." The Mandatory administration had to (Article 6) "facilitate Jewish immigration . . . and encourage . . . close settlement by Jews on the land, including state lands and waste lands. . . ." The Mandatory had to (Article 11) set up "an agrarian system with a view above all to promoting colonization and the intensive cultivation of the land," and organize public works and services, with the aid of the Jewish agency, and develop the natural resources of the country.

In conformity with the Balfour Declaration, the Mandate, in several of its articles, aimed at assuring equal treatment for all inhabitants of Palestine, and forbidding all religious discrimination. Hebrew, Arabic, and English were to be the three official languages. The administration of the *Wakf* (religious holdings of the Moslems) would be carried out according to the laws of Islam.

Article 25, *in cauda venenum*, one of the last articles, allowed the Mandatory "to postpone or withhold" application of the measures provided for in the text if it considered them "inapplicable to the existing local conditions." The reason for this strange arrangement was soon revealed. On September 16, 1922, the British government, invoking Article 25, presented a memorandum to the Council of the League of Nations that said that certain parts of the Mandate were "inapplicable to the territory known as Transjordan," namely, on the one hand, the paragraphs of the preamble pertaining to the Balfour Declaration and to the recognition of the historical rights of the Jewish people, and on the other hand, articles 2, 4, 6, 7, 11, 13, 14, 22, and 23, which is to say all those pertaining to the Jewish national home, the immigration and establishment of the Jews in Palestine, to Hebrew as an official language, and to religious equality. The Council approved this proposition. In effect, it snatched back with one hand what it had given with the other. Historical Palestine, covering an area of about 45,560 square miles, was to have three quarters of its land amputated. Palestine in the new sense of the term was reduced to 10,000 square miles, of which 4,800, forming the subdistrict of Beersheba in the Negev, were barren desert. The Balfour Declaration, though it had been expressly used by the League of Nations as the basis of the Mandate, no longer applied to the greater part of the country.

This first partition of Palestine had even more serious consequences for the future since it seemed to be a retreat before the threats of Arab agitators. New anti-Zionist troubles had burst out in Jaffa in 1921, leaving ninety-five people dead and more than two hundred wounded in the streets. An Arab delegation went to London and in strident terms demanded the annulment of the Balfour Declaration and the end of Jewish immigration. "Had these delegates been the agents of a great power instead of the representatives of a backward population, only lately emancipated from the oppressive domination of the Turks ... the language of their communications could hardly have been more peremptory."[10]

England had been through a long hard war and now had "shed the khaki." Public opinion and Parliament shrank from the idea of maintaining large armies in the East to keep order. Faced with Arab agitation, London preferred partially to sacrifice the Jews. This preoccupation with appeasement was reinforced by the desire to compensate the Hashemite family for Faisal's disappointments in Syria, and to accommodate the French position in the Levant. The emirate, which became the kingdom of Transjordan — a state without historical foundations, political or economic reality — was therefore created under British aegis. Scarcely had the Mandate been written before its purpose changed.

Even before the League had approved the Mandate, Sir Herbert Samuel had been named high commissioner in Palestine to set up the civil government. This liberal, honest, distinguished politician, Jewish and pro-Zionist, disappointed everyone who expected England to apply the Balfour Declaration. Simply because he was Jewish he may well have been affected by a "complex" toward the Arabs. As the representative of the Mandatory power, he did not wish to be accused of partiality toward one sector of the population, particularly the one to which he was tied by origin and by religion. In any case, he constantly gave way before Arab pressures. After the Jaffa riots of May, 1921, he decided, obviously contradicting the principles of the Mandate, to suspend Jewish emigration; he made the mistake of announcing this decision to an assembly of Arab dignitaries at Ramleh. It was also he who took the disastrous step of naming as grand mufti of Jerusalem the unscrupulous chief of one of the great landowning families, Haj Amin el Husseini, who was to earn a sinister reputation as an organizer of massacres, and later, as an agent of Hitler.

Contrary to Article 6 of the Mandate, Samuel refused to let Zionist pioneers into the lands of the fertile valley of Beisan, which was in the public domain as a legacy from the Ottoman state. Giving in to agitations organized by Wadi Boustani, a Haifa lawyer and businessman, he allotted about 120,000 acres of this land to a group of Bedouins especially formed to receive it. After acquiring this acreage for a nominal sum, the Bedouins did not even farm it but sold some of it off at exorbitant prices to Jewish immigrants.

The British government issued the first of a series of White Papers in 1922. Like those that followed it, it was obviously meant to eviscerate the Balfour Declaration and the Mandate. According to the interpretation it gave to the Declaration, the national home was to be nothing more than an enclave within Palestine. All idea of a Jewish state, even in the remotest future, seemed to be excluded. Of course the White Paper conceded that immigration should continue, but "subject always to the condition that it should not exceed the absorptive capacity of the country." This notion of "absorptive capacity," which would provoke unceasing discussion for twenty years and more, was — beneath its apparent technical rigor — utterly imprecise. It was easy to interpret in its most restrictive sense. Should the absorptive capacity of the country be measured by its present miserable state, or by what it would be like after immigrants had reclaimed it?

One can say that in 1921–22, the precedent was set: to every Arab complaint, every Arab act of violence, the administration customarily responded by knocking another hole in the structure of the Mandate. Numerous observers, writers, and politicians have examined this strange phenomenon and looked for the motives: a preconceived hostility of at least part of the administration and the army;[11] policies deliberately designed to gain the support of the Arab world; a desire to avoid dangerous and expensive disturbances at any cost; a conviction that the Jews, like it or not, had to take what was given them, while the Arabs had the power to block England's way in the entire Middle East; and perhaps, simply, in many cases, a lack of vision and long-term conceptions on the part of a regime that was weighed down in the details of daily action. No doubt there was some truth in all this. The fact remains that Zionism, stimulated at first by the promises of England and the League of Nations, was led from one disappointment to another, and that Great Britain not only failed to appease the Arabs but simultaneously squandered the immense capital of good will it had acquired since the Balfour Declaration. Such are the usual results of a policy of appeasement.

The Zionist leaders, headed by Weizmann, reluctantly accepted the White Paper. Faithful to his philosophy of the "possible," and always much attracted by England, where he had played such an important wartime role, Weizmann pointed out that to reject the White Paper would be to jeopardize the Mandate and throw out the good with the bad. At least, he pleaded, the White Paper reaffirmed that the Jews were in Palestine "by virtue of a right and not on sufferance"; as to the absorptive capacity of the country, it was up to the Zionists to colonize and develop it.

It was here that Weizmann's and Jabotinsky's paths parted. Jabotinsky resigned from the Zionist executive committee shortly after the White Paper had been approved. Soon after, he founded the Union of Revisionist Zionists. Although only vaguely aware of what it was doing, official Zionism was returning to the "practical" Zionism of prewar days, while Jabotinsky held high the flag of "political" Zionism, according to Herzl's doctrine.

The Jewish Agency provided for by Article 4 of the Mandate was set up in August, 1929, by a constituent assembly at Zurich. Almost at the same moment, serious trouble broke out in Palestine. The rights of the Jews to meet for prayer before the Wailing Wall had never yet been contested; however, in the previous year several incidents had been provoked by the Arabs at Yom Kippur. In August, 1929, Jews were attacked and driven out of the square in front of the Wall, and the holy books were burned. A few days later, when a fanatical mob seized Jerusalem, the largely Arab police of Palestine[12] refused to protect the Jews. The explosion of violence had been carefully thought out and organized by Haj Amin el Husseini. It soon spread to Haifa, Safed, and Hebron. One hundred thirty-three Jews were murdered and more than three hundred wounded, many of them women and children.

Lord Plumer, who had succeeded Sir Herbert Samuel in 1925, knew how to win the respect of Arab agitators.[13] Sir John Chancellor, who became high commissioner in 1928, did not have the same ability. The grand mufti was all the more quick to profit by the weakness of the administration (for that matter, the outbursts of 1928 had been a test), because he was determined to see that he and his family, the Husseini, would triumph over their rivals, the Nashashibi, who were politically more moderate.

The reaction of the British administration to the riots was pre-dictable: it condemned the excesses committed by the mufti's bands, but it behaved as if the Jews had caused the violence rather than been its victims. A commission of inquiry headed by Sir Walter Shaw reached the not surprising conclusion that the troubles resulted from the development of the national home, from which it followed that to prevent future disturbances, reductions must be made in Jewish im-migration and in land acquisition by the Zionists. In May, 1930, Sir John Hope Simpson was asked to prepare a report on the land prob-lem and the landless Arabs, whose poverty allegedly excused, if it did not justify, the atrocities of August, 1929.

To appreciate fully this turn of events, it must be remembered that the national home had developed very slowly over the course of the preceding years. The Jewish population of Palestine had grown by only about fifty thousand people between 1919 and 1925. Beginning in 1926, the failure of the Polish *zloty* and the exchange restrictions in most Central European countries had seriously slowed immigration. The economic depression in Palestine was so bad that the national home almost seemed doomed.

Moreover, the promise, contained in the Mandate, to let the pio-neers have state-owned or fallow ground had not been kept. Zionists were thus forced to pay higher and higher prices for such sterile dunes and pestilential marshes as the great Arab landowners were willing to sell them, the latter of course being the most violently outspoken against the sale of land to Jews.

According to the most conservative estimate, the maximum area of arable land in Palestine was 6,000,000 dunams, or about 1,680,000 acres, of which the Jews owned only one sixth. The greater part of the land they bought had never been farmed by its Arab owners.

In addition, despite the economic crisis, 80 per cent of all activity in industry, business, transportation, and public works resulted from the Zionist presence. A considerable number of Arab workers were employed by the 2,688 Jewish enterprises that were counted in 1930. At the port of Jaffa, where only Arab labor was used, 75 per cent of the traffic was Jewish trade. In addition, the Jews paid about 70 per cent of the taxes collected by the Mandatory administration; and since the *yishuv* provided for its own hospitals and schools, a large part of this money was used for the benefit of the Arab population.

In spite of all this, the reports of the Shaw Commission and of Sir John Hope Simpson recommended restrictive measures that the

MacDonald government hastened to sanctify with a new White Paper published by the colonial secretary, Lord Passfield (better known as the socialist theorist Sydney Webb). Immigration and land acquisition were suspended. The very tone of the document revealed a deliberate hostility toward the national home. The Balfour Declaration and even the Mandate, by virtue of which the British were in Palestine, seemed to be forgotten. Now everything was done to cater to the Arabs, or at any rate to those Arabs who spoke for the ignorant, starving masses whose poverty they exploited.

The White Paper raised a storm of protest. Weizmann wrote to Lord Passfield reproaching the English government for wanting to "crystallize" the national home and forbid its development. The opposition, led by Winston Churchill, stigmatized the White Paper categorically. In February, 1931, Ramsay MacDonald actually disavowed the White Paper in a letter to Weizmann that ostensibly explained the policies contained in the document. A new high commissioner, Sir Arthur Wauchope, took charge in Jerusalem. In spite of MacDonald's about-face, it was clear that the orientation of the Mandate had subtly changed: originally intended as a means of protecting the national home and helping the Jewish state take shape, it tended more and more to a wholly different use — that of defending the Arabs against the so-called injustice that Zionist colonization was supposedly inflicting on them. That left the Arabs, or more exactly the grand mufti and his gangs, as arbiters of the present and masters of the future. On an economic level, the effect was to subordinate the development of the country to its most backward, feudal faction, to the detriment even of the *fellahin* and the Arab people. The Zionist political goal was receding rather than approaching. Weizmann's plan, to build Palestine "cow by cow, dunam by dunam," was no longer possible.

This was what Jabotinsky had well understood. In 1923, he had created the *Beitar*, a youth organization that would serve as a nucleus for Revisionist Zionism and later for the *Irgun Zvai Leumi*. In August, 1925, a meeting called in Paris founded the World Union of Revisionist Zionists that took up the thread of the Herzl tradition and set as its objective the creation of a state in Palestine based on a firmly established Jewish majority. For ten years the Revisionist Zionists stayed inside the world organization, leading a vigorous opposition that was first directed against Chaim Weizmann.

The seventeenth Congress, held in Basel in August, 1931, passed a resolution calling for the application of Article 6 of the Mandate, which provided for the "intensive colonization" of Palestine. Weizmann resigned as president of the organization and was replaced by Nahum Sokolow. The Revisionist faction then comprised 21 per cent of the delegates. Jabotinsky, as usual, made a lucid speech forcibly restating his essential argument: the aim of Zionism is to obtain by massive immigration a majority on both sides of the Jordan River and definitely to establish a state in Palestine. But the rise of Revisionism in the heart of the organization was cut off by the Arlosoroff scandal.

Chief of the political department of the Jewish Agency, Chaim Arlosoroff was a militant of the socialist left who had often vigorously opposed Revisionist ideas. However, some of his own ideas were not too distant from Jabotinsky's. In a letter to Weizmann in 1932 (published in 1958 by the *Jerusalem Post*) he said he was convinced that immigration and colonization under British control could not alone be the solution, and that thought must be given to a revolutionary period and armed combat — a heretical idea for official Zionism. Be that as it may, Arlosoroff was murdered on a lonely beach near Tel Aviv, and two young disciples of Jabotinsky's, Avraham Stavsky and Zvi Rosenblatt, were accused of the crime. It is hard to imagine today the fury that all this unleashed. While the British police redoubled their efforts, pressure, and false testimony in an unbelievable atmosphere resembling a witchhunt, Jabotinsky and his friends were, so to speak, made outlaws. They were quarantined at the Prague Congress and hardly allowed to speak, and Weizmann was re-elected president of the Zionist organization. The two young men were tried and acquitted. Twelve years later, a Jewish policeman and member of the Mapai proved that Arlosoroff had been killed by Arabs.[14] But this affair left wounds that healed with difficulty, and an enduring bitterness.

Jabotinsky nevertheless tried to reach an agreement with his adversaries the next year, and conferred at London with David Ben Gurion. The two men had mixed feelings about each other, compounded of admiration and animosity. The socialist leader especially had shown uncalled-for hostility toward Jabotinsky, going so far as to call him Vladimir Hitler in a speech he made in Poland. At the same time, he could not help admiring Jabotinsky's fascinating personality. The latter, for his part, thought of Ben Gurion as a true Zionist patriot, and recalled that he had worn the uniform of the Jewish Legion at the end of the war.

After a number of long conversations, the two men signed an agreement. They foresaw a *modus vivendi* between the Revisionists and the Zionist organization, and they forbade attacks and insults against groups or individuals. Jabotinsky's partisans would stop boycotting Zionist institutions, and the Zionists would stop opposing the immigration of Jabotinsky's Beitarim. They even envisioned at a later date reunifying the trade unions and rebuilding the Zionist executive committee and the Jewish Agency to accommodate all political parties.

Unfortunately, though the Revisionist party (*Hatzohar*) ratified these accords, Ben Gurion's troops refused to follow him. After bitter debate, a large majority of the Histadrut voted it down in March, 1935. Personal relations between the two leaders were good even after this setback, but the schism in Zionism had become inevitable. The Revisionists pulled out completely and created the "New Zionist Organization," the N.Z.O., which held its constitutional convention in Vienna in the presence of the delegates elected by 713,000 Zionists.

The N.Z.O. was firmly opposed to what Jabotinsky[15] called little Zionism, meaning the idea that the Jews had to content themselves with an ill-defined "home" and for all practical purposes renounce the thought of a Hebrew state. At this period official Zionism wavered between the Mandatory administration and the Arabs. Sometimes they spoke of a binational state with a "parity" representation of the two communities. The British had often proposed the creation of an Arab agency or a legislative council where Arabs would be in the majority, but instead of taking these opportunities, the mufti and his entourage angrily refused them. They were not going to bargain with Zionism in any way, however small. Their objectives were clear: the elimination of the Jewish presence, the end of the Mandate, and the creation of a purely Arab state in Palestine. Faced with this emphatic position the Jewish Agency tacked about while the N.Z.O. stated its doctrine unambiguously.

Jabotinsky had long before perceived the dangers of Pan-Arabism; as early as 1922, while in Rome, he had written a prophetic letter to Mussolini. Alluding to the fascist plan to support a Pan-Arab, Pan-Islamic movement, he noted, "It is an interesting plan, but I believe that Italy will not profit from it ... [if the plan succeeds] the French will have to leave Morocco, Algeria, and Tunisia, the English Egypt, and then the Italians Libya. Do you not agree?"[16] He had no illusions about the chance of reaching agreement with the Arabs—Faisal's time was past. At the same time, his throat tightened when he thought of the tragic urgency of the Jewish problem in Europe. He saw Hitler's anti-Semitism growing stronger each day. In Poland, three million

Jews had been inexorably condemned to losing their means of liveli-hood and thus to hopeless poverty. "The entire Jewish people is about to slide into an unprecedented world catastrophe," wrote Jabotinsky in 1936. That same year he published a declaration at Warsaw urging "evacuation"—exodus of the Jews en masse from Central Europe, from Germany and Poland, toward the only land where they could rebuild their lives—Palestine. This prophetic vision earned him misunder-standing and hatred in Zionist circles that refused to face the tragic reality. He knew, however, that a massive immigration had to be ef-fected, whatever the cost, against the wishes of the Mandatory, if need be, and despite Arab resistance. In one extraordinarily perceptive analysis,[17] he showed how the "legend of the Islamic menace" had been overestimated and exploited by the British administration in or-der to escape the obligations of the Mandate. He proposed a ten-year plan with the objective of transforming historical Palestine, on both banks of the Jordan, into a state with a Jewish majority, in which the Arabs would "enjoy all the rights that the Jews ask for themselves in other countries," that is, the political equality and cultural independ-ence that Jabotinsky himself had written into the Declaration of Hel-sinki.

The N.Z.O. proposed the creation of an organization democrati-cally elected by all sectors of Jewish opinion to replace the Jewish Agency (which represented Weizmann's position), the Mapai, and the Histadrut. Later, at the outbreak of World War II, the N.Z.O. also called for the formation of a Jewish army, the immediate transfer of a million Central and Eastern European Jews to Palestine as soon as the war was over (the "Max Nordau Plan"), their settlement by means of an international loan, and a "Covenant of Equality" or international treaty designed to safeguard the rights of all minorities and to outlaw religious and racial hatred. This program, which Weizmann disdain-fully referred to as "revisionist illusions," met with a certain inertia in the Jewish communities of the Diaspora, and in Palestine itself with what has been called yishuvism, that is, the natural but self-defeating tendency of the Palestinian community to be wrapped up in itself and to forget that its existence and its fate, however important, were nevertheless only one part of the whole Jewish problem.

The Revisionist movement was colored by the exceptional per-sonality of its chief. This explains much of the misunderstanding and animosity that surrounded it. Completely removed from the ghetto spirit, a philosopher as much as a man of action, Jabotinsky saw be-

yond what he called in Russian *obstanovotshka*, the daily little problems of the community in Palestine. He did not think that colonization
was an end in itself. For him even political action took second place to
what in Hebrew was called *hadar*, a conception of life made up of
chivalric generosity, self-control, energy, and righteousness — the ideal
that he proposed to his Beitarim.

He was sharply reproached for his "militarism," and the first parade of the Beitar at Tel Aviv, on October 13, 1928, was conducted
amid a rain of insults. Yet can anyone deny today that Israel's only
chance for survival lay in its armed forces? In his magnificent novel
about Samson,[18] Jabotinsky shows the Biblical hero answering difficult
questions with the words, "What do you need? Iron, and a king,"
which is to say weapons and a disciplined social structure. His Mapai
adversaries willingly took another short step and accused him of fas-
cism. The adjective has never been less aptly applied than to Jabotinsky. He was "an old-fashioned liberal," as he loved to call himself, profoundly democratic and respectful of human beings.

He certainly did not share the socialist tendencies of David Ben
Gurion and the leaders of the Zionist majority. He thought the kibbutzim had been given an excessive importance in the agrarian program; that such organizations as the Solel Boneh Trust and the Hamashbir, which depended upon the Histadrut, were too complicated
and expensive, and that private initiative and the small artisan had
been allowed too small a role. Even today, twenty years after the foundation of the state of Israel, there are plenty of objective observers who
say that many of his criticisms were well founded. Far from being
reactionary, Jabotinsky, like Herzl, wanted the future nation to be bal-
anced as a state, capable of solving economic and social conflicts, and
of assuring each man a just share. His ideas were already much closer
to modern ones than to the doctrinaire socialism of the early twentieth century. But the Histadrut and the Mapai never forgave him for
his often caustic opposition to their monopoly, or for denouncing the
absurdity of the Orthodox theory of "class war" between Jews who
were trying to build a nation in the teeth of Arab hostility and under
the eye of an unsympathetic Mandatory administration.

The last three years preceding World War II were marked in Palestine by the Arab rebellion. It was no longer a question of sporadic disturbances, revolts, and pogroms, or localized attacks, but of all these at
once, plus incursions by armed bands, prolonged political strikes, and

systematic harassment of communications. The disorders began on April 19, 1936, with a riot at Jaffa, during which nine Jews were assassinated in the street. The next day, a group of Arab leaders meeting at Nablus called a general strike. The Arab Higher Committee was formed amid these events. Its president was Grand Mufti Amin el Husseini, and its secretary was Auni Bey Abdelhadi. One new and important fact: the rival of the Husseini, the Nashashibi family, decided to send as its representative on the committee, Ragheb Bey, an archenemy of the grand mufti. Formerly mayor of Jerusalem, Ragheb had had to resign after a scandal that revealed the corruption of his administration.

The committee sent a relative of the mufti as delegate to London, Djamal el Husseini, and laid down its conditions. The strike, and it was understood, the rest of the troubles, would end only if Great Britain accepted the following conditions: Jewish immigration must be halted; Jews must be prohibited from acquiring further arable land; and an Arab national government must be created for Palestine. They were asking for a definitive end to the policies set in motion by the Balfour Declaration.

The Mandatory administration reacted mildly. It tolerated not only the strike but the incitement of civil disobedience and nonpayment of taxes. To "protect" the three thousand Jews living in Jaffa, they simply sent them to Tel Aviv. On May 18, the British high commissioner announced a sharp reduction in the number of immigration permits; only 4,500 were to be issued during the next six months. He also announced that a Royal Commission of Inquiry—yet another—would be appointed to investigate Arab grievances in Palestine. All this naturally led the mufti and his committee to think that their violence was paying off. From this they drew the logical conclusion that the violence had to be intensified.

That summer bands of opportunists, many of them not even Palestinian, began to demonstrate in the mountainous regions. They were equipped with arms and munitions from neighboring countries, purchased by the mufti with the large funds he controlled as administrator of Moslem religious holdings (the *Wakf*), and with Italian subsidies. In August, Fawzi El Kaukji, formerly an Iraqi officer, then military adviser at the court of ibn-Saud, took command of the rebellion. He had five thousand men at his disposal, divided into *mudjahiddini*, "soldiers in the Holy War" organized in more or less regular units, and *fedayeen*, who were saboteurs, snipers, and killers. There was a general breakdown in security. In the first month of the rebellion, eighty-nine Jews were killed and more than three hundred wounded; harvests, orchards, and dwellings were severely damaged: 80,000 orange trees and 62,000 other fruit trees, and 4,800 acres of grain, among other things, were destroyed.

During this time the Arab Higher Committee, in the words of a British historian[19] "was allowed to continue the abuse of its functions without Government control of any kind, long after it had become apparent that the organization and the funds at its disposal were being used for illegal, seditious and even murderous purposes."

The first phase of the rebellion ended in October, 1936, because of the weariness of the strikers, a proclamation of martial law, and a sort of mediation from the Arab countries. Ibn-Saud, the king of Iraq, and Emir Abdullah of Transjordan actually published an appeal to the Higher Committee on October 10. "We have been deeply afflicted" they said, "by the present state of affairs in Palestine. . . . We request that you make a decision in favor of peace in order that blood may cease to flow. We rely on the good will of our friend Great Britain, which has declared herself ready to see justice done."

The British government not only had not opposed the intervention of the Arab states in the internal affairs of Palestine, which were solely a British responsibility according to the League of Nations, but most probably had prepared this intrusion by backstage maneuvering.

The Royal Commission with Lord Peel presiding arrived in Palestine in November. His report, founded on the testimony of numerous witnesses, both Arab and Jew—among them Haj Amin el Husseini and Weizmann (Jabotinsky was exiled from Palestine but had testified in London)—was published only in July, 1937. During that time open rebellion had ceased but had been succeeded by terrorism. The mufti undertook to have his thugs assassinate those Arab leaders whom he considered too "moderate," and thus Fakhri Bey Nashashibi, the nephew of Ragheb Bey, was attacked in Jaffa.[20] The Nashashibi and their friends left the Higher Committee. But the breakup of this organization did not keep the mufti from pursuing his seditious and racist policies. It was during this period that he began soliciting the aid of Hitler's Germany against the Jews of Palestine, as shall be seen later.

What were the conclusions of the Peel Commission? Essentially, it recommended a partition of Palestine. The Mandate ought to be annulled or rather reduced to a zone under British control. The zone would include Jerusalem and Bethlehem; a corridor between Jerusalem and Jaffa along the road that connects the two cities; the airport of Lod; the port of Haifa; Tiberias, Safed, Nazareth, and Acre. The rest of Palestine would be divided into two states: a Jewish state extending to the Plain of Sharon and Esdraelon, to a part of Galilee and an enclave south of the "corridor." The rest of the country, Jaffa included, would be the Arab state.

In the meantime, the commission recommended that as a palliative "likely to reduce inflammation and to lower the temperature," Jewish immigration be reduced to twelve thousand people annually in the coming years. But it expressed its "firm conviction that the only hope of a cure rested in a surgical operation."

The two elements scheduled for surgery welcomed the idea with the feelings one might expect. The Arabs rejected it unanimously, although Emir Abdullah had semiofficially looked upon it with some favor, seeing an opportunity to annex the new Arab state to his own. The English secret agent Philby, who was a convert to Islam and an adviser to ibn-Saud, fruitlessly urged the king to accept the plan. Jewish reaction was less clear-cut. Weizmann and Ben Gurion were inclined to accept the partition, at least as a basis for discussions, but Jabotinsky refused. The Zionist Congress of Basel, in August, 1937, rejected the Peel plan after a heated debate, but asked the executive committee to explore the partition problem with the British government. A new Congress was to be called to deliberate on the results of these conversations.

In fact, the talks never took place. In April, 1938, the British government sent a new commission to Palestine, headed by Sir John Woodhead. It concluded, in October, that no practical plan could be made for dividing the country between two states. In November, siding with this opinion, London buried the idea of a partition.

All that remained of Lord Peel's inquest was the recommendation to reduce immigration. Once again, the British prepared to retreat before the threats and violence of the mufti and his fanatical supporters. Weizmann, who had always upheld British policies in the face of the Zionists, wrote to the English colonial minister, Ormsby-Gore, that the Mandate had been "undermined" by the administration itself, which had proved to be "inefficient, devoid of imagination, obstructive, and unfriendly," and had given in to the mufti and the nationalist movement, which was supported by Italian money.

However, the Arab rebellion broke out with renewed vigor in the form of assaults, ambushes, and guerrilla warfare. Andrews, the British governor of Galilee, was assassinated at Nazareth on his way to church. The hills of Galilee and Samaria and the Hebron region were infested with bands of terrorists. The mufti had set up general head-quarters at Jerusalem and Damascus. From these cities he directed an increasing wave of daily outrages against the Jews and the British administration.

Only after the murder of Governor Andrews did the British finally decide to take action. They declared the Higher Committee illegal, deposed the mufti, and deported several members of the committee to the Seychelles. The mufti himself escaped from Jerusalem, probably with the complicity of the administration, took a boat near Jaffa, and settled down in Lebanon under the very tolerant surveillance of the French authorities. Franco-British relations in the Levant were then, as always, mutually mistrustful. The mufti was, in theory, confined to his residence, but he was allowed all the visitors he wished, and he continued to direct the rebellion from his retreat. "By October, 1938, a large part of Palestine was physically under the control of the rebels, and almost the entire Arab population was either giving support to, or was dominated by fear of, the rebels."[21]

In November, 1937, a special representative of the mufti, Doctor Said Iman, called on the propaganda minister and the foreign minister in Berlin. He brought proposals from Haj Amin el Husseini. In exchange for "ideological and material support," the Arab nationalist movement would help the Reich in the nine following ways:[22]

1. Propagation of German commerce in the Arab-Islamic world.
2. Creation of a sympathetic atmosphere for Germany that could be most useful in case of war.
3. Diffusion of National-Socialist ideas in the Arab-Islamic world.
4. Opposition to Communism.
5. Boycotts of Jewish merchandise.
6. "The organization of terrorist actions in all territories, colonies, or French Mandates inhabited by Arabs or Moslems, as for example Syria, Lebanon, Algeria, and Morocco."
7. Battle by every means possible against the formation of a Jewish state in Palestine.

8. German cultural propaganda in Arab countries.

9. If the Arab liberation movement were successful, it would call upon German capital and German intellectual potential.

The mufti had unwittingly stepped into a controversy that had long been brewing among the ruling circles of the Third Reich, who were of two minds regarding Palestine. One idea, which had been followed since the coming of Hitler, consisted of "facilitating" Jewish immigration to Palestine (in the same way that Witte told Herzl the Russian government would facilitate it, "with kicks") by making life in Germany less and less tolerable for the Jews. At the same time, an agreement called the Haavara had been made in September, 1933, between the Reich's minister of economic affairs and the *Palästina Treuhandelgesellschaft zur Beratung deutscher Juden*, by which German Jews who wanted to go to Palestine would turn over to the "Paltreu" all the money they had. This money would then be used to finance half the German exports to Palestine, the other half being paid in foreign currency. In return, the Jewish immigrant, once in Palestine, would collect the proceeds of the sale of these German products whose export he had helped finance.[23]

This "arrangement" had not pleased Foreign Minister von Neurath. On June 1, 1937, he sent a telegram to the German consulate general in Jerusalem, among others, stating that "the creation of a Jewish state or semblance of a state directed by Jews under a British Mandate is not in the German interest. In fact, Palestine cannot absorb world Jewry, but instead will be the sort of supplementary legal base to international Jewry that the Vatican is for Catholicism. . . . Consequently Germany has a stake in reinforcing Arabism (*Arabertum*)."[24] However, German policy was still fluid, for in the same telegram von Neurath added that there was no question of giving "precise assurances" to the Arabs.

The consul general of the Reich at Jerusalem, the "comrade of the party," Döhle, was a determined opponent of the Haavara agreement. A small war of notes, memoranda, and replies broke out in the ministries in Berlin. The Nazis protested ever more heatedly against the indirect aid that Germany was giving to the creation of a Jewish state by assisting immigration to Palestine. On June 22, 1937, a long, detailed circular letter was sent out to all the Reich's diplomatic posts insisting upon "the interest of Germany in the Arab nationalist effort," and its hostility to a Jewish state, which was again compared with the Vatican.[25]

Döhle, in a telegram dated July 15, 1937, sent word of a visit he had just had from the mufti,[26] who had "emphasized the sympathies of the Arab world for the new Germany, and expressed the hope that Germany looked sympathetically upon the Arab battle against Jewry." Haj Amin el Husseini asked whether the Reich would be prepared to take a public stand against the establishment of a Jewish state. A few days later the mufti was able to let the German consul know of his "joy and satisfaction" following declarations in the German press against partition and against the Jewish state.

German documents published after the war show that the embassies of the Reich in Arab countries, especially at Baghdad, worked ceaselessly between 1937 and 1939 to build their contacts with Pan-Arab nationalism, and that the Palestinian question was the subject of innumerable conferences among Germans, Iraqis, Saudi Arabians, and so forth. Ambassador Grobba at Baghdad was received by ibn-Saud in February, 1939. The Arab king declared that if "by skill" he cut a good figure with the English, "at the bottom of my heart I hate them and submit only unwillingly to their wishes. . . . Saudi Arabia and Germany have a common mortal enemy, that is to say the Jews."[27] He made the Reich a detailed offer of strategic, political, and economic co-operation.

But this emerging Nazi-Arabian idyll was not without its cloud. Ibn-Saud's undersecretary of foreign affairs, Fuad Hamza, arranged with the Oberkommando of the *Wehrmacht* for a massive purchase of arms destined to go to Palestine via Saudi Arabia. The deal even had the approval of the information service (*Abwehr*). Only at the last minute was Hamza revealed as being in the pay of England.[28]

In any case, although Nazi Germany had at first shown only slight interest in Eastern affairs, preferring to leave them to its Italian ally, it gradually became more involved in them as war approached, partly to undermine British positions in the Levant, and partly because of the obsessive anti-Semitism of the Nazi leaders. The argument that the Arabs repeated a thousand times—"we have a common enemy, the Jews"—could not fail to have its effect. In June, 1939, Hitler received the royal counsellor from Saudi Arabia, Khalid Al-Houd Al-Gargani, at Berchtesgaden. Hitler told his visitor that he could not rest until the last Jew had left Germany. The Arab went him one better: Had not Mohammed himself chased the Jews out of Arabia? There was only one Jew left in Arabia, he added, and he was in jail. "The Führer assured the ambassador of his sympathy"[29] and ordered large credits to be given the Arabs for arms purchases.

As for the mufti, at the first shot of the war he went to Iraq, then Italy, and finally Germany, where he was much involved with the "final solution," which is to say the total extermination of the Jewish population of occupied Europe.

Faced with rising Arab aggression from the beginning of the Mandate to the period just before the war, the Jewish community of Palestine and the Zionist leadership at first reacted only defensively. "Defense" is what the word *Haganah* means, and it became the name of the first Jewish paramilitary organizations. The Arab attack against the colony of Tel Hai, where Trumpeldor was killed, gave rise to what has been called the doctrine of Tel Hai: not one village, not one kibbutz would be abandoned. The earliest nucleus of the Haganah was the *Hashomer*, the federation of guards who saw to the security of the farm colonies, and the soldiers and noncommissioned officers from the demobilized Jewish battalions. In 1920, as has been seen, Jabotinsky took charge of self-defense measures at Jerusalem and was rewarded with a heavy prison sentence. A force for defense had to be created, though it would have to be illegal. The British administration, although incapable of defending Jewish security, would not tolerate the existence of any such force.

In spite of widespread pacifism and antimilitarism in the leftist parties, a conference of labor leaders at Kinneret in June, 1920, adopted the principle of a defense organization. Six months later, the Federation of Trade Unions, the Histadrut, appointed some of its own members to a central committee for defense. The Arab demonstrations of 1921 led the committee to speed up its work. An executive committee was established to buy arms in Austria and send them to Palestine via Beirut and Haifa. The first course in officer training was held during the summer of 1921 at Tel Aviv and Kfar Guiladi. A man of strong personality, Eliahu Golomb, took charge of this embryonic army—a post he would retain until his death in 1945.

In theory, the whole *yishuv* should have contributed to the defense effort. In fact, the Haganah depended mainly on the pioneers from the kibbutzim rather than the few volunteers from the cities. Direction came from the Histadrut, and would later be closely linked to the Jewish Agency, which in turn was dominated by the leftist parties of official Zionism. All the while the Youth Guard, (*Hashomer Hatzaïr*, the seed of the future Mapam) remained hostile to the very idea of armed resistance.

These structural peculiarities in the command of the Haganah contained the germ of future schisms and quarrels. The Jewish Agency, the official organization established by the Mandate, had by definition to co-operate with the British authorities and was thus in an extremely embarrassing position since it could neither openly recognize a paramilitary organization, nor disavow it. The protectorship of the various political parties over a clandestine militia could only lead to disputes, especially because these parties represented only one tendency and excluded the branch of Zionism headed by Jabotinsky.

Besides, from 1921 to 1929, Palestine had been calm. The Haganah had been reduced to tight, ill-armed groups at Jerusalem, Tel Aviv, and Haifa. Many Jews did not even comprehend the necessity for having it. Since England is here to maintain order, they said, why organize a Jewish army despite England? "Protected Jews" (*Schützjuden*) was Vladimir Jabotinsky's sarcastic description of those who left the assurance of their own safety to others, as they had once done in the little German principalities. But official Zionism, partly because of its attachment to the Jewish tradition of nonviolence, partly because it systematically opposed Jabotinsky, condemned his "militarism."

Thus, outside the Zionist organization and even in spite of it Jabotinsky assigned to his youth movement, the Beitar, the essential task of giving military training in Europe to pioneers on their way to Palestine. These Beitarim, who would grow in number until the Second World War, arrived already trained. They were required to devote their first two years in Palestine to working the land, organized in squads (*pelogoth*) that could instantly be transformed into fighting units.

The Palestine pogroms of 1929 destroyed any lingering illusions. A handful of young men managed to repel the attack of thousands of Arab aggressors at Beer Tuvia and Hulda. The Haganah had a few feeble forces at Jerusalem, Tel Aviv, and Haifa, but none at all at Hebron, where the Jewish population was cut to pieces. It was a harsh and bloody lesson. They then undertook to reorganize and reinforce the Haganah, to train officers, to set up munition dumps, to make cartridges, grenades, and other rudimentary weapons, and finally to set up a communications system of messengers—all this, of course, secretly.

From 1931 onward, a growing malaise took hold of the Haganah. A number of leaders criticized the organization for its political character, closely tied as it was to the Mapai and the Histadrut, and called for an activist orientation that would be less purely defensive. The result was the formation at Jerusalem of the Haganah B, commanded by Abraham Tehomi and controlled by a civilian committee made up of Revisionists, general Zionists, and members of the Mizrachi. Jabotinsky, then in Europe, was a member of the committee. Gradually the new force came to be designated as the National Haganah, or the *Irgun Zvai Leumi* (National Military Organization). The latter name (often abbreviated to Irgun, I.Z.L., or Etzel) has stuck to the group and to its actions.

The Irgun first took shape in Jerusalem, where some thirty leaders joined the secession, and in Tel Aviv, where there was a strong group of Beitarim. Anxious to procure arms, Tehomi went to Finland and bought Suomi machine guns, some of them destined for the Haganah. In 1937 Tehomi rejoined the ranks of the Haganah, but after a referendum among the leaders of the Irgun, 65 per cent of them stayed in the new organization. Jabotinsky had broken with official Zionism the year before, and the Irgun looked to him as its spiritual leader.

As Arab aggression intensified between 1936 and 1939, the directors of the *yishuv* were faced with a problem that was not just military or political but moral: how to retaliate against the Arabs. Because of the ethical tradition of Judaism, this was a deeply troubling question. For Jabotinsky it was the theme of a lengthy interior debate. The *yishuv* thought the solution lay in the watchword *havlagah* —"self-restraint." According to what became official doctrine, Jewish forces had to limit themselves to self-defense. They could respond to an act of aggression but could not attack first. Most of the time, this attitude was only grudgingly accepted by the officers of the Haganah, and still less by the Irgun.

However, the Irgun did not at first take a stand against self-restraint and seek reprisals. After Tehomi left, the Revisionist party picked Robert Bitker as the new commander, assisted by Chief of Staff Moshe Rosenberg. As the commander of the Jerusalem region they chose a brilliant young philosopher and mathematician, David Raziel, who devoted himself henceforth to the study of military arts. When Bitker proved unsuccessful, Raziel replaced him. Beside him was Abraham Stern, a complex man full of dreams and violence, a man of letters and a man of action, a poet brought up on Greco-Latin culture and Biblical prophecy.

Jabotinsky "believed that in the end British statesmen would realize that not just honor but self-interest commanded them to keep England's promises."[30] As a politician he shrank from any action that might have provoked a break with England. As a humanist he shrank even more from instigating reprisals that could hurt innocent people. Only in 1937, after an interview at Alexandria with Moshe Rosenberg, Stern, and Shmuel Katz, did Jabotinsky agree to renounce the policy of self-restraint pressed by the officers and men of the Irgun who could no longer leave unanswered the attacks being made on the Jews. And only after many more weeks did he decide to send to the commanders of the Irgun the telegram that gave the go-ahead to the activists: "Transaction completed. Mendelsohn." In any case, there was to be no terrorism and no attacks on individuals.[31] On November 14, 1937, the Irgun launched its first attacks against armed Arab groups and by this action began to loosen the vise of terror that had been clamped in place by the mufti's bands.

However, the extent and growing violence of the Arab rebellion forced the British authorities willy-nilly to utilize any weapon that came to hand, and so they aligned themselves with the Jewish community. An official agreement was concluded with the Jewish Agency. It established the *Notrim*, or Jewish Settlement Police, which was an auxiliary militia, locally recruited, for the defense of the villages. It was armed and equipped by the Mandatory. Later the Notrim were put in charge of patrolling roads and guarding railroads and electric lines. "These units thus served as a legal cover for the activities of the Haganah."[32]

An English officer of energy and imagination, Captain Orde Wingate (he later fought heroically in Burma during the war) managed, despite the passive resistance of headquarters, to form Special Night Squads that he himself led in guerrilla fighting. Nicknamed Ha-Yedid, "the friend," Wingate trained many officers of the Haganah and led his Night Squads in audacious raids against the Arab villages in the hills of Galilee where the mufti's gangs hid out.

During this period the tactic called Stockade and Tower—*Homah u-Migdal*—was perfected. Under cover of darkness, a column of armed pioneers would move into a parcel of land purchased in advance. They would work feverishly throughout the night setting up a prefabricated tower equipped with a searchlight and essential fortifications. By dawn, the little colony would already be entrenched on its hillside with lookouts and guns in place ready to resist any attack. Then they would put up barracks and begin to cultivate the neighboring lands.[33] About seventy colonies were created in this way, ten of them in the Beisan valley and others in Galilee and the Negev. They were all part of the plan: in case Palestine was partitioned, these villages would be not only farms but military outposts. Hanita, near the Lebanese frontier, was attacked the very first night, and the valiant young men and women of the Haganah withstood a siege there of several months' duration. It goes without saying that these activities were expensive. To meet them, a voluntary tax called the *Kofer Hayishuv* ("community ransom") was set up.

In sum, these three years of the Arab rebellion saw the rapid development of Jewish forces. It was then that such military chiefs as Moshe Dayan got their training.

Unfortunately, the Judeo-British honeymoon was short-lived. After the flight of the mufti and the liquidation of the Higher Committee, the British army went into action and a period of calm set in. The peasants and the ordinary Arab people were tired of terrorism and unemployment caused by the economic depression. As soon as the agitation appeared to die down, semiofficial co-operation between the British and the Jewish Agency ceased. Wingate was transferred, and the authorities started throwing members of the Irgun into prison, beginning with David Raziel. There was soon a brutal repression against the Jews.

The young Beitari Shlomo Ben Yosef, an immigrant from Poland in 1937, was a farmer at Rosh Pinna. The colony had been attacked many times, and one day he fired upon a busload of Arabs. No one was wounded, but Shlomo was nevertheless dragged before a tribunal, condemned to death, and hanged in spite of a wave of interventions and protests. This merciless execution, so out of proportion to the crime, made Shlomo Ben Yosef the first Zionist martyr whose death had been decreed by the Mandatory administration. It aroused a deep and lasting bitterness in the Jewish community, particularly in the ranks of the Beitarim and the Irgun.

Besides, when all was said and done, it was obvious that Arab terrorism was rewarded. A new White Paper in 1939 gave in to the mufti's threats on every important point. It granted the Arabs everything they had sought for three years at gunpoint.

Jewish immigration was not to exceed seventy-five thousand people during the next five years, after which all new immigration would depend upon Arab agreement. The purchase of lands was forbidden, except in 5 per cent of the territory, the coastal zone. The White Paper foresaw that in ten years a Judeo-Arab state would be created in Palestine on the condition that internal peace was re-established and that the Jews and Arabs came to some agreement. In practice, this text annulled all English promises since the Balfour Declaration. The future offered to the Jews was the ghetto—a place as the eternal minority in an essentially Arab state.

The Jews of Europe, whose tragic fate was no longer in doubt, were now condemned to stay where they were. This policy of Neville Chamberlain and the colonial secretary, Malcolm MacDonald, offered Pan-Arabism the same "appeasement" they had already shown to Hitler.

Jewish disappointment was boundless. Ben Gurion called the White Paper the "Paper of Treason." In England, Winston Churchill spoke out against it, but the House of Commons nonetheless approved it. The twenty-first Zionist Congress, which met in Geneva in 1939, rejected it unanimously, and the Jewish Agency decided not to co-operate in its enforcement. The Mandate Committee of the League of Nations also rejected it and would have submitted it to the League had not the Second World War broken out in the meantime. According to good legal logic, the Mandate as formulated in 1922 ought to have remained the supreme law as long as the League had not abrogated or modified it. The White Paper, a unilateral statement by the Mandatory government, had no legal value until it was ratified. The twenty-seventh article of the Mandate in fact affirmed that "the consent of the Council of the League of Nations is required for any modifications of the terms of this Mandate." Unfortunately, this was not the attitude of the British administration, which on the contrary insisted on enforcing this illegal policy at the very moment when its most obvious interests —and any possible concern for humanity—should have led it rather to support a solidly Jewish Palestine, strengthened by substantial immigration.

In these conditions the Second World War broke out.

FOOTNOTES FOR CHAPTER 4

1. Aaronsohn died in 1919, at the age of forty-three, when the plane that was taking him from London to the Paris peace conference disappeared over the English Channel.

2. I should like to express my gratitude to Miss Rivka Aaronsohn, the sister of Aaron and Sara, and the only survivor of this episode. Thanks to her I was able to visit Aaronsohn's house at Zikhron Yaakov, where his scientific and political papers are kept.

3. Letter published by the *Jerusalem Post*, April 4, 1958.

4. For more on this subject, see Jacob Tsur. *Prière du matin*. Paris, Plon, 1967, p. 47 (anti-Semitism among Denikin's officers), and p. 64 (anti-Semitism among the Red Cossacks).

5. "All this," wrote John Marlowe (*Rebellion in Palestine*, p. 26), "was quite regardless of the fact that at that time of day nobody cared twopence about the Caliphate, least of all the Moslems themselves."

6. *The Times*, July 23, 1937. Identical information has also been supplied by Sir Ronald Storrs, then Oriental secretary under Sir Henry McMahon, and by William Ormsby-Gore, staff member of the high commission at the time. Cf. Pierre van Paassen. *The Forgotten Ally*. p. 116.

7. Stein. *op. cit.*, p. 294.

8. In accepting this title, Faisal not only broke his promise to Weizmann but also openly countered the theses of the McMahon Letter.

9. Herbert Sidebotham, *op. cit.*, p. 147.

10. Basil Worsfold. *Palestine of the Mandate*. Quoted by Sidebotham, *op. cit.*, p. 149.

11. In July, 1918, this hostility showed itself in an incident that occurred when the foundation stone of Hebrew University was being laid on Mount Scopus. British officials openly remained seated during the playing of the Hebrew hymn *Hatikva*.

12. In 1927, of 132 police officers, only eighteen were Jewish. Total police personnel consisted of 1,213 Moslem Arabs, 502 Christians, and 326 Jews.

13. When a delegation of these agitators declared to him in menacing tones that they "would not guarantee the security of Palestine" if the Mandatory administration did not give in to their demands, Lord Plumer cried, "Who is asking you to guarantee its security? That's what I am here for."

14. The policeman's name was Yehuda Tannenbaum-Arazi. See the *Jewish Herald*, June 24 and July 1, 1955.

15. "What does little Zionism mean?" (in Yiddish). *Morgenjournal*. New York, August 3, 1930.

16. Weizmann met Mussolini a number of times. He thought that the Italian dictator was not fundamentally hostile to Zionism but feared that England wanted to use it to reinforce its own position in the Mediterranean. Mussolini was, however, getting questionable information about Palestine from Count Theodoli, Italy's representative on the Mandate Commission of the League of Nations and a relative by marriage to the Palestinian Arab family of Sursuk. The Sursuks had made a fortune selling land to the Jewish Agency in the valley of Jezreel, and having done so, felt that the Jews had not paid nearly enough.

17. *The Hebrew State* (in Polish). Kraków, 1936.

18. The original was published in Russian in 1926. English translation: *Prelude to Delilah*. New York, 1945.

19. John Marlowe. *op. cit.*, p. 171.

20. Among other Arab victims of terrorism were the mayor of Hebron, who was killed by a bomb, and the mayor of Bethlehem.

21. John Marlowe. *op. cit.*, p. 190.

22. *Akten zur deutschen auswärtigen Politick* (Official Documents of the Third Reich). Vol. V, document #576.

23. Hans Bucheim, Martin Broszat, H. A. Jacobsen, Helmut Krausnick. *Anatomie des SS*

Staates. Vol. II, pp. 319–20.

24. Official documents already cited. Vol. V, document #561.

25. *Akten,* document #564.

26. *Ibid.,* document #566.

27. *Ibid.,* #589.

28. Note of Von Hentig, *ibid.,* #590.

29. *Ibid.,* #541. Von Hentig's trial.

30. Shmuel Katz, quoted from a manuscript in English sent to the author, entitled *Days of Fire* in Hebrew.

31. It is interesting to note that a plan drawn up by certain members of the Irgun to assassinate the mufti in his Lebanese refuge was vetoed by Jabotinsky.

32. From the brochure *Beth-Eliahu, Beth Hagana,* published by the Defense Ministry of Israel, paragraph 12.

33. Arthur Koestler described the establishment of such a colony in his novel, *The Tower of Ezra.*

5
WITH
ENGLAND
AGAINST
HITLER

The war surprised the Jewish community of Palestine and world Jewry at a moment when their moral and political situation looked grave, if not desperate. In Germany, racist taxes and the Nuremberg laws had created a permanent climate of pogrom, and if Hitler won the war, the Jews in the countries he occupied would clearly meet the same tragic fate as the Jews of Germany. The example of Austria after the *Anschluss* proved it. No one had dared to imagine total extermination, but there was already talk of a plan to create a sort of reservation, or gigantic ghetto where all the Jews would be imprisoned.

To make matters worse, England had just affirmed in a White Paper that it would never open the gates of Palestine very widely to persecuted Jews. Renouncing the Balfour Declaration, it dashed all hopes for a national home just when the home offered the only hope of salvation for these threatened masses.

Choosing sides in the war was difficult. However, the great majority of the *yishuv* and the Zionist leaders supported England and the Allies. Naturally, so did Weizmann. David Ben Gurion announced that "we shall fight Hitler as though the White Paper did not exist, and we shall fight the White Paper as though Hitler did not exist."

In 1939, Jabotinsky did not believe that war was imminent — an error he would bitterly reproach himself for later. When Germany invaded Poland, he issued an appeal: "A brutal enemy threatens Poland, the heart of the Jewish world-dispersion for nearly a thousand years, where over three million Jews dwell in loyalty to the Polish land and nation. France, all the world's fatherland of liberty, faces the same menace. England has decided to make that fight her own; and we Jews shall, besides, never forget that for twenty years, until recently, England has been our partner in Zion. The Jewish nation's place is therefore on all the fronts where these countries fight for those very foundations of society whose Magna Charta is our Bible."

"On September 3, 1939, scarcely an hour after England declared war on Germany," wrote Colonel Patterson, "I was called to the telephone:

it was Jabotinsky. He entreated me to co-operate with him, as I had done nearly a quarter of a century before, in the creation not of a legion but a modern, mechanized Jewish army to fight by the side of the Allies."

Jabotinsky spent the first six months of the war in London trying to launch the idea of a Jewish army. It was there, at the beginning of 1940, that he wrote his last book.[1] That spring, the New Zionist Organization submitted to the British government a memorandum drawn up by Jabotinsky. Noting the presence of Czechoslovakian and Polish forces among the Allied armies, he argued that the Jews of Palestine and the Diaspora could bring to the battle against Hitler a moral and material contribution comparable, if not superior, to that of the governments in exile.

Weizmann, for his part, approached the Chamberlain government to suggest that a Jewish unit be formed. But he had to wait until September, 1940, to put the question more effectively to Churchill. The prime minister and the colonial secretary, Lord George Ambrose Lloyd, approved a five-point program: recruitment of the greatest possible number of Jews in Palestine and formation of battalions or larger units; an equal number of Jews and Arabs to be recruited in Palestine; Jewish officers to be trained in sufficient numbers to command a division; creation of a unit for desert warfare; and recruitment of non-British Jews living in England. On the second point Churchill felt he had to give in to demands at the colonial office, which, still haunted by the Arab problem, clung tenaciously to the idea of recruiting equal numbers of Arabs and Jews. But everyone knew that many more Jews than Arabs would volunteer.[2] The program therefore provided that Jews "in excess" would be sent to Egypt or the Middle East. Nevertheless Weizmann said he was satisfied.

Discouraged by the restrained reaction of the British government in 1940, and convinced that the outcome of the war would depend ultimately on the United States, Jabotinsky decided to go to America in March. He was not quite sixty; but worn out as he was by a life of wandering (he had just traveled through Poland and the Baltic countries, organizing clandestine emigration and speaking at innumerable meetings), overwhelmed as he was with personal problems (his wife was ill, and his son Eri was in prison in Palestine), he already had the symptoms of a serious heart ailment. On August 4,1940, during a visit to a group of his Beitarim near New York, he had a fatal heart attack. The news of his death caused deep sadness and even penetrated the walls of Nazi concentration camps, where so many Jews had been incarcerated since the partition of Poland between Berlin and Moscow. The moral stature of this extraordinary man, spiritually a giant, would never cease to grow. When in accordance with his will his body was laid solemnly to rest in Jerusalem near the tomb of Herzl, thousands of people of Palestine joined his funeral cortege.

The last acts of his life were attempts to unite Zionism behind the Allies, despite personal and doctrinal differences. As his last work testifies, Jabotinsky understood that England did not relish the idea of a Jewish force whose presence and action would have justified the inscription of the Jewish state among the war aims of the democratic countries. In his view, the formation and official recognition of such an army was of vital importance, and Zionist unity was a small price to pay to achieve it. On May 18, 1940, when the *Wehrmacht* was already rolling over Western Europe, he had cabled Weizmann and Ben Gurion proposing the establishment of "a single front." Weizmann replied that he was ready to meet Jabotinsky during a forthcoming trip to the United States, but he took care not to give a positive answer, and weeks and months went by. Shortly before his death, Jabotinsky must have realized that his efforts had come to naught. The Jewish Agency, he said, must henceforth take some initiative, if it thought proper.

Meanwhile, Lord Lloyd had been replaced as colonial secretary by Lord Moyne, who quickly disavowed the five-point program Weizmann had accepted. From then on things moved slowly. In spite of the work of committees for a Jewish army in England and the United States, in which such prominent people as Lord Strabolgi, Lord Wedgwood, Robert A. Taft, Harry Truman, Jacques Maritain, and others took part, and in spite of many Parliamentary debates, the creation of the Jewish brigade was delayed until September, 1944. The support of the former captain, now General Orde Wingate was valuable, but the delaying tactics of anti-Zionist elements in the colonial ministry and the war office succeeded in wasting four years.

This is not to say the Palestinian Jews did not participate in the war effort—quite the contrary. But as was indeed the intention of those responsible for the delay, their participation was, so to speak, drowned in the British war effort, and Zionism was unable to profit from it politically.

Beginning in September, 1940, Palestinians of all origins were allowed to enlist. The number of Arab volunteers was negligible, in contrast to the one hundred fifty thousand Jewish volunteers, of whom fifty thousand were women, who flooded the recruitment offices. Despite everything, several hundred Jews had previously managed to join the British military engineers; they fought in Flanders, and at Saint-Malo they were among the last to be pushed off the continent by the German advance. From the moment that they were officially accepted, the Palestinian volunteers, under the British flag and in British uniforms, took an active and often glorious part in the Middle Eastern campaign. It was a Jewish suicide task force under the command of Major Osterman-Averni that infiltrated Bardia by sea, thereby permitting the British infantry to seize the fortress and nine thousand prisoners without firing a shot. A Jewish commando force of German origin, wearing Nazi uniforms, was assigned by Montgomery to create a diversionary action in Rommel's rear. The mission was accomplished, but half the unit never came back.

In June, 1942, when the heroism of the Free French at the battle of Bir Hacheim astonished the Germans and the rest of the world, a Jewish company of the King's West African Rifles drove back a similar siege by Rommel's armor and Junker Stukas. This was at Mekili, about eighty miles east of Bir Hacheim. The commanding officer of that unit was Major Felix Liebman of Tel Aviv. For many days his five hundred men fought on foot against the tanks, and were pounded by enemy planes. There were only forty-odd left when the column led by Koenig joined them on July 2.

The white and blue Zionist flag flew over the camp all during this nightmare. As the survivors were preparing to retreat with the Free French, a Jewish soldier lowered the flag, saying, "We are not permitted to fly that flag. It's against regulations." "I don't give a damn for regulations," replied Koenig, and ordered his legionnaires to salute the flag of David.[3]

In 1941, the pro-German revolt of Rachid Ali el Gailani in Iraq, supplied with arms from Vichy-controlled Lebanon and Syria, provoked the intervention of the British and the Free French, and was finally settled by the armistice of Saint John of Acre. Palestinian commandos took an active part in reconnaissance work and fighting. Young Moshe Dayan, the future commander in chief of the Israeli army, was wounded at Fort Gouraud and lost his eye.

A Jewish regiment from Palestine, numbering twenty-three thousand men, was created in August, 1942. Other Jewish contributions to the war effort have been enumerated by Pierre van Paassen:[4] Jewish units took part in the defense of Tobruk, then in the recapture of that city, as well as in the conquest of Sidi Barrani, Salum, and Fort Capuzzo. A hundred speedboats of the Jewish coast guard plowed the Mediterranean from Palestine to Egypt, Libya, and Cyprus. Two thousand five hundred Jews served as pilots or bombardiers in the Royal Air Force, and six thousand in ground crews at air bases in Egypt. The Jews of Palestine put communications systems into operation between Lebanon and the Red Sea, built the fortifications at El Alamein and the bridges over the Euphrates, manned antiaircraft batteries in Palestine, and defended the coasts. A Jew from Haifa, General Kisch, successfully organized Montgomery's supply lines from El Alamein across Libya to Bizerte, where he finally met his death. Suicide commandos fought in Eritrea and Ethiopia; others in Greece. The brigade that was organized so late in the war nevertheless arrived in time to distinguish itself on the Italian front and in the invasion of Germany.

Special mention must be made of the heroic adventures of the young people who parachuted inside German-occupied territory in Central Europe. Volunteers for these missions, which led to almost certain death, were assigned to make contact with what was left of the Jewish population (particularly in Hungary) and the nucleus of partisan forces in order to create resistance and sabotage networks. The name of Hanna Senesh, a girl who was tortured and shot at Budapest, will live as the symbol of these fighters, who were the veritable elite of the Palestinian community.

In the realm of civilian activity for the war effort, the work of the *yishuv* cannot be ignored. They made war matériel, serums, vaccines, uniforms, shoes; organized hospitals and ambulance units; opened up new farm lands around the Bay of Haifa and in the Lake Huleh and Lake Beisan regions. The entire Israelite population of Palestine mobilized just as devotedly as the British at home.

The Irgun, following the direction Jabotinsky had given it in 1939, decided to subordinate everything to the fight against Hitler. Released from prison by the British, David Raziel undertook a mission in Iraq to sabotage pipelines. He was accompanied by Yaakov Meridor, but Raziel never returned. Meridor succeeded him as the head of the Irgun.

But Jabotinsky's decision was not approved by all the leaders of the secret organization. Shortly before the war began, Abraham Stern had quarreled with Jabotinsky in Poland. He maintained that the Jews should not give up their anti-British activity, and that if the chance arose they should try to obtain permission from the Axis for the emigration of Jews who had to stay in Europe because the British would not admit them to Palestine. Stern exercised an extraordinary magnetism on the men around him, and when he split with the Irgun he took with him such distinguished personalities as Itshak Yitzernitsky (Shamir), Nathan Friedmann-Yellin (Yellin-Moor), and Dr. Israel Scheib (Eldad). This was the origin of the Stern group, which would later be called Lehi, the abbreviation of *Lohamei Herut Israel*, meaning "fighters for Israel's freedom." But hunted as he was from refuge to refuge, isolated with only a handful of partisans, and cut off from the Jewish community, Stern lasted only until 1942. He was arrested by the British police in a little room under the eaves in the modest Tel Aviv house where he was hiding; he was shot, according to the official story, "while trying to escape." He himself had told Shamir a short time before that he was sure he would be shot if he were ever caught.[5] Most of his companions were arrested and either imprisoned or interned in camps, notably at Latrun. However, this was not the last of the Stern group.

Before Stern's tragic death, he had sent two emissaries to Syria, whence they were to try to get to the Balkans and take every measure to facilitate Jewish immigration to Palestine, with the aid of the Axis authorities if necessary. Neither of them succeeded in getting out of Lebanon. One, Friedmann-Yellin, was imprisoned when he returned to Palestine.

In 1942, Rommel's apparently invincible advance toward Egypt, coupled with the *Wehrmacht's* march toward the Caucasus — a gigantic pincer movement — seemed close to assuring the fall of Alexandria and the Suez Canal to the Nazis. Palestine was in danger of becoming the front line and doubtless would soon be invaded. The Arab population awaited the Nazis with an apathy that scarcely masked their jubilation. In their minds they were already dividing up the Jewish houses and goods. The Jewish community, on the contrary, could expect a general massacre.

The strategy of the British high command had designated the Holy Land as indefensible. If Rommel reached the Canal, there would be nothing to do but evacuate Palestine and retreat into Mesopotamia. Rumors were flying and the *yishuv* was expecting an invasion. Some Jews provided themselves with poison, preferring to die rather than fall into the hands of the Germans. With the approval of the British military authorities, the Haganah and the Irgun prepared themselves for a desperate defense. Special Haganah units of elite commandos, called the *Palmach*, were created to defend the kibbutzim. Haganah headquarters were set up under the command of Yaakov Dori, who was to become, after independence, the first chief of staff of the Israeli army; Eliahu Golomb remained the supreme commander of the Haganah, in direct liaison with the Jewish Agency. The Irgun, turning the exceptional quality of its recruits to advantage, organized "German" and "Arab" units, made up of Jews who spoke one or the other language perfectly and who would stay in Palestine if it fell to the Germans and conduct guerrilla warfare.

The Arab nationalists now placed all their hopes on an Axis victory. In September, 1940, the mufti, Haj Amin el Husseini, sent his private secretary, Osman Kemal Haddad, to Berlin. "With the approval of the Iraqi government — except for Nouri Said — and the Saudi government," he asked the Axis powers publicly to recognize the independence of all Arab states and "the right of the Arab states to solve the Jewish problem in the national and the people's interest (*im nationalen und völkischen Interesse*) according to the German and Italian model." In exchange, Haj Amin el Husseini promised a "declaration of strict neutrality" for Iraq, Syria, and Transjordan, with the corollary that British and Allied troops would be forbidden to cross these territories. He also envisioned a widespread anti-British rebellion, thanks to French armaments already in Syria, and provided that the Axis would finance the rebellion up to a monthly sum of twenty thousand pounds in gold. All this, he said, could be accomplished if Nouri Said, the Iraqi foreign minister who was known to be pro-British, was dropped from the government.[6]

The secret papers of the foreign ministry of the Reich published after the war show that the German government did not wish at this time to get involved in the Middle East without the approval of the Italians. When Ambassador von Mackensen approached him, Count Ciano answered that the mufti had for years had access to considerable funds provided by the Italian government and that thus far "the giving of these millions had been of no special importance."[7]

At the same instant, Franz von Papen, ambassador to Ankara, notified Berlin that the Iraqi minister of justice, Nadji Shawkat, had told him of a plot to get rid of Nouri Said and provoke an insurrection in Palestine.[8] This plan was carried out during the next year, and it nearly succeeded. The overthrow of Nouri Said and the declaration of Iraqi "neutrality" were accompanied at Baghdad by pogroms in which one hundred twenty Jews were murdered.

In 1940, as has been seen, the mufti's proposals aroused enthusiasm neither in Berlin nor in Rome. Ciano pointed out to the Germans that Iraq was not strong enough to lead a widespread insurrection in the Levant. He added, however, that "it does not seem desirable completely to drop the proposals that have been made to us." He concluded that they should "adopt a delaying attitude toward the Arabs," and "respond positively to the mufti's request for financial aid," in order to enable him to resume the raids and sabotage on the pipelines.[9]

The mufti, frustrated by the attitude of the two Axis powers, next resorted to blackmail. At the end of September he let it be known through his private secretary that although the Arabs had no sympathy for Communism, they would align themselves more closely with Soviet Russia if Italy tried to threaten their independence, "since obviously they would enjoy greater sovereignty as a Soviet republic than under Italian domination."[10] The wily el Husseini knew very well that Italy, dreaming of being the "protector of Islam," had been responsible for slowing down the negotiations, so he turned most of his efforts toward Germany. During a conversation with von Weiszäcker on October 18, the mufti's secretary declared that "the enemies of Germany and the Arabs are the same: that is to say, the English, the Jews, and the Americans." The German diplomat told him about a projected announcement on the subject of German sympathy "in complete agreement with her Italian ally" toward Arab efforts for liberation. This rather academic text apparently satisfied the Arab.[11]

It is unnecessary to go into all the details of the various negotiations that led to a slow change of German policies toward Arab nationalism. The decline of Italian influence was naturally a major factor. On January 20, 1941, the mufti wrote Hitler a long letter in French,[12] in which he completely explained the Middle Eastern question and emphasized the common interests of the Arabs and Nazi Germany against the English and the Jews. This letter amounted to a veritable charter of the common "war aims" of Nazism and Arabism.

Haj Amin el Husseini managed to flee Iraq after the failure of Rachid Ali's pro-German coup. The *Völkischer Beobachter* of October 28, 1941, carried a lyrical article praising the mufti who then went to Berlin by way of Albania and Italy. On December 8 he was personally received by Hitler and von Ribbentrop. According to the official statement, his conversation with the *Führer* was "full of significance for the future of the Arab countries." This interview was but the first in a series. The mufti began to make speeches in Arabic over the Reich broadcasting system exalting the "fantastic victories of the Germans and Italians . . . against Jew-allied England." He also distributed tracts throughout the Levant containing inflammatory appeals to the Arab population. This propaganda activity continued until 1944.

Supported by the Nazi foreign policy office — of which the director was Rosenberg — and by Himmler's S.D. (*Sicherheitsdienst*), the mufti undertook to organize a Moslem legion in Croatia. Although the Croatian dictator Pavelitch did not look favorably upon the mufti's meddling[13] and the *Wehrmacht* was even less enthusiastic, el Husseini went to Bosnia with SS Gruppenführer Berger and several other members of the SS and the Gestapo. He made a grand tour of Zagreb, Banja Luka, Sarajevo, and then went to Vienna, where Baldur von Schirach received him in April, 1943. Wherever he went in Bosnia he organized the leaders of Moslem communities. In a report addressed to Himmler, Berger concluded, "It has been proved that the mufti has an excellent information organization at his disposal and that he enjoys extraordinary prestige in the Moslem world." Following his trip, the SS Division of Moslems of Bosnia (13th SS Division) was created on the orders of Himmler. "For the rest of the Arab world, this Moslem division will be the example and the torch illuminating the battle against the common enemies of National Socialism and Islam."[14]

Since he took an interest in anything that concerned Arabs and Moslems, the mufti intervened with Berger on behalf of North African Moslems being held in France. He suggested that some of these men might be used to fight against the Allies.[15] The mufti maintained a frenetic pace on all fronts, especially where the persecuted Jews of occupied Europe were concerned. A number of times he intervened with Ribbentrop and the Bulgarian and Rumanian governments to oppose Jewish emigration to Palestine.

In a letter to the Bulgarian foreign minister, dated May 6, 1943, he expressed strong opposition to the emigration of four thousand Jewish children and five hundred adults. After a diatribe on the "Jewish peril," "world Jewry," and the dangers of creating a Jewish state against the wishes of the Arabs "who everywhere support the Axis powers," he demanded that these unfortunate people be deported to Poland. He also assigned a member of his entourage, as well as a representative of Rachid Ali (the ex-premier of Iraq, who had also fled to Germany), to train as SS men and to visit a concentration camp and "decide whether the plan of such a camp could serve as a model."[16]

"Since its foundation," Himmler declared in a letter addressed to the mufti, "the National-Socialist movement has made it a point to battle against world Jewry. For this reason, we have always watched with special sympathy the struggle of the Arabs who have been deprived of liberty, especially in Palestine, against the Jewish invaders. The recognition of this enemy and the common fight against him forms the powerful basis of the natural alliance between Greater Nazi Germany and the Moslems."

As his reward for all this activity, Haj Amin el Husseini got special funds from the German government, amounting to fifty thousand Reichmarks, plus twenty-five thousand Reichmarks in foreign currency, rent-free residences (he seems to have occupied two at once), all expenses incurred by himself and his visitors at the Hotel Adlon, maintenance for a "Jewish Institute" he had founded on the Klopstockstrasse, and the salaries of his domestic help and his chauffeur. The grand total was some one hundred thousand Reichmarks per month.[17]

It is interesting to note that the mufti was closely allied with the exterminator of the Jews, Adolph Eichmann. Their relationship dated from before the war. In the fall of 1937, in fact, Eichmann and Sturmbannführer-SS Herbert Hagen had gone to Palestine. British police surveillance prevented their meeting the mufti, but they contacted him through an Arab journalist at Jerusalem. Thenceforth their steady correspondence was conducted through the head of the German press agency at Jerusalem, Dr. Reichert. Shortly after the mufti arrived in Germany he visited Eichmann in his Berlin office at number 116 Kurfürstenstrasse. Eichmann gave him a "complete and detailed explanation of the solution to the Jewish question in Europe." Very favorably impressed, the mufti made Eichmann promise to send a representative to Jerusalem "when he [the mufti] returned there after the victory of the Axis powers." When one knows what the SS meant by the "solution to the Jewish question," one shudders at the idea of what a personal representative of Eichmann could have done in Jerusalem under the protection of el Husseini.[18]

In his blind and maniacal anti-Semitism, in his total adherence to the most inhuman aspects of National Socialism, the mufti was the perfect representative of the Pan-Arabism that opposed England and the Jews. By a disconcerting paradox, British policy, rather than taking these facts into account, was from the start of the war oriented against the Jews, the very people who would have been their natural and effective allies. Instead, the British sought to please the Arabs, who at the best of times did nothing to aid them, and usually hoped to see them defeated.

As is often the case with so-called realistic policies, this one was proof of a basic irrationality. Like the hostile attitude taken by Great Britain toward the French presence in Lebanon and Syria, it arose out of a fantastic overestimation of the capabilities and the importance of the Arab masses. It was a continuation of the romantic dream of Lawrence and Saint-John ("Abdullah") Philby, seasoned with a varying but persistent degree of anti-Semitism. It was a vision of an Arabic East that would remain medieval, in striking contrast with the dynamic modernism of Zionism.

Goebbels' propaganda seems also to have scored a point. By saying over and over that this was a "Jewish war," he succeeded in giving even the British a sort of complex that kept them from realizing the truth, which was that the Jews were in the front rank of peoples victimized by the Nazis, that consequently they were allies, and that the solution of their age-old problem should have been a war aim of the democracies, like the liberation of countries occupied by the Germans. But instead, the subject seemed to be unmentionable, as though, in Jabotinsky's word, it was "pornographic."[19] And so the Jewish contribution to the Allied war effort was never publicized; indeed, it was "the best-kept secret of the war."[20]

FOOTNOTES FOR CHAPTER 5

1. *The Jewish War Front,* published in June, 1940, and reissued in 1943 under the title *The War and the Jews.*

2. Weizmann. *Trial and Error.* p. 521.

3. Van Paassen. *The Forgotten Ally.* p. 197.

4. *Op. cit.,* p. 225.

5. Statement of Mr. Itshak Shamir to the author.

6. Telegram in code from the Reich foreign minister, von Weiszäcker, dated September 9, 1940, to the ambassador at Rome, von Mackensen. Published in *Akten zur deutschen auswärtigen Politik,* series D. Vol. XI-I, document #35.

7. *Ibid.* Document #40. Telegram from von Mackensen dated September 10, 1940.

8. *Ibid.* Document #51.

9. *Ibid.* Document #58.

10. *Ibid.* Document #134.

11. *Ibid.* Document #190.

12. Published in *Akten zur deutschen auswärtigen Politik,* Series D, Vol. XI, pp. 957–60.

13. Ladislaus Hory and Martin Broszat. *Der Kroatische Ustascha-Staat, 1941–1945.* Deutsche Verlags-Austalt, Stuttgart, pp. 156–57.

14. *Histoire et création de la . . . 13th division SS.* Document from the office of the Reichs-führer-SS, November 30, 1943. This text and the Berger report cited above are part of a series of documents in the archives of the SS.

15. Certain Algerians agreed to commit acts of espionage and sabotage in North Africa on behalf of the *Abwehr* or the *Sicherheitsdienst.* One of these was Mohammed Said, future "historical" chief of the F.L.N. and member of the G.P.R.A.

16. The paper and others quoted in this passage come from the Office of Chief of Counsel for War Crimes.

17. Declaration under oath, October 5, 1947, by Carl Rekowski, former consul at the Reich Ministry of Foreign Affairs. Office of Chief of Counsel for War Crimes, document #NG–5461.

18. Testimony at Nürnberg of Dieter Wislieceny, Haupsturmführer-SS, Eichmann's personal friend and collaborator at the heart of the "special commando" for the extermination of the Jews. This same document shows that the mufti enjoyed Himmler's confidence and frequently influenced him to step up anti-Semitic measures.

19. *The War and the Jew.* p. 31.

20. Pierre van Paassen. *The Forgotten Ally,* p. 175.

6
THE
GATES
ARE
CLOSED

Of all the tragedies of the Second World War, none is more atrocious than the extermination of the Jews of Europe. It is the greatest crime in history. Its horror lies not only in its unprecedented scope but also in the cold, implacable organization that presided over the "liquidation" of an entire people. It was a monstrous perversion of a civilization descended from the triple treasure of Athens, Rome, and Jerusalem. This civilization—depraved—turned its efforts to scientific massacre. Compared with the men behind this industrial butchery, the ruffians of Assyria and Tamerlaine's hordes were mere journeymen. The death camps represent reason perverted, progress deflected from its proper object, culture transformed into a savagery that no savage would dare to imagine. The annals of humanity, rich though they are in cruelty, have never presented a more dreadful and degrading spectacle.

During the years preceding the conflict, the Jewish population of Western and Central Europe could be divided into three categories: first, there were the Jews in the Western democratic countries, England, France, Holland, and Belgium. Some of these belonged to long-established families or communities, while others had come more recently from Eastern Europe. Some had been largely assimilated since their emancipation during the French Revolution; others remained more firmly attached to their traditions. Only a minority were active in Zionist organizations. The Algerian Jews—French citizens since the Crémieux decree of 1870—and Italian Jews up until the start of the war must be included in this group. In fact it was not until 1936—37 that Mussolini, under the pernicious influence of his German partners, began to introduce anti-Semitic racism into a country that had always resisted it.

With the exception of violent but short-lived outbreaks of anti-Semitism, such as the Dreyfus affair (which had been forgotten by the end of World War I), anti-Semitism in the Western countries was not virulent. It existed in the form of prejudices, varying with social class and education, but it was not an imminent threat.

In the second category were the two hundred thousand German and the one hundred thousand Austrian Jews. Nothing could be more erroneous than to imagine that Hitler and his supporters imposed anti-Semitism on a society otherwise free of it. Jabotinsky rightly remarked that "there [in Germany] and not elsewhere was the discovery made and the principle proclaimed, that the objection to the Jew is not religious but racial, and that he must therefore be persecuted even if baptized. There and not elsewhere was anti-Semitism sublimated to the rank of a scientific philosophy."[1] Remember, too, the anti-Semitism of such famous Germans as Schopenhauer, Feuerback, Dühring Treitschke; and the prestige that the English racist H. S. Chamberlain enjoyed in Germany; and the election to the Reichstag, as early as 1893, of representatives of the Anti-Semitic party; and in Austria the triumphant rise to power of Karl Lüger, mayor of Vienna in 1895, thanks to a "program" whose alpha and omega were anti-Semitic hatred. All this happened long before anybody had heard of Adolf Hitler and the National Socialist German Workers' party.

But in spite of this endemic anti-Semitism, German Jews did not really suffer before the advent of the Nazis. As we have seen, many of them thought of themselves simply as Germans professing the Jewish religion. Zionism did not attract them in great numbers. Among the Jews of Germany were many professors, scholars, and doctors who never realized, or only realized too late, that the political evolution of the country was leading them inexorably to ruin, degradation, and death. Nothing is more pathetic than to reread the innumerable testimonials of this period that show how these men — devoted to their nation and their professions — were pressed harder and harder, dismissed from their university chairs and their laboratories, but still refused to break with their past and flee Germany, until the hour when the Gestapo led them off to a death camp. The Nazi vise closed in on them and on other victims, too. The two hundred thousand Jews of Czechoslovakia were delivered to their executioners by the appeasement policies of England and France (the Jews of the Sudetenland in 1938 at Munich, those of Bohemia and Moravia and Slovakia in 1939).

In Poland — and this is the third category — things were very different indeed. The three million three hundred thousand Jews there represented 10 per cent of the total population, and 33 per cent of the urban population. In the province of Lublin, 43 per cent of the urban population were Jews. There, and in Lithuania and Byelorussia, the heart of the Diaspora had lived since the Middle Ages, made up of thriving communities nourished by traditions and reflection, with their *yeshivot* where sages and mystics taught, with a Yiddish literature that ran from popular tales to theological discussion, and with a keen sense of national and spiritual identity. As to their politics, some Polish Jews belonged to the Bund or Socialist party, others to "orthodox" Zionism, and others to Revisionist Zionism. There, from Warsaw to Brzesc (where a young militant named Menachem Beigin commanded the local Beitari group), Jabotinsky found enthusiastic support among the masses, particularly among the young people.

The predicament of Polish Jewry had steadily worsened during the quarter-century before World War II. Making his customary effort to be objective, Jabotinsky did not blame this state of affairs on the Polish people or their statesmen. Certainly, he said, it was undeniable that there was "anti-Semitism of men" in Poland, meaning discrimination and hatred; but worse than that was "anti-Semitism of things," or "the force of circumstances," which inevitably tended to exclude from economic and political life an ethnic and religious minority that had become too numerous. In his book *The Hebrew State*, published in Kraków, Poland, in 1936, Jabotinsky showed that the modernization of the Polish economy, industrialization, and the advent of a technical era were bringing country people to the cities in greater and greater numbers; that the fight for jobs was growing more and more bitter, and that "inevitably the first victim must be the Jew."[2] Four years later, he traced the development of the co-operative movement in Poland as an example of this problem: in 1938 there were 3,207 rural consumers' co-operatives, 1,475 dairy co-operatives, and 453 general marketing co-operatives, which were inevitably "killing the Jewish traders *en masse*."[3]

In fact, on the eve of the war one third of the three million Polish Jews were unable to earn even a subsistence income. Shut up in lugubrious urban ghettos, they constituted a *Lumpenproletariat* living in hopeless poverty. Their presence presented an economic, political, and moral problem for the Polish authorities, and made them an easy target for the anti-Semitism that emerged there just before the war.

As for the Jews of the Reich, that is to say those in Germany proper, in Austria, in the Sudetenland, in the protectorate of Bohemia-Moravia, and in the Slovakian satellite, it is clear that the attitude of the Nazi directors toward these five hundred thousand Jews had varied over the years, and that conflicting tendencies had cropped up even in Hitler's entourage.

Since the credo of the Nazi faith was hatred for the Jew, who was said to be the antithesis of the Aryan "culture carrier" and a corrupting influence that should be destroyed, the question confronting the Nazis when they came to power was what to do with the Jews of the Reich.

Their first response was two series of measures designed to provoke and accelerate emigration. From 1933 onward, they began to dismiss Jews from the universities, administrative positions, and liberal professions; to boycott their businesses, to exclude them from theaters, cinemas, concerts, and spas in accordance with the demented anti-Semitism of Julius Streicher. At the same time, emigration was made easy for the Jews who, seeing themselves restricted within the German community, wished to flee to Palestine. In short, the essential was to "purify," to clear the Reich of its Jewish population.

After a lull in 1934 (several thousand Jews who had fled Germany even returned to their homes), the Nürnberg laws of 1935 defined the Jews according to purely racial criteria and turned them into a caste of pariahs and untouchables. They were beaten and brutalized in the streets. A permanent, feverish anti-Semitic campaign, in which Streicher's obscene magazine, *Der Stürmer*, played a large part, set public opinion against them. Joseph Goebbels, the minister of propaganda, ranked among the most violent, pitiless anti-Semites.

However, not all the important Nazis shared these views. Hermann Göring, as director of the economy, wanted to leave the Jews to their own pursuits in certain sectors, at least for a while. The S.D. (*Sicherheitsdienst*), which had a "Jewish Section" (*Judenreferat*), stated its disapproval of Streicher's excesses in its official organ, the *Schwarze Korps*, and tried to speed up Jewish emigration to Palestine. The chief of the Jewish Section was an SS man named von Mildenstein. He thought that the only solution to the Jewish problem in Germany was to organize emigration. He followed the work of the Zionist attentively, going so far as to have his collaborators draw graphs to show Zionist progress in German-Jewish circles.[4] As we shall see later, when emissaries from the *yishuv* tried to rescue their brothers, von Mildenstein encouraged them, not out of humanity, to be sure, but to hasten the expulsion of the Jews from Germany.

One of von Mildenstein's collaborators was a young SS officer named Adolf Eichmann. Von Mildenstein, now adjudged to be too friendly toward Zionism, was replaced by the SS *Oberscharführer* Herbert Hagen, and Eichmann was put in charge of the "Zionist" bureau. Hagen and Eichmann realized that emigration would reinforce Jewish colonization in Palestine. Would this not help to create a Hebrew state that would, in its turn, protect scattered Jewish minorities? "Germany," said Hagen, "can in no way approve of the formation of such a monster-state: it is entirely possible that one day the mass of stateless Jews will start demanding Palestinian nationality."[5]

The S.D. chiefs seemed for a long time unable to find a way out of this dilemma. Eichmann continued to specialize in more or less forcible emigration, first in Berlin, then in Vienna. He affected the use of Hebrew and Yiddish expressions, and demonstrated an amazing knowledge of the Zionist movement, of Palestine and its inhabitants. The rumor went around that he had himself been born in Palestine in one of the German colonies, such as Sarona or Wilhelma, which had been founded in the nineteenth century. In September, 1937, in the guise of correspondent of the *Berliner Tagesblatt,* he spent a short time in Palestine and Egypt during which he made contact with emissaries of the mufti, as we have seen, and with an officer of the Haganah.

After the *Anschluss,* Heinrich Himmler, chief of the SS, and Reinhard Heydrich, head of the Gestapo, asked Eichmann to organize the emigration of the Jews of Austria. He set up his office in Vienna at the Rothschild house, and recruited a team whose principals — Novak, the Brunner brothers, Erich Rajakowitsch — would one day figure along with Eichmann among the most notorious war criminals. Under his direction, the Austrian Jews were more and more brutally pressed. Ruined by the confiscation of their possessions and businesses, hounded by the police, subjected to a thousand annoyances and brutalities, the Jews had no choice but to flee. Forty-five thousand left the country between the *Anschluss* and the autumn of 1938.

Eichmann, however, had managed to find someone who was more inhuman and anti-Semitic than he himself: Julius Streicher thought that the borders should be closed, not opened. He called upon all European nations to refuse entry to the "World Enemy Number One."

On October 28, 1938, Heydrich ordered the arrest of seventeen thousand Polish Jews living in Germany. They were thrown into cattle cars and transported to the Polish border, where the Polish police were in no hurry to let them in. These poor people remained in no-man's-land, deported by the Reich, and refused entry by Poland. Among them was a tailor from Hanover named Grynszpan. His son Herschel, who lived in Paris, learned about his father's fate from a radio newscast. Driven wild by the news, he bought a revolver and killed the third secretary at the German embassy in Paris, Ernst vom Rath, by firing five bullets into him.

This occurred on November 7th. On the 9th, Goebbels made one of the most violent speeches of his career before an assemblage of Nazi dignitaries at Munich that was presided over by Hitler. This unleashed a pogrom. Synagogues were burned all over Germany, Jewish stores were destroyed and looted, many Jews were killed or wounded, others were arrested and sent to the camps.

Now even the blindest Jew saw that the only chance for safety was exodus. In 1939, seventy-eight thousand Jews left the Reich and thirty thousand fled from Bohemia-Moravia. Heydrich and Eichmann collaborated with the emissaries of the Mossad, the Zionist organization in charge of emigration, and during the summer of 1939 actually authorized them to use Hamburg and Emden as ports of embarkation.

But 1939 was also the year in which the British government decided to give in to Arab threats and close the gates of Palestine. The White Paper and Nazi anti-Semitism thus converged to crush the Jews between the Reich, which threw them out, and Great Britain, which refused them entry to the Promised Land. The English fleet in the eastern Mediterranean gave chase to immigrant boats, and on July 21, 1939, the colonial minister of the Chamberlain government triumphantly announced in the House of Commons that in the space of two months the navy had turned back 3,507 illegal immigrants.

The torrential exodus of persecuted Jews created an international problem. Roosevelt called a world conference on German and Austrian refugees at Évian in July, 1938, followed by a second meeting in Washington in October, 1939. These meetings, as so often happens, degenerated into futile chatter, with Britain refusing to open Palestine and the majority of the Commonwealth countries, as well as Latin America and the United States itself, unwilling to lower the immigration barriers imposed by law. So these men and their families were squeezed between the hatred that exiled them from Europe and the cold inflexibility of governments and administrations incapable of responding to their despair with a human gesture.

The war broke out. The Jews of the Reich and its satellites all found themselves trapped. The Zionist emissaries had to leave Germany and Austria. Then events took the course that is known too well. The number of Jews subjected to Hitler's slavery grew each day: two million in the part of Poland occupied by the *Wehrmacht*; sixty thousand in Holland; fifty thousand in France. After the partition of Poland between Hitler and Stalin, the Jews in the Russian zone came under the rule of the Soviets, who treated them little better than did the Germans. The NKVD hunted down Zionism, which was considered a "petit-bourgeois, nationalist deviation allied with British imperialism," as energetically as did the Gestapo. Menachem Beigin, who had first been imprisoned at Vilno, was condemned as "an individual dangerous to society" and deported to Siberia, inside the Arctic Circle, as were many other Polish Jews.[6]

After the first victories of the *Wehrmacht* and its advance to the East, the Jews of the Soviet zone—White Russia and the Ukraine, Rumania, the Balkans, and Hungary—a total of more than three million five hundred thousand people, were ground up in their turn by the hellish machine. No longer was there any question of expulsion. Annihilation—*Vernichtung*—was the order of the day.

As Jabotinsky in particular noted, massacres of several hundreds or thousands of people began in Poland in the regions of Katowice, Łódź, and Warsaw as early as 1940. A "death march" claimed more than one thousand three hundred victims in four days at Chełm and Hrubieszów. However, official Nazi doctrine of the period still called for concentrating all German and Polish Jews in a "reservation," a gigantic ghetto, in the province of Lublin. Mass executions began with the Russian campaign. Entire communities, whipped and threatened with guns, were herded to the edge of vast pits. Then men, women, and children were ordered to take off their clothing and shoes (which the meticulous military administration retrieved), and were mowed down by machine guns; earth was thrown over these slaughterhouses while some of the victims were still alive.

But this was only the beginning. The decision to apply to the Jewish question what was called in Nazi jargon the "final solution" (*Endlösung*) appears to have been made by Hitler in November, 1941, on a proposition by Goebbels. Himmler, according to recollection of his personal physician Kersten, is said to have disapproved for a long time of this measure, but he applied it with a ferocious energy that is well known. According to Rudolf Diels, former chief of the Gestapo, Himmler and Heydrich first had the idea of the "final solution." In any case, Heydrich claimed it as his own and presented the plan on January 20, 1942, at a meeting on the Wannsee, where he specified that the *Endlösung* ought to be applied to about eleven million people. Thus the industry of death got underway. Shootings and hangings gave way to gas trucks, which gave way to gas chambers and crematories; prussic acid was preferred to carbon monoxide.[7]

Although they undertook to exterminate twenty-five thousand persons a day at Treblinka, it was undoubtedly at Auschwitz that the Nazis achieved their highest degree of efficiency. According to the testimony of Rudolf Hess, who was camp commandant from May 1, 1940, to December 1, 1943, at least two million five hundred thousand people were killed during this period alone, and another half a million died of sickness, hunger, and misery. Four hundred thousand Hungarian Jews perished there during the summer of 1944.[8] In addition to these death factories, extermination camps (*Vernichtungslager*) were operating in Lithuania, the Ukraine, and Poland. These were less highly perfected, as for example Fort #9, near Kaunas, where at least twenty-five thousand Jews from that city were put to death, plus ten thousand victims from Germany, Austria, and Czechoslovakia, and an unspecified number of other Jews.[9]

The figure of six million dead, which has been challenged sometimes since the war, undoubtedly in an attempt to attenuate the horror provoked by Nazi crimes, is only too well justified. Here we have the logical consequence of the application of modern industrial methods to the pitiless destruction of a human group. Alas, it is an irrefutable demonstration of the naïveté of those who look only to scientific and technical progress, to "development" as it is called, for the constant betterment of the human condition. Technical progress and moral progress are two very different things, and when the former is not guided by the latter, it can easily lead to the most atrocious tragedies.

Jabotinsky long before had sensed that this holocaust of European Jews was in the making. He saw but one way to escape it—hasten emigration to Palestine. Since the Mandatory gave in to Arab agitation and limited the number of "certificates" it would give to the Jewish Agency, the only solution left was illegal immigration. In an article on "adventurism" in March, 1932, Jabotinsky urged European Jews, especially the young ones, to forget the rules and break with legality. "One thing should be perfectly clear," he wrote, "which is that a nation, especially its youth, must not bow its head and sigh, 'since the police have barred our way to safety, we must resign ourselves and wait obediently. . . .' Where has it been written, where has it been said, that adventurism may not be one of the weapons in our fight?"[10]

Beginning in the early thirties, the trend to illegal immigration strengthened. Denied certificates by the British administration, Jewish "tourists" would arrive in Palestine with a temporary visa and then disappear into the farming colonies. Students who had finished their studies stayed on in Palestine without authorization. More than twenty thousand illegal immigrants arrived like this in 1932 and 1933. Most of them were Revisionist Zionists from Poland. Small groups also succeeded in infiltrating through the Lebanese border. During the summer of 1934, a 2,000-ton ship, the *Vellos,* chartered by the Zionist pioneers (*Hehalutz*) of Poland left Piraeus with three hundred visaless Jews on board, led by the young Levi Schwartz. It managed to land its passengers on the coast not far from Tel Aviv and to return to Greece for another voyage.

The directors of the Jewish Agency, such as Menahem Ussischkin and David Ben Gurion, still placed all their hopes on a change in the British attitude. What good does it do, they thought, to run the risks of illegal crossings in leaky ships to bring a few hundred immigrants into Palestine when we might be able to persuade Britain to increase substantially the number of certificates? Ben Gurion was sure that if he went to London he could get forty thousand immigration permits. He was soon disabused, because his attempts met a stone wall.[11] Nevertheless, many years passed before official Zionism began actively to organize clandestine immigration. The second voyage of the *Vellos* failed. The ship was driven back by the British navy and returned to Greece; the unfortunate passengers had to go back to Poland.

When Jabotinsky spoke of adventurism he was referring to the criticism that Zionist leaders usually made against illegal immigration. The Jewish Agency feared that the British authorities would react to illegalism with even more restrictive measures. Two other factors to some extent explain the hostility of official Zionism toward what Jabotinsky called the national sport of the Jews of the Diaspora. The Jewish Agency and the union of kibbutzim hoped for selective immigration, made up essentially of young people with some education who would one day become useful partners in the Palestinian economy. The Revisionists, on the contrary, were aware of the mortal danger Judaism faced and they wanted, in Jabotinsky's words, "to transplant all the Jews — the great writers and the most creative talents, but also the man in the street, the ordinary Jew of the Diaspora."

In the second place, there were political considerations. The parties that dominated the Jewish Agency did not care to see Revisionist tendencies reinforced in Palestine; they preferred to control the issuing of certificates to exclude as many Beitari and members of the

New Zionist Organization as possible.

Even after official Zionism began to assist illegal immigration, the quarrel between the Jewish Agency and the Revisionists continued to rage. The Revisionists were accused of extorting large sums of money from the emigrants they brought to Palestine, or of making them face needless danger in unseaworthy "coffin-ships," or of bringing in prostitutes and other undesirable elements. Jabotinsky protested strongly to Ben Gurion against these sectarian allegations.[12] Even after World War II began, the quarrel continued.

Thus, in February, 1940, the vice president of the United Jewish Appeal in the United States wrote to a rabbi in Maryland that the Revisionists, instead of "selecting" immigrants, recruited them on a "purely money basis . . . at random and irresponsibly," bringing criminals and protitutes into Palestine.[13]

However, ever since 1934 Jabotinsky and his cohorts in Europe had been operating the *Aliyah Beth*, "Immigration B."[14] Reifer and Schwarz in Vienna, Joseph Schechtman in Poland, Oskar Rabinowicz in Czechoslovakia, and Dr. Reuben Hecht in Basel were among the directors of these operations between 1935 and 1938. In Poland, the Revisionists managed to get official co-operation, and the Rumanian ambassador at Warsaw agreed to furnish the illegal immigrants with transit visas allowing them to embark at Constanta.

From 1938 on, the organization of the *Aliyah Beth* was divided between the Beitari and the Irgun: the Beitari were in charge of transporting the emigrants and putting them aboard ships, and the Irgun was to "receive" them on their arrival in Palestine, look to their safety, and see that they got settled in the country without the knowledge of the British authorities. This arrangement caused trouble between the two organizations, especially when Abraham Stern, who had gone to Europe on behalf of the Irgun, tried to "short-circuit" the Beitari and Jabotinsky himself. But despite these internal difficulties, illegal immigration to Palestine increased. To aid it, the labor leaders of Palestine and the head of the Haganah, Eliahu Golomb, decided in 1937 to create the Mossad.[15]

On the eve of World War II, Colonel Wedgwood told the House of Commons that there were thirty thousand illegal immigrants each year, of whom nearly half (46 per cent) arrived through Revisionist efforts, 30 per cent through official Zionist activity, and the rest on individual initiative. During the summer of 1939, representatives of Weizmann and Jabotinsky conferred with a view to co-ordinating the two movements for the collection of funds and the organization of clandestine transportation. Unfortunately, they never reached an agreement. Eliahu Golomb himself said to Jabotinsky that the Haganah would never accept any agreement as long as the Irgun stayed "outside of Zionist discipline," and that the Haganah could not approve of the entry into Palestine of "people who will increase anarchy and commit actions that we consider to be dangerous."[16] The *Aliyah Beth* thus had to depend on two sources of leadership separated by an airtight compartment.

In 1938 two emissaries of the Mossad, Pino Ginsberg in Berlin and Moshe Bar-Gilad in Vienna, made contact with the Gestapo and the S.D., and with Eichmann in particular. This was the beginning of the strange and paradoxical "collaboration" between the Jews and their most ferocious enemies. It was of short duration, for in May, 1939, Eichmann had Bar-Gilad expelled from Austria and all Reich territories. The SS had realized that organizing transportation to Palestine could be quite profitable for them. They decided to take over the business, and created a central office in charge of emigration that was chiefly intended to extort money from Jews fleeing from persecution and the concentration camps. Bar-Gilad and Ginsberg were able to get a reprieve by playing on personal and official rivalries between the Gestapo and the SS, but then the war began and all these operations came to a halt. The Mossad had nevertheless succeeded in sending several ships to Palestine, among them the *Colorado* and the *Dora*, each with four hundred or five hundred passengers. In 1938 and 1939 they succeeded in evacuating about seven thousand people:[17] a modest number, even a ridiculous number when compared with the millions condemned to death.

And yet what courage, ingenuity, and patience was brought into play to save these lives! Everything conspired against those who tried to flee Europe. Each emigrant was the subject of endless negotiations and interminable red tape to obtain visas from Latin American and Balkan countries. Substantial bribes had to be paid. Boats had to be bought or rented, convoys provided, and often, after so many efforts, the ships met a moving wall barring the Palestine coast. The Royal Navy stopped the ships, imprisoned captains and crews, and interned the passengers. But does not the salvation of even one life from hell justify every effort and every sacrifice?

As has been noted, in 1936 Jabotinsky launched his campaign at Warsaw for the evacuation of the Polish Jews, beginning with a million people whose income had fallen below the subsistence level and who were languishing in the ghettos without jobs, resources, or hope. This realistic stand stirred up a tempest in the Polish Zionist press, which attacked Jabotinsky violently in Yiddish and in Polish; in the United States, where Rabbi Stephen Wise called him an "apostate"; in Palestine, where the Mapai daily paper, *Davar*, accused "the *führer* Jabotinsky" of wanting "to expel the Jews from Poland to Palestine with the help of Polish anti-Semites." They condemned the head of the Revisionist party for having negotiated with Colonel Jósef Beck, the Polish foreign minister, and Marshal Smygly-Rydz, which is exactly the kind of negotiation the Mossad itself would undertake two years later with such men as Eichmann and Heydrich, who were much more virulent anti-Semites than the Polish leaders.

Jabotinsky tried in vain to show that Herzl himself had developed similar ideas in his famous work on the Jewish state. Herzl had called for an organized exodus of the Jews of Central and Eastern Europe and co-operation with all governments, even "under anti-Semitic pressure." Jabotinsky also recalled that Max Nordau, who was among the most eminent founders of Zionism, had published in 1920 a series of articles in Paris proposing a plan for the mass emigration of six hundred thousand Jews.

In any case, Jabotinsky braved the storm of protest, and negotiated in Warsaw with Colonel Beck, Prime Minister Skladhowski, and Marshal Smygly-Rydz. He got them to promise that Poland would urge emigration to Palestine at the League of Nations. Above all, he persuaded them to supply governmental and military aid to create military training camps in Poland where Jewish soldiers of the future could take two-month courses under the direction of Polish officers.

Abraham Stern and one of his aids, Strelitz, journeyed from Palestine, where they were part of the Irgun command, and took charge of secret liaison with the Polish army. Gradually a plan evolved to arm and instruct ten thousand young men in Poland and land them on the coast of Palestine at the same time that the Irgun unleashed widespread disturbances in the countryside. They hoped that in this way the restrictive measures imposed by the British administration would collapse. The Poles would furnish not only instructors but arms, too—five thousand rifles and some machine guns. The war began before this plan could be carried out. In September, 1939, the camps were dissolved and most of the young men who were in training succeeded in getting to Palestine.

Jabotinsky used the following analogy to make his thoughts clear: when a Swiss village at the foot of a mountain is threatened with an avalanche, it is "evacuated." If the avalanche occurs before evacuation, the catastrophe is all the more atrocious because it could have been at least partially averted. But in such cases there is always more than one person to blame. And certainly the British government chose to bear a heavy share of guilt when it shut the gates of Palestine to Jews who had managed to flee fom Europe.

The more the Nazi regime hardened and the more desperate the Jewish situation became, the more these unfortunates tried to escape and the more the English authorities tightened the blockade. The colonial minister, Malcolm MacDonald, made increasingly indignant speeches before the House of Commons in the summer and fall of 1939, against what he called a widespread attempt to violate the law. The British government brought more pressure to bear on Greece, Rumania, Yugoslavia, and Turkey to bar the passage of the immigrants to Palestine. Agents of the Intelligence Service, some of them chosen for their knowledge of Yiddish, combed the ports of the eastern Mediterranean and the Black Sea. The coast guard was reinforced with Anglo-Arab patrols.

In June, 1939, two ships with a total of over sixteen hundred passengers, among them several hundred old people, women, and children from Germany, Czechoslovakia, and Danzig, were intercepted by the British navy. Another ship burned in July between Rhodes and İstanbul. On September 2, 1939, the second day of World War II, the British coast guard fired on the ship *Tiger Hill* coming from Bulgaria, and killed two passengers. The others were arrested as they disembarked on the beach near Hayarkon Street in Tel Aviv and were put behind barbed wire in the Sarafand Camp.[18] The Jews, who were Britain's natural allies against Hitler, were treated as enemies when they sought to escape Hitler's domination!

During the autumn and winter of 1939, two thousand refugees from Germany and the occupied territories found places on board four small steamships and riverboats that had come down the Danube to Rumania, where they were stopped. The Revisionist organization had helped the passengers escape from Hitler's hell, but since they had no visas they could not disembark on Rumanian soil and were thus forced to remain on board under frightful conditions, without food or medicine, in the middle of a severe winter. In London, Jabotinsky pleaded the cause of these poor people. Secretary MacDonald was unmoved: he would not authorize these Jews to go to Palestine, and if they got there in spite of him, he would intern them. Jabotinsky's son Eri, who directed the *Aliyah Beth* in Rumania, chartered a Turkish ship, the *Sakaria,* which arrived in Haifa in February, 1940. In the end, the British let the passengers disembark—but the Mandatory annulled a corresponding number of immigration visas. Eri Jabotinsky was sentenced to a year in prison.

Another Danube adventure was that of the Kladovo group. The Mossad had arranged for the emigration of eleven hundred young people. The Yugoslavian government stopped the three little riverboats that carried them, and refused to let them pass the frontier city of Kladovo unless a Mossad ship came to take them to Palestine. It took too long to locate a ship, so the emigrants stayed on board their own icebound ships, where fortunately they were cared for by the Jewish community of Yugoslavia. At last they had to disembark. When the *Wehrmacht* invaded Yugoslavia the following spring, the Nazis massacred all of them.

On November 20, 1940, the Mandatory government announced that any refugee who entered illegally would be deported to Mauritius, an island in the Indian Ocean. "Their ultimate fate will be decided at the end of the war," the official declaration added, "but it is not expected that they will remain in the colony where they are to be sent, *nor that they will go to Palestine.*" The Holy Land was to be denied them forever.

This new policy seemed designed to drive the emigrants to despair. After the exodus, deportation forever! Is it surprising that the emigrants and the entire Jewish community contemplated violent revolt? Even the most moderate political leaders could hardly stand by while the *Aliyah Beth* died. As for the activists of the Haganah and the Irgun, they deduced from the British attitude that on this point at least, armed conflict was inevitable and necessary. Of course England was fighting Hitler, but it was also fighting the victims of the German dictator. This tragically erroneous policy had to be stopped.

In November, 1940, three ships loaded with illegal immigrants, the *Atlantic,* the *Pacific,* and the *Milos,* steamed into the port of Haifa. Their three thousand five hundred passengers came from Germany, Austria, and Czechoslovakia. The Palestinian government, acting on orders from London, decided not to let them disembark but to deport them to Mauritius. For this purpose, the authorities readied an 11,700-ton ship the *Patria,* upon which they loaded nineteen hundred of these unlucky people. The Mandatory's decision provoked an intense reaction in Palestine. The Jewish Agency pressed the government, and many protests were registered. All to no avail. The deportation order was carried out inexorably.

Shaul Avigour, a member of the Haganah high command whose specialty was illegal immigration, took charge of a special group assigned, at any cost, to keep the *Patria* from weighing anchor. During a meeting held in a restaurant in Arlosoroff Street in Haifa, he decided to put a large enough bomb on the ship to prevent her from sailing. A young volunteer, Munya Mardor,[19] disguised as a dock worker, managed to board the ship with a time bomb he had hidden in his lunch bag. The explosive was calculated to "blow a hole in the ship that would immobilize it for a few weeks." Two immigrants, one of whom was a girl, hid the bomb in a sandbag in the ship's hold. On the morning of November 25, a little past nine o'clock, it exploded. But either the charge was too big, or else the *Patria's* hull was too fragile. The ship began to take on water, list, and sink rapidly near the breakwaters of the port. Immediately, dozens of small boats rushed to save the passengers. Harbor workers knocked holes in the hull to rescue them, but the ship sank fast and two hundred fifty people perished. The survivors were then transferred to Atlit, where an internment camp had been set up.

Early in December these internees learned that they were to be put in two ships and taken to Mauritius. The political directors of the Jewish Agency refused to let the Haganah use force to stop this deportation. On December 8, a combined army and police detachment took possession of the camp, locked up the Jewish policemen who normally belonged to the guard, and tried to load the deportees into trucks. They met desperate resistance, even among the women and children. Such heartbreaking scenes took place that certain British police officers, among them one Constable Taylor, refused to carry out this inhuman task. After hours of struggling, sixteen hundred fifty people were loaded forcibly on two ships that sailed at once for Mauritius.[20]

The immigrants at Atlit who were not put on the ships obtained permission to stay in Palestine "as an exceptional act of humanity," and a corresponding number of immigration certificates were canceled. However, they were not let out of the internment camp until much later, in February, 1942.

As the war widened and the successes of the German army carried the swastika farther and farther eastward, the situation of European

Jews became ever more desperate and escape ever more difficult. In Rumania, the Iron Guard tried hard to emulate the racist excesses of the brown shirts: pogroms broke out at Bucharest, Iaşi, Brăila, and Galaţi; the entire Jewish population was forced to wear yellow stars; the Jews were deported all along the Dniester River and throughout the Ukraine; all manner of cruelty and humiliation were inflicted. The young Ruth Klieger, the Mossad's representative in Rumania, had to flee the country after one of her aides was murdered.

One little ship, the *Salvador,* which had left a Bulgarian port carrying no lifeboats, disappeared bag and baggage in the Dardanelles with three hundred refugees on board. Another, the *Struma,* chartered by the Irgun, managed to leave Constanta in December, 1941. She carried 769 emigrants, of whom seventy were children and 250 were women. Rumanian customs officers had taken everything the passengers owned when they sailed, including their meager provisions for the trip. Driven by an ancient engine, the *Struma* took four days to get to İstanbul, where the passengers were hoping to disembark and go overland to Palestine. They were met with the inflexible refusal of the Turkish authorities, on whom Lord Moyne had put great pressure in the name of the British government. His pretext was that enemy agents might have slipped in among these wretches. Short of food and water, without medicine or heat against the intense December cold, the *Struma* emigrants remained in the port of İstanbul for a month and a half, forbidden to set foot on land, and prey to disease, hunger, and despair.

During this time the Jewish Agency did all it could to persuade British authorities to grant legal entry to these emigrants to Palestine, even if it meant canceling an equal number of immigration certificates. To the "enemy agents" argument, the Agency replied that the passengers on the ship could certainly be interned and "filtered" when they arrived. Besides, it was highly unlikely that *Abwehr* spies could have infiltrated these Jews from Bucovina and Bessarabia, where communities were homogeneous and everyone knew everyone else. But all these efforts were in vain. The British government insisted that the *Struma* take to the sea with its pitiful cargo.

On February 3, 1942, eighty Turkish policemen took possession of the ship over the protests and resistance of the passengers. A tugboat towed the *Struma* into the high seas and abandoned her. The ship sank the next morning. According to David Stoliez, the sole survivor, she was hit by a torpedo. According to the Turks, the ship hit a mine.

It is worth noting that the *Struma* flew the flag of Panama. Germany and Italy had been in a state of war with Panama since 1941, and there was no lack of Axis submarines in these waters. In any case, there was only one survivor. By a tragic twist of fate a telegram authorizing the children to disembark and come to Palestine reached the British consul in İstanbul—after the ship was already at the bottom of the sea.

This disaster aroused deep indignation in Palestine. The whole Jewish community, regardless of party, felt plunged into a common mourning. Chaim Weizmann was then in England (his son, Michael, an RAF pilot, died in action about this time), and expressed his disapproval of the inhuman attitude of the British. With the sinking of the *Struma* the naval operations of *Aliyah Beth* came to an end for a while. Besides, all of Europe had been invaded, and the massive extermination of Jews who had been caught in the trap was accelerated with each passing day. The Mossad emissaries to Europe had returned to Palestine. The officers of the Beitari were scattered either in German-occupied territories or in the immensity of the Soviet Union, where those who were Polish citizens joined the Polish army that was being recruited according to the agreement between Stalin and General Sikorksy. The uprising in the Warsaw ghetto, the resistance of the Kaunas ghetto, the battle of the Jewish partisans in the forest of Byelorussia—these were the last desperate convulsions of a people unwilling to die. But the inexorable machine of destruction mounted by National Socialism was too colossal to be stopped by armed resistance. The great mass of unarmed Jews was engulfed in "the night and fog" of the concentration camps.[21]

It is hard to say when the atrocities of the final solution came to be generally known. The Allied governments were probably aware of them by the middle of 1942. On December 16, 1942, Anthony Eden denounced the massive extermination of the Jews in a speech to the House of Commons. The Allies and the National French Committee solemnly condemned this barbarity. But the policies of the White Paper remained unchanged. In a letter to Lord Moyne dated April 18, 1943, Winston Churchill defined the White Paper as a "gross failure to keep our word"; the British government, he added, could no longer give it a "positive endorsement." But, he concluded, "it remains in effect until it is replaced."

And so Great Britain stubbornly opposed every attempt to save a few thousand or tens of thousands of Jews by opening Palestine to them. In March, 1943, a plan worked out by the World Jewish Congress was submitted to the English and American governments. It advocated the "purchase" of seventy thousand Rumanian Jews by depositing ransom money in Switzerland to the account of certain Nazi leaders, who would only be able to draw on it after the war. Washington was reluctant to deposit money to Nazi accounts, but finally agreed to the idea. The ministry of economic warfare in London vetoed the plan, and the foreign office let it be known that it was "seriously concerned about the difficulty of receiving a considerable number of Jews." During a conference held in Washington during the Roosevelt presidency, at which Cordell Hull, Sumner Wells, and Harry Hopkins represented the United States, and Anthony Eden, Lord Halifax, and William Strang represented Great Britain, Hull raised the question of the sixty thousand Jews of Bulgaria who might still be saved. Eden replied that there were not enough ships, and that German agents could infiltrate Palestine this way. Every plan failed, one after the other. The Anglo-American meeting in Bermuda in April, 1943, was a fiasco. England clung to the White Paper, and the United States did not want to modify its immigration laws. The result of this debate was "brutal and cruel: nothing could be done," according to the American undersecretary of state, Adolph A. Berle.

During the summer of 1944, a Hungarian Jew, Yael Brand, appeared with an extraordinary proposal from Eichmann: the exchange of one million Jews for 1,000 tons of tea, 1,000 tons of coffee, and 10,000 trucks.[22] Brand conferred with the Jewish Relief Committee at İstanbul. He told them that Eichmann had given him two weeks to return to Budapest. Otherwise the extermination of Hungarian Jews would begin at the rate of twelve thousand per day. If Brand brought back a favorable response, Eichmann promised to free one hundred thousand Jews immediately.

As strange and, in some senses, repellent, as this offer was, could anyone afford to pass up even this feeble chance to rescue a few people from a death sentence? The Jewish Agency appealed to the British high commissioner MacMichael, who promised that Brand could enter English-controlled territory, although technically an "enemy subject," and that he could also return to Budapest. In fact, Brand went to Syria and met Moshe Shertok (later Sharett), was arrested by the British police, and imprisoned in Cairo. The massacre of the Hungarian Jews began, just as Eichmann had said it would. Every day twelve thousand men, women, and children were loaded into cattle cars, each containing eighty to one hundred twenty people, and sent to Auschwitz.

Some of them died en route from thirst and asphyxiation. Of those who reached the camp, 95 per cent went directly from the train to the gas chambers and the crematories. The rest died within an average of one month. On June 20, 1944, the BBC broadcast an embarrassing announcement: two emissaries of the Hungarian government had come to Turkey to propose that "the Jews still alive in Hungary be authorized to leave in exchange for a certain quantity of medicine and trucks from England and America. A promise was made that this matériel would not be used on the Western Front. Authoritative British circles," the communiqué went on, "regarded this offer as a clumsy attempt to weaken the Allies, whose sympathy for the Jews of Hungary is well known."

Well known as that sympathy was, it never assumed any concrete form. Perhaps Lord Moyne's reaction was less "sympathetic" but more typical of authoritative circles when he exclaimed: "A million Jews? What could we do with them?"

If the Allies did not help the Jews to escape, it would seem that they might have systematically bombed the railroads used by the death trains, and the gas chambers at Auschwitz. In July, 1944, Weizmann made just such an appeal to Eden. Fifty-seven days later, the foreign office answered that these bombing raids were "technically" impossible.

Given the conditions created by the war, nothing could have saved *all* the Jews condemned to extermination. But some of them could have been snatched from genocide, if someone had only wished to do so. The conclusion is inescapable that this will did not exist in high Allied political circles.

Lives can be saved even with very limited means. During the summer of 1943, the colonial minister, Lord Cranborne, sent the British ambassador in Turkey the following confidential instructions: the Jews of occupied Europe were not to be encouraged or aided in leaving the Continent, but if, despite everything, some managed to get to Turkey, they would be authorized to proceed to Palestine.[23] These secret instructions soon came to be known to the Intelligence Service of the Haganah. A center for the Mossad was set up at İstanbul, of which one participant was Teddy Kollek, the present mayor of Jerusalem. In spite of the Nazi occupation, small ships, fishing boats, and caïques sailed from Greece and Rumania to Turkish ports. Several hundred Jews from Greece and four thousand from Rumania arrived this way in spite of some tragic accidents. A German destroyer sank the ship

Mefkure and machine-gunned the survivors. Only five out of three hundred ninety passengers survived.

The Swiss and the Red Cross made every effort to help certain Jews, especially children condemned to a terrible death. In 1943 the Swiss minister plenipotentiary Feldscher held a series of talks with the Reich in an attempt to get permission to evacuate five thousand Jewish children from occupied Eastern Europe. The Swiss legation at Sofia asked the Bulgarian government to allow five thousand Jews to go to Palestine. The International Red Cross asked the German Embassy at Ankara to guarantee safe passage for one thousand Jews who were sailing to Haifa from a Bulgarian port. According to official documents[24] the Swiss efforts had the approval of the British government. Minister Feldscher also intervened on behalf of French and Dutch Jews. As one might expect, the Reich either delayed or refused. The Nazis said they would exchange the Jews in question for an equal number of German nationals; they stipulated that the refugees could not be sent to Palestine, "which belongs to the Arab world." The mufti, of course, opposed any project that might have saved a few victims, and he used all his influence with German, Italian, and Bulgarian officials so that no one be allowed to escape.[25] He wrote to Joachim von Ribbentrop, the minister of foreign affairs, on May 13, 1943: "The Arabs look upon Jewish immigration as a menace to their vital interests. . . . Your friend the Arab people has, by reason of our common interest in the battle against Communism and the Anglo-Saxons, unhesitatingly aligned itself on the side of the Axis powers. From these friends—the Axis powers and their allies—we expect a solution to the problem of world Jewry. . . . [if the Jews are allowed to emigrate] they will be even more dangerous and harmful than before. I therefore wish to implore Your Excellency to do all in your power to see that Bulgaria, Hungary, and Rumania will oppose this Jewish-American-English plan." In another letter to von Ribbentrop dated June 10, 1943,[26] he enumerated at length all the information he possessed on emigration plans already underway: seventy-five Jews had left Bucharest for Palestine; two hundred seventy young people from Rumania and Hungary had reached Turkey; seven hundred Polish women and children with relatives in Palestine had been given immigration permits; the Swiss consulates in Bucharest and Sofia would issue visas for Palestine. "I find it necessary to let Your Excellency know," he continued, "that the Arabs, sincere friends of the Axis as they are, feel deeply wounded when they see their friends, the allies of the Axis powers, facilitating these Jewish-British enterprises and helping transport Jews, who are the agents of the British and the Communists and the enemies of the Arabs and of Europe, to Arabian Palestine."

Haj Amin el Husseini's frantic denunciations were only too well heard. In April, 1944, at last the German government announced that the British response to its demands, through the Swiss minister, was unsatisfactory. The talks were broken off.

In spite of the good will evident in these efforts, diplomacy proved to be disappointing. But illegal immigration, using the means at hand, achieved some notable results in spite of the Nazi occupation in Europe and the blockade of Palestine by the Mandatory. It could have been transformed into something much vaster and more effective if Great Britain had not obstinately applied the White Paper of 1939, even though it was itself illegal since the League of Nations had never approved it, and even though it made no sense in face of the tragic conditions that the inhumanity of the Nazis had created in Europe. England, to its credit, brought its influence to bear in the well-intentioned, although unsuccessful, efforts described above. But such gestures could not satisfy the Jews of Palestine who knew that thousands of their relatives and friends were being swallowed by the crematory ovens each day. What they themselves saw were the ships being turned away, the illegal immigrants interned, and Palestine subjected to a regime so paradoxically anti-Semitic.

One of the most absurd aspects of British immigration policy was that the famous "certificates" were not even all used. The White Paper had in fact provided seventy-five thousand for the five-year period 1940–45. But in four years there were only thirty-two thousand authorized immigrants, instead of the legal sixty thousand.[27]

Evaluating the exact success of the *Aliyah Beth* is difficult, but it did not even reach that figure. It would therefore have been possible to "legalize" almost all the immigrants, rather than going to such lengths to run them off, to intern them at Atlit, or to deport them to the Indian Ocean (and in so doing tie up shipping that was desperately needed for the war effort). It would be hard to find a more stunning example of administrative bungling coupled with a perfect disregard both for humanity and for common sense.

Errors like these, which are common within military or civil bureaucracies in all countries, were nevertheless part of a larger policy. The key to this policy was the "Arabism" of British ruling circles. Lawrence's dreams still wrought their havoc, which was further intensified by Franco-British rivalry in the Levant. Disappointed by the Hashemite dynasty, Churchill pinned his hopes on ibn-Saud. "I want you to know," he said to Weizmann in March, 1942, "that I have a plan. . . . I would like to see ibn-Saud made lord of the Middle East— the boss of the bosses—provided that he settles with you. It will be up to you to get the best possible conditions." Some time previously "Abdullah" Philby, ibn-Saud's confidant, had made similar proposals to Weizmann.[28] Needless to say, this plan, like all the other grandiose proposals by the agents of the colonial office in Arab countries, evaporated like a mirage in the desert. But the grand design of a great Arab union allied to Great Britain never ceased to haunt Whitehall. On February 19, 1943, Eden made a major speech in the House of Commons on the subject of Arab unity, and the Arab League was proclaimed in October, 1944, with England's benediction. The first act of the Arab potentates and dictators (who throughout the war had gambled on a victory by Hitler) was of course to turn against the English.

Thus did the British manage to execute the tour de force of alienating not only the Jews, who had been their active allies since the beginning of the war, but the Arabs as well, of whom the best that can be said is that they did nothing to assist the war effort.

The Jews of Palestine understandably passed from their deep, almost passionate Anglophilia of 1917 (Weizmann never completely recovered from it) to a "marriage of convenience" in 1939, then to active hostility. The pro-Arab policies of the thirties had tarnished English prestige with the *yishuv*. But the terrible drama of the gates that clanged shut while six million men, women, and children burned in German furnaces caused a dreadful emotional reaction. What manner of men could keep from rebelling when they saw the flesh of their flesh die in agony under the indifferent eye of the power that was supposed to be protecting them? Already in 1939–40, the hard core who joined Abraham Stern had refused to postpone armed conflict against England. Neither the mass of the Palestinian community, nor the Haganah, nor even the Irgun had ever approved of Stern and his men or followed them. But as time went on and the horrors perpetrated in Europe became widely known, while the Mandatory authority inexorably maintained the rule of the White Paper, despair gave birth to a new will to fight. It is surprising that officials in Jerusalem and London did not realize that the crucible of Palestine had been heated white-hot by the fires that consumed the Jewish people of Europe and that it had to explode, particularly if all the safety valves remained closed.

The story of illegal immigration did not end with the Second World War; the White Paper remained the supreme law—always to please the Arabs—even after the defeat of the Axis. But from then on, illegal immigration became a part of the history of armed resistance.

FOOTNOTES FOR CHAPTER 6

1. *The War and the Jew.* p. 57.
2. Text in Italian in *Verso lo Stato.* p. 260.
3. *The War and the Jew.* p. 73.
4. Heinz Höhne. "Die Geschichte der SS," *Der Spiegel.* December 19, 1966.
5. *Ibid.*
6. Menachem Beigin. *Hamered* (Revolt) in Hebrew. Translated into Spanish as *La Rebelión en Tierra Santa.* Buenos Aires, 1951. Beigin recounted his memories of deportation under the title *White Nights.* London, MacDonald, 1957.
7. Jacques Delpeyrou. *Combat.* July 17, 1967. Heinz Höhne, *op. cit.*
8. William Shirer, *Berlin Diary*, Italian edition, *Diario di Berlino*, Torino, Einaudi, 1967, pp. 586–87.
9. Abraham Golub. "The Escape from the Ninth Fort," *Extermination and Resistance. Historical Records and Source Material.* Published by the kibbutz "Lohamei Haghettaot" (Ghetto Fighters), near Haifa, p. 141 ff.
10. *On Adventurism,* in Yiddish. *Morgen Journal,* New York, March 8, 1932.
11. Jon and David Kimche. *The Secret Roads.* pp. 20–22. This book is concerned almost exclusively with illegal immigration as it was organized by official Zionism, and it reflects that point of view.
12. Schechtman. *The Jabotinsky Story.* Vol. II, p. 428.
13. Shmuel Katz. *Day of Fire* (in Hebrew). Manuscript translation into English given to the author by Mr. Katz.
14. The word *aliyah*, "ascent," in Hebrew, traditionally designates the return to the Holy Land. *Beth* is the second letter of the alphabet.
15. Kimche. *op. cit.,* p. 23. See also Mardor, *Strictly Illegal.*
16. Golomb. *The Hidden Strength*, Vol. II, p. 98. Quoted by Schechtman. *Fighter and Prophet*, p. 429.
17. Bracha Habas. *The Gate Breakers.* p. 109. The exact figure given by this author (of Mapai tendencies) is 6,821.
18. *Ibid.* p. 103.
19. Cf. Munya Mardor. *Strictly Illegal.* London, Robert Hale, 1957, p. 56 ff.
20. 130 of them never returned. The others lived for five years in an ancient fortress dating from the French occupation and at last returned to Palestine after the war.
21. Cf. Sarah Neshomit. *Beginnings of the Partisan Movement in the Kaunas Ghetto.* Immanuel Ringelblum. *Notes from the Warsaw Ghetto.* Samuel Bornstein. "Dr. Yehezkel Atlas, Partisan Commander," in *Extermination and Resistance,* Kibbutz Lohamei Haghettaot, 1958.
22. Ben Hecht. *Perfidy,* New York, Messmer, 1961, p. 212.
23. Jon and David Kimche. *op. cit.,* p. 66.
24. Documents of the Office of Chief of Counsel for War Crimes, Doc. #NG–4786.
25. *Ibid.* #1309, NG–2757, 1310.
26. *Ibid.* #1311.
27. Vera Weizmann. *op. cit.,* p. 194.
28. Weizmann. *Trial and Error.* pp. 427–28.

7
ARMED
RESISTANCE

With the exception of the Stern group, which had been virtually paralyzed by the death of its chief, all the Jewish paramilitary organizations in Palestine had decided to fight at the side of the British and
help defeat Hitler.

David Raziel met his death in Iraq on a dangerous mission for the
English. Yaakov Meridor, his companion, came back safe and sound
and succeeded him as the chief of the Irgun Zvai Leumi.

When Rommel threatened Egypt, the British high commissioner
warned the Jewish Agency and the Vaad Leumi (National Council)
that if Alexandria fell, Palestine would have to be abandoned. The
Haganah, especially the Palmach commandos, and the Irgun prepared
themselves for this eventuality. An accord between the two organizations seemed highly desirable. A meeting was arranged at the home
of Moshe Sharett between Meridor, who represented the Irgun, and
two Haganah delegates, Eliahu Golomb and Moshe Sneh. They never
reached an agreement.[1]

Although times were grave, an abyss separated the disciples of
Jabotinsky from the leaders of official Zionism. The ideological conflict
was artificial, for Jabotinsky's political thought, whatever could be
said of it, was in no way conservative and certainly not reactionary.
What really separated them was the temperamental incompatability of
the activists of the Beitar and the New Zionist Organization and the
partisans of a prudent and gradual approach. The former believed that
the ultimate aim of Zionism — the creation of a Jewish state — would be
achieved only by a hard fight; the latter, in fact renouncing Herzl's
doctrine, were content with an ill-defined "home" within the framework of the British Empire.

It would be a mistake to believe that the Jewish Agency and the
Haganah presented an absolutely united front. Chaim Weizmann, for
example, never stopped saying, "Our only hope is England"[2] and "It
would be folly to risk a breach with England."[3] Ben Gurion, who was
the most influential leader of the Zionist institutions within Palestine,
responded to the pressure of events. In his testimony before the Peel
Commission on January 7, 1937, he declared: "We have never said that
we wish to establish a Jewish State in Palestine. We did not say it then

[at the origins of Zionism], and we do not say it now. . . . For the solution of the Jewish problem, and for our free national future, Palestine
need not be set up as a separate state. We would be only too glad if in
the future, when the National Home is completely established, Palestine, eternally and completely free, could be part of a larger unity, the
British Commonwealth."[4] Five years later, on May 9–11, 1942, the Biltmore Conference took place at the New York hotel of that name;
several hundred American Zionists and sixty-seven Zionists from
other countries, including Weizmann and Ben Gurion, took part. The
Biltmore Program they adopted called for the creation of a Jewish republic in Palestine, which was a return to the position of the Revisionists. Weizmann approved it, perhaps against his better judgment,
while Ben Gurion wanted to get American help for a "rapid and revolutionary" change in Palestine, whether England agreed or not. This
was the beginning of a certain estrangement between Weizmann and
Ben Gurion.[5]

By rallying to the idea of an independent Jewish state, Ben Gurion departed from both the pro-British moderates like Weizmann and
the anti-imperialist left-wing that favored a binational Judeo-Arab
state. This latter tendency was that of the *Hashomer Hatzaïr*, then influential among some of the kibbutzim. Rather than a Jewish state of
all of Palestine (as Jabotinsky had wanted), or a partition of the country between Jews and Arabs (as proposed by the Peel Commission),
the *Hashomer* wanted to seek an agreement with the Arabs for a state
common to both peoples. This idea, with its pacifistic overtones, was
obviously utopian in nature.

Furthermore the Haganah, though within the political institutions
of the Jewish community, was by reason of its very function a crossroads for activist currents. The mood of the members of this organization and of its elite, the Palmach, was quite often close to that of the
Irgun. This was especially true among the youth. With the ghastly fate
of the Jews of Europe imprinted on their minds, they reproached the
Haganah and even the Irgun for what they thought was timid procras-
tination. In the kibbutzim, the co-operative villages, the schools and
colleges of Tel Aviv, Jerusalem, and Haifa, boys and girls fifteen years
old boiled with impatience and rebelled against the policy shared by
the Haganah and the Irgun of collaborating with England in the face of
the Nazi peril.[6]

But at the bottom of all this, the main obstacle to unity (which in
fact was never completely overcome) lay in two conflicting conceptions

of the relationship that should properly exist between the political organs of the Jewish community and its army. The Jewish Agency looked upon itself as a "State in the process of being created," with civil powers to which the military ought to be subordinate. The Agency felt it inconceivable that there could be two or more "secular arms." Thus, anything that was not part of the Haganah, anything independent of the authority of the national council and the executive committee was considered "dissident" and severely condemned as undermining discipline. More than twenty years later, in 1966, at the symposium arranged by the newspaper *Ma'ariv,* the spokesmen of orthodox Zionism, even those who had in the meantime become Communists, such as Dr. Sneh, or dissidents, such as Shimon Peres, staunchly upheld the thesis that even if the institutions (The Jewish Agency and the Vaad Leumi) were sometimes mistaken, and even if they sometimes hampered the Haganah, it was they and they alone that were qualified to direct the paramilitary organizations. Dissidence was blameworthy in and of itself and ought to be curbed. Although the state did not exist, this was a state policy.

The position of the Irgun was quite different. While Jabotinsky was alive, his matchless personal prestige united the Revisionist party, of which he was president, the Beitar, of which he was the chief, and the Irgun, command of which he delegated to such men as Raziel. But it was indeed a personal union around an uncontested leader rather than a real subordination of the Irgun to the party (although even before the war, Stern and Israel Scheib had, as they say, "kicked in the traces"). After Jabotinsky's death, relations between the military command of the Irgun and the directing committee of the party became more and more strained, for it is hard to tie an illegal activist movement to a legal political authority.

Being strictly dependent on the institutions, the Haganah found itself oriented inevitably toward the acquisition and conservation of power. The Irgun, an autonomous combat wing, did not fight for power but for the creation of a democratic state where the people would decide what forms power would take and what groups or persons would wield it. This disinterest could have been called naïve, but it did not overcome the trust of the orthodox Zionists, who always feared the Irgun and doubted the sincerity of its detachment with regard to the problem of power. Such were the tensions and the hidden motives, naturally complicated by personalities and by memories of the years of bitter struggle, that divided the political and the military staffs while the course of events tended to "radicalize" the positions of the members of the community and while the horror of the European holocaust weighed more and more heavily on them.

At the end of 1942 and the beginning of the next year, many of the Revisionist Zionists, notably Hillel Kook (Peter Bergson), Shmuel Marlin, and Arieh Ben Eliezer, seeing that they could expect nothing from an England obstinately attached to the politics of the White Paper, tried to arouse American public opinion. They established a Committee for the Rescue of European Jews in New York, whose work soon had resounding effects. At the same time, Menachem Beigin, the former chief of the Beitar in Poland, had been let out of prison in Siberia through the Russo-Polish accords, and was on his way to Palestine in the ranks of the Polish army. When he reached the Holy Land, he soon impressed the leaders of the Irgun as the most capable leader they had seen. Yaakov Meridor was the first to ask him to assume command.

Beigin was ready for such responsibility, provided that the Irgun would reverse the line it had taken at the start of the war. The defeat of the Axis had been assured since El Alamein, Stalingrad, the French landing in North Africa, and the fall of Mussolini. It was no longer tolerable to sacrifice the aims of Zionism's war to a British ally that took no account of the martyrdom of European Jews. Now they must wage armed resistance against Great Britain without waiting for the war to end.

Menachem Beigin could easily have deserted the Polish army, but for many reasons the idea repelled him. Returning from the United States, Ben Eliezer persuaded the Polish military authorities to release Beigin to serve on the Committee for the Rescue of European Jews. So Beigin left the Polish army in good order and entered the clandestine life. From the summer of 1943 until May, 1948, he was to lead the Irgun from dangerous and threatened hiding places, sometimes in Jerusalem, sometimes in the rural surroundings of Petach Tikvah, sometimes in a secluded house near the River Yarkon, sometimes in the very center of Tel Aviv. Beigin disguised himself as a studious lawyer or a bearded Talmud scholar and assumed such names as Ben Zeev, Sassover, Halperin, or Koenigshofer while dodging the thousands of police who pursued him relentlessly.

In January, 1944, Beigin sent a call to rebellion throughout the land in the name of the Irgun Zvai Leumi. "Four years have passed since the war began," he said, "and all the hopes that beat in your hearts then have evaporated without a trace. We have not been accorded international status, no Jewish army has been set up, the gates of the country have not been opened. The British regime has sealed its shameful betrayal of the Jewish people and *there is no moral basis whatsoever for its presence in Eretz Israel.*

"We shall fearlessly draw conclusions. There is no longer any armistice between the Jewish people and the British administration which hands our brothers over to Hitler. Our people is at war with this regime — war to the end. . . . This then is our demand: Immediate transfer of power in Eretz Israel to a provisional Hebrew government!"[7]

Begin's first decision was to remove the Irgun from the guidance of the Revisionist party. This guidance was not very strict, but Dr. Altman and the directing committee of the party had often during 1943 tried to restrain Meridor. Begin thought it would be better for the legal and "open" party if it could pursue its course without being compromised by the illegal and clandestine movement. It would be better for the illegal movement not to be hampered by the normal scruples of the party.

At the same time, the command of the Irgun laid down its principles; its aim, unalterable according to the teachings of Jabotinsky, was to establish the Jewish state — the only solution to the appalling tragedy taking place in occupied Europe. Methods had to be adapted to situations, but from the onset the Irgun forbade any recourse to terrorism against individuals. It set its own war objectives. While the war against Hitler continued, it limited its attacks to whatever represented the Mandatory power in its administrative and policing aspects — police stations, immigration bureaus — with the exception of military installations and anything else that might affect the war effort against Nazi Germany. In effect, it enforced a form of *havlagah,* or voluntary moderation, at the heart of the offensive it was opening against Great Britain.

This is the difference between the Irgun and the Stern group. "Yaïr's" comrades, who had been arrested and thrown in jail after his death, were regrouping. Yitshak Yitzernitsky escaped from the Mirza camp. Then Nathan Yellin-Moor and twenty of his friends managed to tunnel out of the Latrun camp under the noses of the British guards. Israel Scheib, who had been wounded in his first escape attempt, was carried on a litter to a Jerusalem clinic. A nearby "patient," moaning under a blanket, suddenly pulled a revolver and fired at the English subaltern who was watching Scheib. Then a Stern commando disarmed the police guard, grabbed Scheib, and put him into a car that pulled away like a shot. Yellin-Moor, Yitzernitsky (now under the name of "Rabbi Shamir"), and Scheib (who became "Dr. Eldad") formed the central committee of the revived Stern group. The organization took the name of Lohamei Herut Israel—"Fighters for the Freedom of Israel," abbreviated to Lehi. It soon became evident that there was scarcely any ideological unity within this movement where opinion ranged from the biblical and romantic nationalism of Eldad to the left-wing anti-imperialism of Yellin-Moor. But it was cemented during the years of combat by the necessity to fight to the death with whatever means came to hand, including terrorism. The effective force of the Lehi never numbered more than hundreds while those of the Irgun were counted in thousands. Their very numerical weakness obliged them to take limited but daring action. It is only fair to say that they pushed the spirit of self-sacrifice to rare heights.

The three members of the central committee complemented one another admirably. Shamir, the organizer and man of action; Eldad, the theoretician, propagandist, and poet; Yellin-Moor, an intellectual and a keen analyst, endowed with a talent for diplomacy and negotiation. Shamir recruited and trained small armed teams. Eldad explained the ideas of the movement in a multitude of articles, tracts, and undercover newspapers (their "official" publication was Hehazith, "the Front"). They started a clandestine radio to supplement their written propaganda, and their announcer was the young Yemenite girl Gueoula Cohen. Yellin-Moor found himself in charge of liaison between the rival paramilitary organizations. He maintained personal relations with such Haganah directors as Eliahu Golomb and stayed on good terms with Menachem Beigin, whom he had known in Poland at the time of Beigin's arrest by the Russians. Yellin-Moor himself had succeeded in escaping from the N.K.V.D. and returning to Palestine. He hoped to bring the three armed organizations together, and he worked to that end.

When Menachem Beigin took charge of the Irgun, it was commanded by Meridor—disguised as "M. Honig," a peaceable businessman in transportation. His colleagues were Arieh Ben Eliezer, a sabra, born in Palestine; Eliahu Lankin, a Chinese, that is to say a Jew from the Russian colonies of Harbin and Shanghai; and Shlomo Levi, who came from a pioneer family in Petach Tikvah. British reprisals occasionally created gaps in this staff. Meridor was arrested in February, 1945, and imprisoned in Palestine, in Cairo, and then in concentration camps in the Sudan and Kenya. Ben Eliezer, captured shortly after Meridor, was deported to Eritrea, as was Lankin. Shlomo Levi was also sent to East Africa. They escaped from their prisons, however. Other leaders joined Beigin to work and fight: Yeroham Livni, called Eitan, or Uncle Moshe, was captured at Bat-Yam following a sabotage operation; Amilai Peglin, called Guiddi, a former Haganah militant (his older brother had been a member of the Mapai and the Night Patrols of Captain Orde Wingate and had died serving under the British flag in Syria in 1941) was the most daring fighter, and the most cunning inventor of a thousand devices made up from the materials at hand. Chaim Landau, called Avraham, was a tireless and efficient organizer; Yaakov Amrami, called Yael, was a skilled member of an intelligence service that frequently trumped its British counterpart; Shmuel Katz, a writer and journalist from South Africa, was spokesman for the Irgun. There were many others. As partisans of the French resistance said, every man who fell was replaced by another who emerged from the shadows.

The organization of the Irgun was simple. The command on the one hand administered finances, propaganda, liaisons, social services (for prisoners and families), and the information service known as *Delek* (Inflammable), and on the other, the fighting units. In 1943 Meridor had the idea of a "secret within a secret." Certain elements of the Irgun would disappear, "desert," and make a show of abandoning their comrades and the fight. Actually they became the nucleus of the *Yehidot Mahatz*, or shock troops, shortened to Yam, also called the Red Company. This top-secret unit, the first to conduct armed resistance, was composed mainly of Arab-speaking youths, with Oriental looks— often of Yemenite origin (though many of them were pure Ashkenazim from Central Europe)—that gave rise to the legend that the Irgun appealed chiefly to Eastern Jews. Under the command of Livni, the Yam eventually became part of the combat force, *Hok*. Finally the *Tsom*, a sort of reserve, was created, but not until the end of the period of secrecy when the Irgun integrated with the regular army to fight in broad daylight against the Arab invaders.

Command decisions were taken after group discussion. The prestige of Menachem Beigin, with his ardor, intelligence, sense of humanity, and unshakable resolution, allowed him to fully exercise his function as the rankless "commandant" of this shadowy army, where the highest post was that of *seren*, or captain. Among themselves the Irgunists called Menachem "the old man"—he was not yet thirty-five.

The Irgun was simultaneously an army, an embryonic state government, and a family. The reigning spirit of confidence and comradeship was such that provocation and treason, which are the common scourges of secret organizations, were almost unknown in the Irgun. The exceptional case of Hilevitch threw an interesting light on the attitude of Beigin, the "terrorist" chief. Hilevitch, who occasionally helped the Irgun but was not a member, told the British policeman Catling where Beigin's home was in Jerusalem. Beigin escaped the search by pure luck, and his comrades demanded that the traitor be summarily executed. Beigin staunchly refused because of a lingering doubt. Hilevitch fled to Egypt under British protection and went from there to the United States. "Those who fell and degraded themselves were the exception, while those who were elevated by their heroism were too numerous to count."[8]

A clandestine radio station and a secret press are among the basic needs of a resistance movement. The secret transmitter was installed in the home of Esther Raziel, David's sister, but after a few broadcasts it was detected. The police raided the house and seized it. Esther was sent to the women's prison at Bethlehem and her husband was deported to Africa. But another transmitter was set up, and the Irgun announced that this one would be defended by force. There was no further attempt to silence it.

The printing press was moved many times before being finally installed in a stifling-hot cellar under a carpenter's shop. The carpenter's truck, coming and going with planks, joists, battens, and furniture, would also deliver posters, tracts, and the magazine *Herut* (Liberty) to the distribution centers of the propaganda service.

And the battle was on. The immigration bureaus in Jerusalem, Tel Aviv, and Haifa were bombed simultaneously. Income tax officers of all three cities, as well as police headquarters in Jerusalem, Jaffa, and Haifa, were attacked. During this last operation the first deaths occurred, one in the ranks of the Irgun, and six Englishmen.[9] On Yom Kippur, 1944, the Irgun warned the authorities that if they tried, as they had done the year before, to molest believers on their way to the Wailing Wall and to keep them from sounding the shofar, or ram's horn, there would be a fight. The authorities took them at their word, and the sound of the shofar was heard by the faithful.

All these actions were partly symbolic—attempts to repudiate the Mandatory power by attacks on the agencies that refused to open Palestine's gates: the offices collecting taxes that were partly used for the good of the Arabs, and the police. They kept the Mandatory at bay where it attacked Jewish traditions and faith. It was not terrorism, strictly speaking, but political warfare, in which every act was planned and its significance weighed. The Irgun worked tirelessly to explain the sense of their violent actions to local and world opinion. They were not shooting for the sake of shooting, but as a demonstration — by force, since the Mandatory administration had left them no other choice.

Such explanations were all the more necessary because the Irgun aroused conflicting feelings in the Palestinian Jewish community — approbation and enthusiasm (particularly among the youth), fear of reprisals, moral outrage among the traditionalists, the anger of the "institutions" faced with "dissidence." The old ghetto spirit persisted with a number of Jews: resignation and nonviolence, although they knew the Polish ghettos had resisted. The pious trembled before this rise in violence. Just before Yom Kippur, the rabbinate of Jerusalem issued a statement saying that to sound the shofar at the Wailing Wall was a praiseworthy custom but not a religious obligation. Thus they implicitly disavowed the Irgun.

The leaders of the Mapai and the Histadrut, and the Haganah general staff that was tied to them, looked to England for everything and hoped for a change in the Cabinet and in the elections of 1945. They expected the Labour party to win. Had not the Labour party, ideologically close as it was to the Palestine socialists, denounced the White Paper dozens of times? Had it not repeatedly stood up for Zionism? And besides, Churchill had promised Weizmann, in the course of a particularly friendly talk, that when the war was over England would partition Palestine and the Zionists would receive the "biggest plum in the pudding." Ben Gurion, Moshe Sharett, and Golomb reasoned that either Churchill would stay in power after the elections and, as he had promised, would give them their state "on a silver platter," or else their friends the Labourites would win and would certainly institute new policies favoring Zionist aspirations.

Events would soon prove that the moderates were living in a dream world. Meanwhile, they utterly opposed what the Irgun was trying to do. However, some of the Haganah troops and officers realized the importance of the violent resistance. Moshe Dayan went to see Beigin secretly and told him, "You have already accomplished an historic act, you have proved that it was possible to attack the British."[10] The standard argument of the moderates consisted in saying that to attack the mighty British Empire would be not only wrong but also mad.

In the fall of 1944, Menachem Beigin, Moshe Sneh, and Eliahu Golomb met secretly. Despite an apparent politeness—they greeted one another with the usual *shalom*—the discussion was tense and disappointing. Golomb demanded that in the name of the "institutions" and of discipline the Irgun cease its actions. "Don't you want to fight?" asked Beigin. "All right. Do as you like, but let us alone. You could even make political use of our actions. You could tell the English that you don't agree with us but that these are signs of a revolt that they should take into consideration." But agreement was impossible. Golomb walked out of the meeting with the threat, "If you don't stop, we shall finish you."[11]

On November 6, 1944, in Cairo, two young men from Palestine, Eliahu Bet Zouri, aged twenty-two, and Eliahu Hakim, aged seventeen, fired three pistol shots at the Right Honorable Walter Edward Guinness, Lord Moyne, who died a few hours later. Arrested immediately, the two young men made no attempt to defend themselves. On the contrary they claimed full responsibility for their act, which they had carried out on the orders of the Lehi, or Stern group.

The supreme triumvirate of the Lehi had condemned Lord Moyne to death[12] as much for his dominant role in repressing illegal immigration as for his status as Britain's representative in the East. He was in fact a member of the British Cabinet resident in Egypt. The two Eliahus had lived through the drama of the *Aliyah Beth* in Tel Aviv and Haifa, had taken part in demonstrations that were broken up by the police, and at last had joined the Lehi. In Cairo, under assumed names, they carefully planned the assassination, aided by an officer and an ambulance driver, both of them members of the Stern group.

In the Egyptian court that tried the young Sternists, Bet Zouri calmly explained the reasons for what he had done. It had nothing to do with Zionism, he said. "We don't fight for the sake of a National Home. We fight for our freedom. In our country a foreign power rules. ... If we have turned to the gun, it is because we were forced to the gun!" He added that millions of men and women had died, and the Mandatory government had closed the doors of escape to them. The alternative was to "tear it out by the roots and throw it away."[13]

Sentenced to death, the two Eliahus might still have had their sentence commuted, but on February 24, 1945, the Egyptian prime minister, Ahmed Maher, was assassinated by another Egyptian whose political motives had nothing to do with Palestine. In a speech to the House of Commons, Churchill declared that ". . . security measures in Egypt require considerable tightening; above all that the execution of justice upon men proved guilty of political murder should be swift and exemplary." The fate of the young men was sealed. They mounted the scaffold on March 22, 1945, with a courage that made a profound impression upon those present at the execution.

In Palestine the assassination of Lord Moyne had aroused intense emotions. Weizmann announced that the death of the British minister had grieved him as deeply as the death of his own son. The *yishuv* feared further reprisals. The British police had already begun mass arrests of the activists; 251 members of the Irgun and the Lehi had been deported to camps in the Sudan, shortly before the death of Moyne. After November 6, a general campaign of denunciation against the "dissidents" was launched by the leaders of official Zionist organizations. At the sixth conference of the Histadrut, Ben Gurion stated that they had to choose between "terrorist organizations" and an "organized *yishuv*, an organized people, and an organized labor movement." The choice, he added, was clear. From this he concluded that anybody belonging to or sympathizing with the "dissidents" must be turned out of his factory, his office, his school, or his college. And since there was as yet no Jewish state, everyone must "collaborate with the British authorities and police in whatever measures they choose to take against terrorism. We can never liquidate this scourge without the help of the authorities and without helping the authorities."

Thus began a terrible period of the struggle: it was generally known by the English word "season," even by those who spoke Hebrew. It was open season on "terrorists."

Nathan Yellin-Moor then had a talk with Eliahu Golomb. As an indication of the atmosphere at the meeting, the Sternist leader began by taking a revolver out of his pocket and putting it on the table. Golomb asked sadly: "Have we lost confidence in each other to this point?" "Under present conditions I can be sure of nothing," Yellin-Moor replied. He demanded the immediate liberation of one of his men, who had been seized by the Haganah and detained in a kibbutz. He threatened Golomb and his men with reprisals.

But the big guns of the "season" were trained upon the Irgun. Meridor and Lankin were denounced and identified by Haganah agents. Many other Irgun members were forced to spend weeks and months imprisoned in kibbutzim, where they were threatened and abused.[14] Others were turned over to the British police.

The resentment that this offensive provoked in the ranks of the Irgun is easy to imagine. It was perhaps the first and only time that Menachem Beigin disagreed profoundly with his comrades. They were demanding reprisals. Beigin said there would be no reprisals. "Civil war in Palestine? Never!" Looking beyond this demoralizing crisis, he foresaw a time when all the Jewish forces in Palestine without exception would have to unite in a common battle. How would they accomplish it if a river of blood separated the Haganah and the Irgun? And this certainly would be the case if the Irgun demanded an eye for an eye. He therefore ordered his men to avoid searches, interrogations, and arrests as often as they could, and to resist the English police, but not to fight other Jews. His men reluctantly gave in. The next year's events were to bear out the "commandant's" clairvoyance.

The official organizations of the *yishuv* were far from being of one mind in this sad business. In the executive committee's secret debate before the "season" opened, representatives of the Mizrachi, or religious party, and the general Zionists, opposed the very idea of any "crusade against the dissidents." Leftist elements came out in favor of battling the Irgun and the Lehi but were vehemently opposed to collaboration with the British. Moshe Sneh stood against the official line but finally gave in. In the final analysis it was not the Haganah, as a unit, that hunted down "terrorists," but "volunteers" who took the task upon themselves.[15] But admittedly these volunteers from the Mapai and the *Hashomer* were numerous and so well organized that their actions closely resembled an official offensive enjoying the support of Zionist institutions.

Every day brought bad news to the command of the Irgun. Young people were expelled from their schools; men and women fired from their jobs; Irgun militants were kidnapped. Anger increased in the ranks of the organization, but Beigin stood his ground. During this time the Lehi was left more or less alone—paradoxically enough, since the pretext for the "season" had been the assassination of Lord Moyne. Doubtless this was because the size of its effective force did not greatly alarm the official leaders of the *yishuv*. Yellin-Moor met frequently with Dr. Sneh and Israel Galili, who replaced Golomb when the latter died of a heart attack. He tried to convince them that the moderation of the Irgun could not last forever, and that one day there would be a fratricidal war. Yellin-Moor also kept in touch with Beigin. Both of them thought that the situation, as it was evolving, obliged them to work together in the resistance.

And in fact that was how it worked out. The advent of Clement Attlee's Labour government in 1945, with Ernest Bevin in the foreign office, had been welcomed in Palestine. But it quickly became evident that this government intended to maintain the policies fixed by the White Paper of 1939. Tel Aviv realized that the Labour party's solemn promises while it was the opposition did not bind it as the party in power. Bevin looked more and more like a hardened anti-Semite[16] perhaps because of his troubles with Jewish Labour intellectuals, such as Harold Laski. He knew nothing about the Middle East and depended entirely upon his advisers, particularly Harold Beeley, who was known to be anti-Zionist and pro-Arab.

This was a great disappointment. Weizmann and Ben Gurion had hoped that at the very least a large number of supplementary immigration permits would be granted to alleviate the misery of the tens of thousands of European Jews—perhaps a hundred thousand—who remained behind barbed wire even after Hitler's defeat and their theoretical "liberation." It seemed both reasonable and humane to turn liberation in principle into a fact, and to open Palestine to the wretches who had escaped the great massacre so that they could rebuild their lives. But Bevin categorically rejected this solution, and always for the same reason: the Arabs must not be offended. Interestingly enough the Arabs had abstained from all activities and demonstrations since the Irgun and the Lehi had taken up the fight. Because the mufti had had to flee as a war criminal, the leadership of the movement was neutralized.

When the Labour government came to power, Beigin published a manifesto that said in substance: "A new government is in power. Its members made many promises while they were part of the opposition. We cannot count on them. Experience teaches us that such hopes are baseless. But if there are those among the *yishuv* who believe we still can count on them, well, let us wait a few weeks. We shall see whether or not they keep their promises."

The Irgun and the Lehi working together between May and October, 1945, had sabotaged a certain number of railroads and bridges, especially in the south, and the two groups remained closely allied. Moreover, Yellin-Moor stayed in touch with Sneh and Galili. Through him, the Haganah high command asked Beigin if he would agree to meet them. The leader of the Irgun answered that he would, provided they released Eli Ferstein (Tavin), the head of their information section who had been imprisoned in a kibbutz for several months. Tavin was set free—they let him go near the *Habima* theater in Tel Aviv—and the first meeting took place between Yellin-Moor, Beigin, Sneh, and Galili.

Their discussions were predictably bitter. "We are the representatives of the organized *yishuv*," said Sneh and Galili, "and of the future state. This state has decided that the Haganah must lead the fight. Dissident organizations no longer have the right to exist. You must disband and join the Haganah." To which Beigin replied: "You don't recognize our right to exist. It is regrettable, but we do exist. We were right, and we are right. We want national unity but without disbanding our organization. We will not join the Haganah as a unit or as individuals. What we want is a united front. If the Haganah fights on, unity will be maintained. If not, we shall fight on alone."

After a number of meetings, an agreement was reached on this basis. The united front of the three organizations took the name *Tenuat Hameri*—"resistance movement." They agreed that the principle of all undertakings would be discussed by representatives of the three groups, and that the Haganah would retain the veto over proposals of the Irgun and the Stern group. The Haganah representatives had to submit proposals to a secret committee, called the "X" Commission, made up of delegates from the various parties of the Jewish Agency. This was a cumbersome procedure and hardly conducive to secrecy. Once the higher echelons had made decisions, a unified general staff would carry them out. It was composed of Yitshak Sadeh for the Haganah, Livni and Guiddi for the Irgun, and Yaakov Banai for the Lehi. The agreement left up to each movement the so-called recuperation of funds, and particularly of arms and war matériel, which was an Irgun specialty.

The *Tenuat Hameri* lasted nine months, from November, 1945, to August, 1946. The first joint action took place on November 2 (the anniversary of the Balfour Declaration), when the Haganah blew up a number of railroad lines, and the Irgun and the Lehi attacked the Lydda railroad station, which was an obligatory stopping point for all military trains traveling between Egypt and the Levant. Since May 8, 1945, military installations had of course no longer been off limits.

Co-ordinating the activity of secret movements is always extremely difficult; trouble is bound to occur. For example, on one occasion, either the Haganah or the Irgun unwittingly endangered an arms depot of the Lehi by making a raid in the vicinity and attracting the attention of the British police to the vulnerable spot. The Stern group, although it usually worked with the Irgun, had a tendency to sally forth alone; once, they mounted an unsuccessful attack on the Haifa refinery. Once when two Irgunists, Simhon and Ashbel, were condemned to death by an English tribunal for taking part in a raid to "recuperate" armaments at Sarafand, the Irgun kidnapped a group of British officers and held them until the two condemned men were pardoned. But the Haganah made an ill-advised announcement that almost gave everything away.

Political differences and suspicions persisted. Although Beigin swore time and again that the Irgun had had no candidate for power since the death of Jabotinsky, and although he promised to support Ben Gurion provided the latter would fight to establish the Jewish state, the Jewish Agency continued to fear that the Irgun's true objective was a takeover. Besides, the Agency's situation was growing uncomfortable, for although it pretended to know nothing about the activities of the Haganah, let alone the agreement among the three movements, nobody was fooled, least of all the British authorities.

At any rate, the *Tenuat Hameri* developed in an atmosphere of near unanimity. Most of the population encouraged, aided, and supported the resistance. They knew that its battle was theirs. At Tel Aviv, sixty thousand people went to funeral services for four resistance fighters. New blows fell each day on the British administrative and military establishments in Palestine: radar installations were attacked, including Mount Carmel's; airplanes were destroyed on the ground (thirty-nine in one day, including twenty Halifaxes and eight Spitfires); a military train carrying £35,000 was intercepted; bridges and railroads were cut off; three coast guard boats were scuttled; police stations and camps were attacked. Of course the British did not stand idly by, and losses were often heavy among the resistance.

In April, 1946, a hundred or so Irgunists under Livni's command mined the railroad between Tel Aviv and Ashdod and blew up some of the stations and locomotives. The operation took all night. In the morning the saboteurs split into three groups and started back to Tel Aviv. But they were exhausted, many of them dropping in their tracks from fatigue. A British military plane spotted them. Soon surrounded, they fought back courageously. Livni was captured and sentenced to fifteen years in prison. He escaped the next year. A young girl named

Dvora Kalfus received the same sentence.

Significantly, the men of the Irgun, returning from the landing fields at Lydda and Kastina, where they had turned a number of heavy bombers into scrap metal, were given a triumphal welcome not only in the Jewish villages but in Arab villages as well. The debate in the House of Commons was acrimonious. British public opinion became more and more critical of the policies of the Attlee-Bevin government.

The twelve-member Anglo-American Committee was created in November, 1945. It was to report to London and Washington on the situation of the European Jews in the displaced persons camps and on the possibility of admitting some of them to Palestine. This committee was set up on the initiative of President Harry Truman. He had in fact drawn Clement Attlee's attention to the plight of those who had managed to survive the concentration camps, and had asked whether the immigration restrictions decreed by the White Paper of 1939 might not be removed or at least modified. Attlee and Bevin no doubt looked upon the committee as a means of stalling. However, Bevin told the commissioners explicitly that if their recommendations were unanimous, he would see that they were carried out. The six Englishmen and six Americans who made up the committee[17] acted in good faith. Knowing nothing of the problem, they undertook to gather information honestly. They went to Germany and other countries in Central Europe and held a session in the United States to hear representatives of Jewish organizations, whether Zionist or not; they also went to Egypt and, finally, to Palestine.[18] They took into account oral testimony and documents by the thousands. In the calm of Lausanne, Switzerland, they reached a unanimous decision in spite of serious differences of opinion (Crossman, for example, was convinced that Palestine had to be partitioned between the Arabs and the Jews, an opinion most of his colleagues did not share). They affirmed that the plight of Central European Jews still detained in camps was intolerable and recommended that one hundred thousand immigration certificates be issued for them immediately. They also suggested the repeal of the law that forbade Jews to buy arable lands in the greater part of Palestine. This report seemed to open the door, at least a little way. The Jewish Agency had Dr. Sneh request the secret organizations to undertake no further operations if the recommendations of the committee were adopted, particularly the one dealing with the one hundred thousand immigrants. Although they were skeptical, the Irgun and Lehi leaders agreed, and the clandestine radio station Kol Israel announced a conditional "truce."

The skepticism of Beigin and Yellin-Moor proved to be justified. When Truman publicly expressed his satisfaction about the one hundred thousand immigrants, Bevin "flew into one of the blackest rages" of his life[19] and Attlee responded bitterly before the House of Commons. Emphasizing the "technical difficulties" of transferring these immigrants, he added a "precondition": the disarming and liquidation of the "private armies."

The remarks effectively torpedoed the committee's report and by the same token administered a death blow to the moderate policies of Chaim Weizmann. Most Zionists already opposed him and now the British government made him look ridiculous. During the weeks that followed, the Cabinet did not examine the committee's report, but rather a memorandum from a committee of civil servants and military men. These were exactly the same men who had obstinately defended the White Paper at both Cairo and Jerusalem![20] In the end, the report met the same fate as all those drawn up by various royal commissions between the two wars — and it was forgotten.

Events in Palestine were taking an increasingly tragic course. The Haganah, disillusioned, went back to fighting, as did the other two movements, and in June launched a broad-based attack on all bridges in the north, east, and south that linked the country to the outside world. This brilliantly successful operation was the most spectacular of the period;[21] it was also the last that the Haganah conducted.

June 29, 1946, was a Saturday. This Sabbath has gone down in history as "Black Saturday." In the early morning hours, tens of thousands of soldiers and police occupied the Jewish Agency building in Jerusalem and the official Zionist offices at Tel Aviv and elsewhere, arrested all the directors of these "institutions" and of the Haganah, and searched the kibbutzim. Sneh and Galili managed to escape, as did Ben Gurion, who was then in Paris, but Sharett, who directed the political section of the Agency, Remez, the president of the Vaad Leumi, and many others were interned, as well as a large number of officers of the Palmach and the Haganah.

The Irgun immediately proposed a nine-point plan of action including the proclamation of a provisional government, the creation of a liberation army, a national treasury into which all taxes would be paid, a call for help from all free peoples, the publication of a declaration of independence, and the outlines of a constitution guaranteeing liberty, equality, and social justice.

Dr. Sneh believed that military action could and should continue.[22] He proposed to the "X" Commission (whose chief members were Rabbi Fishman, Yaakov Riftin, and Levi Eshkol) a plan to recapture the arms that the British had seized in a kibbutz at Yagur—10 machine guns, 325 rifles, 96 mortars, 425,000 cartridges, and more. The commission agreed. But Meir Weissgal, Weizmann's envoy, visited Dr. Sneh in his hideout. He brought an ultimatum from the Zionist leader. Weizmann told Weissgal to say that as president of the Zionist organization he had never meddled in Haganah affairs; that nevertheless, if the Jewish state existed, he as president would be the supreme commander of all armed forces; that at the present juncture the decision under discussion was of capital importance politically; and finally, that if the Haganah persisted in armed warfare against the British, he, Weizmann, would resign. Overwhelmed, Sneh recalled the "X" Commission, explained the situation to them, and stated that in his opinion, armed fighting ought to continue. Finding himself in the minority, he resigned as Haganah commander.

However, the secret meetings of representatives of the three military organizations were not called off. Before June 29, they had considered a daring move together—to blow up the King David Hotel at Jerusalem, which was occupied by the secretariat of the Mandatory government and by the police. This operation, *Malonchick* (little hotel), was put off several times on the request of Israel Galili, who represented the Haganah. But on July 1, he insisted that they carry it through as soon as possible, partly because the Haganah felt it necessary to strike back hard after the massive arrests of Black Saturday, and partly because he knew he had to destroy compromising papers that the English had seized during their search of the Jewish Agency.[23] The Irgun put Guiddi in charge of the operation.

The stated objective was to destroy the building and its archives without loss of life. To accomplish this, they planned to give advance warning, followed by a sufficient delay to permit evacuation of the hotel. Guiddi suggested a delay of forty-five minutes, but Sadeh, in the name of the Haganah, objected that this would allow enough time to remove the papers, too. He suggested a quarter of an hour. They finally agreed upon half an hour.

The plan they adopted was to put explosives inside innocent-looking milk cans that "porters" would bring in the hotel. In order to scatter passers-by they would throw a harmless but very noisy smoke bomb into the street in front of the hotel. Warning would be given by telephone to the hotel, to the newspaper *Palestine Post,* and to the French consulate, which was near the King David.

On July 22, at noon, the plan was carried out in every detail, the only variation being a brief exchange of gunfire in the basement between the Irgunists and some British soldiers. The shooting and the smoke bomb scared pedestrians away—the street was deserted. At 12:10, Guiddi made the three telephone calls. A little after 12:37 a colossal explosion shook all Jerusalem. The entire six-story wing of the King David occupied by the British services was destroyed.

But for reasons that remain a mystery to this day, the hotel was not evacuated. There is no doubt that the phone calls went through. Sir John Shaw, secretary general of the Mandatory, is said to have exclaimed, "I am here to give orders to the Jews, not to take orders from them," and no doubt thinking it was a bluff, he apparently refused to give the evacuation order. Police officer Taylor, testifying before the coroner, stated that the alarm bell at the King David rang at 12:15, but at 12:31, inexplicably, the all-clear sounded. Many people testified that they had wanted to leave but were stopped by guards. Unfortunately ninety-one people were killed, of whom about a dozen were Jewish civil servants, among them members of or sympathizers with the resistance. Many more were wounded.

The Haganah command now adopted an equivocal attitude. Those Zionist circles that had always opposed armed struggle seized this opportunity to mount a violent campaign against the men who blew up the King David, and the Haganah tried to disassociate itself from the affair. It even published a communiqué denouncing the "heavy loss of life caused by the dissidents."

Moshe Sneh, who had secretly left Palestine, went to Paris to see Ben Gurion and other Zionist leaders. Questioned about the King David affair, he made this odd statement: "The Haganah high command approved the operation but this cannot be proved, because the approval was given in the form of an unsigned, typewritten note."[24]

In Paris, Ben Gurion declared himself in favor of continuing to fight within the framework of the *Tenuat Hameri.* But he finally agreed to carry the question to the Zionist Congress that was to meet in Basel in December, 1946, the first Congress since the end of the war. The Haganah meanwhile stopped all armed action, except in connection with clandestine immigration.

At the Basel Congress, Weizmann—"half-blind, old, heavy of heart"[25]—clung pathetically to his old viewpoint. He was aware of the absence of any confidence and even of any hope in the British government among a great number of delegates, and of their inclination to resort to methods that had never been sanctioned by Zionists before the war. For him, "resistance," "activism," and even "defense" were "non-Jewish, demoralizing" notions.[26] The majority of the Congress, led by Rabbi Silver of the United States and Ben Gurion, stood up to him and refused to send delegates to London for a conference on Palestine scheduled for January, 1947. Disowned, the old man retired to Rehovot in Palestine, wishing to devote his remaining strength to founding the scientific research institute that bears his name.[27]

During this time Sir Evelyn Barker, the commander of British forces in Palestine, issued an order to his troops, couched in racist and insulting language, which forbade any contact between British soldiers and any Jew whatsoever. This caused some embarrassment even in London. Secretary General Shaw, who had escaped unharmed from the King David explosion, and General Barker were transferred shortly thereafter. A vast mopping-up operation was begun in Tel Aviv. All houses were searched and identification papers of all citizens were checked. Menachem Beigin spent four days in a secret closet that had been built in his apartment, and he was not discovered. Shamir, of the Stern group, was arrested and deported to East Africa, but Yellin-Moor managed to slip through the net.

The united front of the three organizations of the *Tenuat Hameri* was not dissolved immediately after the King David affair. As late as August 17, 1946, Israel Galili wrote to Beigin that "I insist once more that we must give maximum attention to the Luntz affair."[28] The "Luntz affair" (from the English word "launch") was the code name of an Irgun plan to sink a coast guard ship at Haifa. But a *de facto* truce, accepted by the Jewish Agency, spread when the prisoners at Latrun were liberated after three months' detention. The Haganah's armed resistance came to an end; the only illegal activity it took part in was immigration, the *Aliyah Beth*. But the Irgun and the Lehi fought on.

Illegal immigration by sea had been stopped, as we have seen, in 1941. During the rest of the war, some twenty thousand unauthorized immigrants (*ma'apilim*) got into Palestine through Turkey, Syria, and Iraq, and some even came through Persia, with the help of an underground set up by the Haganah and the Irgun.

The advance of the Soviet armies into Rumania and the fall of the pro-Hitler regime in Bucharest in August, 1944, knocked the first breach in the wall of Fortress Europe. The rescue committee created at İstanbul could now send emissaries to Bucharest. Finding the offices of the Red Cross abandoned, they set up shop in them without further ado. It was a chaotic situation. The Russians seemed to pay no attention to the problems of the three hundred fifty thousand Jews still living in Rumania. The new Communist masters, led by Anna Pauker, who was Jewish but fiercely anti-Zionist, had other things to worry about. Between November and December, 1944, the "Red Cross office" managed to send several thousand refugees to Turkey. But the waiver granted by Lord Cranborne was annulled by the British authorities, and the Turkish government announced that it would accept no more refugees from the Balkans.

At Bucharest the Palestine emissaries made their first contact with the representatives of the Jewish partisans who had fought in Poland and the Baltic countries. A young girl named Rushka told them the story of the revolt of the Vilno ghetto and the activity of the Jewish partisans, in which she had played a role. She told them that she and her comrades had fought the Germans and the Lithuanian and Polish anti-Semites and that they had come back to Vilno with the Russian army and found a handful of Jews, who by some miracle had escaped extermination and "began to crawl out of the holes where they had been hiding for three years."[29] Not one Jewish family had survived intact at Vilno, and it was the same at Ravno, Lvov, and Stanislav. The extent of the disaster that had overtaken the European Jews gradually became apparent. Of 600,000 German Jews, 20,000 were left. Of 200,000 in Vienna, 4,000 remained. Of 3,500,000 Polish Jews, scarcely 300,000 were still alive: 80,000 in Poland, 75,000 in displaced persons camps in Germany, and the rest wandering through Russia, Poland, Austria, and Bavaria. Those who returned to their own villages or cities found only ruins; their families had vanished, their possessions had been confiscated, sold, or destroyed. If they tried to claim restitution or indemnification, they met renewed anti-Semitism. There was even a pogrom at Kielce. Most of them were so disillusioned and desperate that they simply went back to their former camps.

By the end of 1945 two new facts had to be taken into account. First, the conscience of America was fully aroused by the tragedy of the European Jews, quite apart from any religious or political considerations. Americans had at first known nothing about the holocaust, and when they did hear of it they could hardly comprehend the horror. But the G.I.'s wrote home to their families and, when they returned, told them about the gas chambers and the crematories, the cadavers piled up like stacks of firewood, the living skeletons swathed in striped pajamas, the stockpiles of gold teeth and human hair collected with hellish efficiency. The shock of these revelations deeply moved the American soul. The American Jews, thanks to the committee founded by Peter Bergson and Arieh Ben Eliezer, were overwhelmed by this ghastly drama and Zionism found a powerful new impetus. That is why President Truman had insisted so forcefully that London immediately issue at least one hundred thousand immigration permits.

The second new fact was that the survivors who were in D.P. camps, whether they had formerly been Zionist, anti-Zionist, or indifferent, knew that their only hope for the future lay in Palestine. The British Parliamentarian Crossman, a member of the Anglo-American Committee, observed that out of every one hundred displaced persons of Jewish origin (there were ninety-eight thousand in German camps), fifteen wanted to join relatives in the United States or in Commonwealth countries; fifteen simply wanted to leave the accursed continent where their wives, sisters, or children had vanished in the flames of the holocaust; seventy, particularly the young ones, "wanted Palestine and nothing else."[30]

These men and women had undergone such moral and physical suffering, had witnessed so many atrocities, and so deeply resented the injustice of their fate that the idea of staying in Europe filled them with anger and hatred. A speech by Clement Attlee proposing that they be put to work "reconstructing" their native countries struck them as a bitter joke. Rebuild an anti-Semitic Poland, Communist or not, which wanted no part of them? Rebuild a Germany whose people had followed Hitler and shared the responsibility for the massacre? As they passed some ordinary-looking citizen in the street, would they not wonder whether he was the executioner who had thrown their parents, their sons, into the furnace? Truly Hitler had triumphed in death: Central Europe was still hostile territory to the Jews. After a tragic delay, Jabotinsky's watchword of "evacuation" became the only hope for the survivors. Zionism was the only way.

The drama of this era was that the British government failed to understand the explosive forces building up behind the walls of the camps. The "experts" of the colonial and foreign offices "hoped to divert the [Arabs'] hatred of foreign imperialism away from the British against the Bolsheviks and the Zionists. If . . . despite American and

Jewish pressure, Great Britain stuck to the 1939 White Paper, she could achieve a firm alliance with the Arab League. In return for that concession to Arab nationalism, it was only reasonable that Britain should retain a permanent military base in a Palestinian Arab state."[31]

On the American side we have seen the position President Truman adopted. But his attitude was not always shared by influential Americans. Before his death, Roosevelt had assured ibn-Saud that he did not favor Zionism. Functionaries in the State Department were more often than not anti-Zionist, and businesses tied to the big oil companies thought it was dangerous to annoy the Arabs, who were sitting on the richest oil fields on the planet.

Immigration laws — the quotas — were very restrictive. Only 4,767 displaced persons were admitted to the United States in 1946, and it was not until June, 1948, that Truman won approval for the Displaced Persons Act, providing for the admission of 202,000 immigrants above the quota.

While the Anglo-American Committee laboriously looked for a solution, the rescue work of the *Aliyah Beth* increased daily. Its general headquarters was in Paris under the command of Shaul Avigour and Ehud Avriel. The Mossad began operating again. Thanks to Jan Masaryk, who was still a member of the Czech government, the authorities in Prague did not interfere with the regrouping and transport of emigrants. In Warsaw, the coalition government of Mykolayczik and Gomulka did likewise. Trainloads of emigrants with fictitious Greek visas or Latin American visas obtained in one way or another, left for Greek, Yugoslavian, and Italian ports. Most impressive of all was the spontaneous exodus. By the dozens, the hundreds, and the thousands, like rivers flowing downhill, the refugees went southward, any way they could, often on foot with just a few necessities, on their way to the Mediterranean Sea, which washed the distant coasts of Palestine.

It took British authorities some time to learn of this massive migration and to realize its importance. First the Austro-Italian border was closed. Then the British made diplomatic overtures to various governments. Surveillance of the coast was increased from Acre to Gaza. The emissaries from Palestine, with the financial help of American humanitarian organizations, enlarged their underground networks, multiplied their secret hiding places and their transit camps, and purchased or chartered more ships.

Despite all the efforts of the foreign office, the French governments of 1946–47 did not look unfavorably upon the Zionist enterprises developing in France. Many Jews from D.P. camps in western Germany escaped to France for a brief period before setting sail from Marseilles or Sète. Requisitioned villas were even put at their disposal for use as transit camps along the Mediterranean coast. The French had a deep feeling of compassion for Hitler's victims, and at the same time, admittedly, a certain ill will over English actions in Syria and Lebanon in 1945. In any case, the French police did nothing to interfere with the offices for illegal immigration in Paris, nor did they bother the Irgun, which had also chosen Paris as headquarters for its European activities.

Things were more difficult in Italy, where a number of British forces had remained, exercising considerable influence over the local authorities. But among the British troops were some Palestinian units. Infiltrated by the Zionists, they furnished the ideal cover for transporting, sheltering, and feeding the *ma'apilim*, who frequently crossed Italy eating military rations in His Majesty's trucks fueled with British army gasoline. When these units were recalled to Palestine, the ingenious Yehuda Arazi of the Palmach set up a fictitious transport company in Milan early in 1946, with barracks, trucks, jeeps, insignias, and excellently forged papers. He even recalled demobilized Jewish soldiers from Palestine to round out his unit.

This unusual scheme was discovered only in April, 1946. A convoy of refugees arriving at La Spezia under the command of a Jewish sergeant, who for the moment went under the name of Major MacIntosh, ran into a road block manned by Italian police who were looking for fleeing Fascists. After long discussion, the 1,014 emigrants were allowed to board the *Fede* in the port of La Spezia, but the "transport unit" had to terminate its activities. The British were alerted and forbade the ship to sail. Thus began a strange test of strength between the British Empire and a thousand refugees from hell, led by Arazi, who had boarded the ship. Major Hill of the Intelligence Service ordered Arazi to make the passengers disembark; otherwise they would be forcibly removed. Tanks and infantry were ranged on the land side of the port, and an Italian gunboat dropped anchor under the *Fede's* bow. Arazi replied that if they tried to remove the refugees he would blow up the ship: the explosives were already in place.

Then he called a hunger strike. Press agencies throughout the world and Italian, French, English, and American newspapers followed the story hour by hour. The blue and white Zionist flag flew from the mast and on deck refugees could be seen staggering and falling, exhausted by fasting. The population of La Spezia sided with the passengers of the *Fede,* and little by little so did world opinion. The Italian chief of state, Alcide De Gasperi, sent a message of sympathy to the passengers. A British proposal for transferring the refugees to a "convalescent" camp in Italy where they could wait for immigration permits was rejected.[32]

After the hunger strike had gone on for seventy-five hours, Harold Laski, president of the Labour party, arrived in La Spezia with representatives of the British Embassy in Rome. He first tried to persuade the refugees to wait in camps for their permits. Arazi explained the mood of the immigrants to him — they would die rather than return to camps or stay in Europe. And they were ready to prove it. Ten of them had agreed to commit suicide publicly on the bridge of the ship, and ten others would follow them each day that the ship was not allowed to weigh anchor.

The stupefaction and distress that this declaration aroused is easy to imagine. Laski pleaded with Arazi to let him negotiate with Attlee and Bevin. A truce was reached. On May 19, the day the truce was to expire, London had a new suggestion. It would deliver 679 certificates now and the rest the next month. This offer too was rejected, and at last the 1,014 passengers sailed for Palestine together after thirty-three days of defiance. More decisive than the salvation of these thousand people was the impression the affair made on world opinion. Nobody could understand or approve the obstinate decision of the Attlee-Bevin government to limit immigration to fifteen hundred Jews per month — the official quota at that time — while one hundred thousand unfortunate souls were packed into displaced persons camps. Above all, incidents like those at La Spezia constituted real battles in a psychological war. The British position was growing untenable.

However, the British Cabinet had no intention of changing its policy. Instead it stepped up its fight against illegal immigration. Special agents kept all Mediterranean ports under surveillance, a naval contingent was sent out to intercept ships, and most of the immigrants, arrested as soon as they set foot in Palestine, were sent to the camp at Atlit. But even so, escapees from Auschwitz and Bergen-Belsen preferred a camp in Palestine, where at least they could hope one day to be set free.

In August, 1946, the English announced that illegal immigrants would no longer be interned in Palestine but deported immediately to Cyprus, where special camps would be set up for them. The first ship to reach Palestine after this order went out was the *Katriel Yaffé*, carrying six hundred men, women, and children. Intercepted by a destroyer, the ship was brought to Haifa. But when the British tried to transfer the passengers into the cages that awaited them on the deportation ship, a spontaneous revolt broke out. (Klein, who commanded the *Katriel Yaffé*, had been ordered by the Haganah not to resist.) Armed with bottles and pieces of wood the emigrants fought back. Tear-gas bombs had to be used to break their resistance, and they had to be carried off one by one. Once on board the prison ship they managed to damage it badly and delay its departure for several days.

Others followed their example. Henceforth violence occurred each time a ship was intercepted and its passengers transferred to Cyprus. The Palmach, commanded by Yigal Allon, carried out bombing attacks on the deportation ships and the coast guard. However, "the Jewish Agency leaders refused to sanction attacks against British warships or planes."[33]

A total of 23,000 illegal immigrants left Europe for Palestine in 1946, 44,000 in 1947. Of these, 52,000 were taken to the camps in Cyprus.[34] A few ships, such as the *Chaim Arlosoroff*, managed to run aground on the coast and some of their passengers were able to scatter into the countryside before the British arrived. Others were escorted to Famagusta by British destroyers and gunboats. But whatever the luck of a given operation, illegal immigration was an important demonstration of the fact that Palestine was indeed the land of the Jewish people and that there was no force on earth that could keep them from returning to it. The legitimacy of British power was called into question and diminished with every shipload of tattered, hungry refugees, drawn to the country by the unconquerable hopes of two thousand years.

The story of *Exodus–1947* is well known. It overwhelmed world opinion. This decrepit American river steamer crammed with forty-five hundred passengers, nine hundred fifty of them children, sailed from Sète in July and was intercepted by the cruiser *Ajax* and five destroyers. About twenty-five miles from the Palestine coast, before the *Exodus* had even entered territorial waters, the warships opened fire, sprayed the deck with machine-gun fire, and sent out a boarding party. After a three-hour battle, in which a crewman of the *Exodus* and two refugees were killed and many wounded, the *Exodus* was taking water through several holes in her side and the destroyers forced her into the port of Haifa. The *ma'apilim* were immediately loaded onto three prison ships. But this time, rather than setting sail for Cyprus, the ships returned to Europe, for the Cabinet had decided to "make an example" of this incident by simply sending the forty-five hundred "illegals" back to their point of embarkation.

Palestine reacted with anger and violence. There were mass demonstrations in the cities. The Irgun and the Stern group blew up military installations in Jerusalem; the Palmach destroyed the radar station on Mount Carmel, and its frogmen scuttled a prison ship at Haifa.

On July 28, the three deportation ships dropped anchor at Port-de-Bouc, but the refugees refused to disembark. French authorities announced that they would allow anyone to remain in France who wished to do so, but they would force no one. The administrator of the Bouches-du-Rhône district, François Collavéri, went on board and was shocked by the intolerable conditions imposed on the passengers.

Three weeks went by, during which tensions mounted, and as at La Spezia, world opinion turned more and more against the Labour government. On August 21, that government announced that the refugees must disembark at once and that if they would not comply they would be forcibly taken to the British zone of occupation in Germany. This was a serious psychological error, as Sir Alan Cunningham, high commissioner in Palestine, understood. He begged the Cabinet to revoke its decision, as much for its own self-interest as for reasons of humanity. His appeal was ignored. On September 9, the three ships reached Hamburg, and while the world watched, passengers were violently removed from the ships in spite of their strenuous resistance and locked up in prison trains to be taken to two concentration camps. It is not known whether Arab nationalists (whose interests were constantly invoked in London to justify such measures) were pleased, but Great Britain's moral position was certainly damaged more by this episode than it would have been by Arab displeasure if the passengers of the *Exodus* had been allowed to enter Palestine.

The *Exodus* affair was not the last. Early in 1947, Zeev Shind, one of Avigour's collaborators, bought two 4,500-ton ships in the United States, the *Pan York* and the *Pan Crescent*. Duly fitted out, these ships could each carry more than seven thousand passengers in conditions of extreme discomfort. The *York* put into Marseilles and the *Crescent* went to Venice for repairs. While this ship was in Italy, the hull was damaged by a mysterious explosion, attributed by some to Arab terrorists, and by others to British agents. But in September the two *Pans* met at Constanta and about twenty thousand Rumanian Jews "signed on" for the trip to Palestine.

The organizers of the trip faced two obstacles. First, the British government launched a violent propaganda offensive. According to an editorial in *The Times* on October 15, which was echoed in innumerable articles, a "wave of illegal immigration" was about to overtake Palestine, and the worst of it was that ten thousand Communists would get into the Middle East this way. Second, the Jewish Agency, then engaged in delicate negotiations with the United Nations at Lake Success on the partition of Palestine, was under intense pressure and asked for caution.

During this time, the English minister at Bucharest, Adrian Holman, worked on Anna Pauker. The Russians complained about the presence of the two ships at Constanta, which was then a Soviet base. They did not want to give the impression of taking any responsibility for the operation. Avigour, Bar-Gilad, and Moshe Sneh went to Rumania to discuss the situation with Anna Pauker. They ended up by choosing a Bulgarian port of embarkation, Burgas, which was acceptable to the government at Sofia as long as a "transit tax" was paid for each emigrant.

The foreign office published daily bulletins about the preparation of ships loaded with "Communist spies." At the instigation of the British ambassador to Washington, Sir Oliver Franks, the American secretary of state, Dean Acheson, told Moshe Sharett at Lake Success that if the Zionist delegation wanted the continued support of the United States, he must see that those ships did not sail.

Sharett sent word to Ben Gurion at Tel Aviv. An argument followed. Weizmann advised them to cancel the voyage, and the majority of the executive committee felt the same, despite the dissent of Sneh and Ben Gurion. The passengers had been ready for months and had already been brought to Burgas on special trains. What would become of these unfortunates who no longer had homes or means of earning a livelihood? On December 21, Ben Gurion, in the name of the Jewish Agency, ordered them not to sail. "I will obey any order from you except this one," Avigour answered. The *Pans* weighed anchor on Christmas Day.

The last act of the drama was played out on January 1, 1948. Surrounded by three cruisers and three destroyers, the ships were taken to Famagusta and 15,169 people disembarked. Newspaper dispatches affirmed that there were numerous Communists among them, as well as sympathizers of the Stern group, and that hundreds of Rumanian Communist party cards had been found in the hold. But by some strange error this report appeared in *The New York Times* on December 31, which was *before* the boats reached Cyprus. At any rate, the Cyprus camps were now strained beyond their capacity, and England was preparing to abandon Palestine. But the blockade of the Palestine coast was maintained until the very last moment.

Can we agree with Moshe Sneh[35] that the illegal immigration was in itself a war and that it forced Britain to surrender? Such a statement is doubtless excessive. Armed resistance, in the first place, resulted in the liquidation of the Mandate because it proved that England could no longer exercise the powers of the Mandate against stubborn opposition. The truth is that the *Aliyah Beth,* through the global emotions it aroused, and through the vivid and pathetic light it threw on the human aspect of the Jewish problem, partly created the moral conditions for its solution. Even if the *Aliyah Beth* was able to satisfy only a part of the vast needs created by wartime genocide, it nevertheless rescued tens of thousands of desperate people. That is reason enough to regard it as one of the finest pages in the history of Israel.

A volume could hardly recount the adventures of captured Jewish freedom fighters — their lives in prison or in camps and their escapes. Thousands of them at one time or another saw the inside of prisons in Jerusalem, Bethlehem (for women), Acre, and the camps at Mirza, Latrun, Rafa, etc. As the battle grew longer and more bitter, and as illegal immigrants kept arriving, British authorities had to set up internment camps in distant African territories — Sudan, Eritrea, Uganda, Kenya. Some of them, particularly those at Cartago in the Sudan, Sambal in Eritrea, and Gilgil in Kenya, specialized in members of the Irgun and Lehi, or suspects interned by an administrative decision. Others, like Soroti in Uganda and Bombo in Kenya, held an odd population of displaced persons judged undesirable in Palestine, including refugee Jews from Europe and Asia, Maltese, Italians, and even pro-Hitler Germans, whose confinement with the Israelis produced predictable incidents.[36]

How curious that in the middle of the war the Germans at the farming colony of Sarona, all of them dedicated Nazis, were simply restricted to their comfortable quarters (where they listened religiously to Radio Berlin) under the command of a local *führer,* Herr Wagner.[37]

Accounts that some prisoners and political deportees have given of their experiences tend to show that with a few rare exceptions[38] the British officers and enlisted men in charge of the prisons and camps

155

acted without brutality or hatred. Some of them showed a humanity that could hardly have been expected under the circumstances. They generally carried out their orders to the letter. The camps in the Sudan, Eritrea, and Kenya were nothing like the German and Polish ones. The prisoners' lives were seldom threatened, though once at Sambal in January, 1946, some native guards killed two Jewish prisoners and wounded twelve in a fit of savagery. The deportees did not have to struggle against extermination but to try to get out and go back to Palestine to take their place in the fight. To the impassive but efficient administrative machinery they exhibited an amazing tenacity and ingenuity.

Arrested in February, 1945, Yaakov Meridor,[39] then second in command of the Irgun, joined Eliahu Lankin and Arieh Ben Eliezer in the camp at Cartago, in the Nubian desert. Within five months, aided by a veritable underground of Irgunist prisoners, and with the complicity of Sudanese, Arabs, and even a Scottish sergeant, the three men managed to fabricate false papers identifying them as Polish officers in the service of His Brittanic Majesty, to obtain uniforms and admirably realistic wooden pistols, and to escape from the camp in a water truck. Once in Port Sudan they realized that their presence there was arousing curiosity. They boldly paid a visit to the British governor, presented their "documents," and requested that their "mission" be kept secret. But they failed to find a ship that would take them to Aqaba. They had to leave Port Sudan and, seeking an escape route, ended up being recaptured. They were sent to Eritrea.

In November, 1945, Eliahu Lankin escaped with three other members of the Irgun. Two of these, disguised as veiled Moslem women, fled to Ethiopia and were imprisoned by local authorities. Lankin and his companion stayed at Asmara where they established permanent contact with the camp of Sambal, about two miles from the city. Meridor organized an escape committee in the camp to attempt a massive flight. The prisoners performed prodigies of invention and skill, dug a tunnel, manufactured uniforms, sword belts, unit insignia (with the initials J.R.F.I.E. — for Jewish Resistance Forces in Exile), even compasses and military police hats. By June, 1946, all was ready. Sixty prisoners escaped and "requisitioned" a bus, which unfortunately broke down. Some twenty got to Asmara, where they went into hiding. The others were captured by native villagers and turned over to the British. The leaders, among them Meridor, were sent to the fortress of Baldizera, where they immediately began to dig another tunnel.

Following his third escape, Meridor joined the small clandestine community at Asmara, which was kept hidden by some local Jews and Italians. In September, 1946, the police broke into their hideout and took them all back to Sambal, where, of course, security measures were tightened around them.

But in spite of increased surveillance they dug another tunnel, in broad daylight, under the very eyes of their guards, whose attention they distracted in various ingenious ways. In January, 1947, four Irgun members, among them Meridor and Ben Eliezer, and Shamir from the Stern group, succeeded in escaping to Asmara, where they were hidden by an Italian. Lankin had left for Addis Ababa and Ben Eliezer also went to the Ethiopian capital, where he passed himself off as a rich American and rented a house. Meridor managed to join him after a terrible trip inside a camouflaged compartment of a water truck. But their troubles were not over.

Lankin succeeded in getting to Djibouti and then to France, but Ben Eliezer and Shamir were arrested in French Somaliland in the truck in which they were hidden. The governor, Siriex, ordered them turned over to the British authorities in Somaliland, but after a lively legal fight led by a French judge who took an interest in their fate, they were allowed to stay at Djibouti — in prison. Only in May, 1948, did the French government allow them to board a warship going to Toulon.

During this time, Meridor was arrested by the police of His Majesty Haile Selassie and taken to the border, where he was turned over to the British police. After a stay in the Asmara prison he was sent to Gilgil in Kenya, where he found a number of his Irgun comrades — and a tunnel already well under way.

At Gilgil, the captive Jewish resistance fighters heard about the historic decision of the United Nations to partition Palestine into a Jewish state and an Arab state. Certain that this plan would not be carried out without bloody fighting, they were all the more eager to regain their liberty. This time they profited by the help of the Irgun representative in Nairobi. Carrying false passports from El Salvador (all the stickers and visas had been designed in camp), Meridor and five other deportees escaped on March 29, 1948, and went into the Belgian Congo, where Irgun agents met them. They flew from Leopoldville to Brussels and then to Paris, where they rejoined Eliahu Lankin and, shortly after, Shamir and Ben Eliezer. Paris was then Irgun general headquarters for Europe. Shmuel Katz joined the escapees. The

Mandatory administration was about to leave Palestine, and guerrilla fighting had broken out between Jews and Arabs. They had to find volunteers and arms in a hurry. To this task they turned all their energies.

On the question of escapes, one cannot fail to mention that of the young Sternist radio announcer, Gueoula Cohen.[40] She was arrested on February 17, 1946, as she was finishing a broadcast. She had just read the text of an appeal when she heard a noise at the door and cried out, "What's happening?" This phrase was picked up by the microphone and heard by thousands of listeners to the clandestine station. What was happening was that the police had surrounded the building. Arrested and sentenced to nine years in prison (the courtroom spectators sang the Hebrew hymn *Hatikvah* when the sentence was pronounced), she remained a little more than a year in the Bethlehem prison. The Lehi planned her escape with the help of Arabs from the village of Abu Gosh, near Jerusalem, who had long sympathized with the Zionist cause. Following a minutely worked out plan, two of the Arabs started a commotion in the corridor of the hospital where Gueoula was sick with pneumonia. Under cover of the diversion, she got up and dressed herself in Moslem costume, which had been hidden by a Lehi agent in a prearranged spot. With tremendous effort, she ran veiled down the corridor, left the hospital, and found one of her Sternist comrades waiting for her in a car not far away. All this time the two Arabs from Abu Gosh flailed away at the police who had come to investigate the uproar. A few moments later the escape was discovered and sirens screamed, but Gueoula was already safely hidden. She had to convalesce for a few days but soon, with Dr. Eldad's help, she was able to resume broadcasting with the same phrase that had involuntarily been her last on the day she was arrested. "What's happening?"

Of all the escapes in this period of clandestine opposition, none is more spectacular than the one from Acre. It was an extraordinary feat, as much for the minutiae of the preparations as for the daring of the execution.[41] It all began on April 23, 1946, at Ramat Gan in the suburbs of Tel Aviv. An Irgun group attacked the British police station in order to "recover" arms and ammunition. The Irgun leader, Gad, disguised as an English noncommissioned officer, presented himself at the entrance to the heavily guarded post with a dozen handcuffed Arabs. He was coming, he said, to turn these thieves over to the competent authority. Scarcely had the fake officer and the fake Arabs been admitted to the station than they threw away their false handcuffs, and opening their ample jellabahs, pointed their revolvers at the police. The arms were seized and the Irgun truck was starting to leave when agents began firing from the rooftops. Two Irgun men were killed. Another, badly wounded in the jaw, fell to the ground. He was a young man of twenty-eight, originally from Hungary, called Dov Grüner. He had served in the British army during the war.

Dov spent eight months in the hospital. When he had recovered he was tried and sentenced to death on January 1, 1947. General Barker, the same officer whose anti-Semitic orders had raised objections even in England, confirmed the sentence on January 24. The Irgun responded by taking two hostages on January 26 and 27, one of them a judge. Barker allowed a stay of execution "to permit Grüner to appeal." On January 28, the Irgun released the two Englishmen. The judge declared that he had been courteously treated, had been given good meals, cigarettes, and even a novel by Arthur Koestler to read.[42]

But three months later, on April 16, Dov Grüner and three other young Jews, Dressner, Elkahi, and Kashani, were hanged at dawn in the prison at Acre without even a rabbi being allowed near them in their last moments. And on April 21, two other condemned men, Meir Feinstein (of the Irgun) and Moshe Barazani (of the Stern group) escaped the hangman by blowing themselves up in their cells at Jerusalem with hand grenades their comrades had smuggled into them among some oranges.

The attitude of Dov Grüner and his friends was impressively dignified right up to the end. In the cell where he awaited death one can still see the Irgun emblem[43] that Dov scratched on the wall. Shortly before his execution he wrote to Menachem Beigin, with whom he corresponded thanks to a relay system set up by Madame Tamir, Jabotinsky's niece. It was a long letter in which he calmly and lucidly summed up his reasons for fighting and dying. "I am writing this," he ended, "while waiting for the hangman. At such a time one cannot lie. I swear that if I had to live my life over I would choose the same path, whatever the consequences might be." He signed himself, "Your faithful soldier, Dov."

These cruel and useless executions, which served only to rally the Jewish community more strongly than ever around the young martyrs, set off a wave of operations and attacks by the Irgun and the Lehi. Above all else the ancient fortress of Acre stood in the imagination of Palestinians as the very symbol of the domination they hated, and the

Irgun decided to attack this symbol audaciously.

Livni, former chief of Irgun operations who had been captured at Bat Yam and condemned to fifteen years in prison, was serving his time at Acre. He asked Beigin for a certain quantity of explosives and detonators. This material was brought into the prison little by little by innocent-looking visitors. Livni managed also to let his comrades know that a certain window opening on the outside could be used for an escape.

Beigin had asked Guiddi, Livni's successor as chief of operations, to draw up a plan of attack on the fortress. At the Ministry of Public Works in Haifa, Guiddi got hold of detailed plans of the old city of Acre, which was a labyrinth of tiny streets and covered passages in the middle of which sat the prison, close by the mosque. He studied the plans with Dov Cohen, called Shimshon, who was to lead the attack. Disguised as Arabs, the two of them took long strolls through the quarters, apparently deep in discussion, and in fact taking note of every detail. Shimshon, thirty-two years old and a native of Kraków, had come to Palestine in 1938 to study philosophy at the Hebrew University in Jerusalem. In 1940, he joined the British army and fought in Eritrea, Libya, Tripolitania, and Italy. He was discharged with the rank of sergeant major and held the Military Medal. Once free he joined the Irgun. Thick-set, blond, and blue-eyed, he was known for his daring and calm.

While Livni, on the inside, planned every detail of the operation with a small staff (five Irgun men, three from the Lehi) and Guiddi drew up the over-all plan of action and obtained the necessary supplies, Shimshon set up a base at Binyamina, in Samaria, about thirty-five miles from Acre. With four assistants, he made a thorough reconnaissance all around the prison. The attacking column would be composed of thirty-four men riding in three military trucks and a jeep. Shimshon would wear the uniform of a captain in the Engineers.

The plan called for three main operations. First, a diversionary attack would be staged on a battalion three miles from the fortress. Then, the fortress itself would be cut off by mining the approach roads and by stationing two groups of three men each around it. Finally, a hole would be dynamited in the wall opposite the window Livni had pointed out as a means of escape.

The plan went off like clockwork. At 4:22 P.M. on May 4, 1947, a violent explosion shook the whole fortress: eighty-eight pounds of dynamite blew a yawning hole in the wall. Livni's men immediately blew open the doors that separated them from the wall. The bars and padlocks shattered. In the midst of clouds of smoke and dust, the forty-one political prisoners ran toward freedom, some of them igniting torches and setting fires to cover their retreat, as planned. Chaos and panic broke out in the ancient prison. The terrified Arab prisoners screamed; the guards fired shots at random. In the general confusion more than two hundred Arabs fled, only to be recaptured shortly afterward.

The Jewish resistance fighters made it to the trucks, and by then the British had begun to react. In the violent exchange of gunfire Shimshon and five of the escapees were killed; seven others were wounded and recaptured. Three Irgunists who had taken part in the assault fell into British hands. The other members of the attacking force and the remaining escapees managed to get away. Hidden first at Nahalat Jabotinsky, near Zikhron Yaakov, they disappeared into the countryside. Livni, whom Guiddi took to Tel Aviv, left secretly for Europe.

This audacious and successful attack upon a supposedly impregnable fortress astonished the world. More than any other action of the resistance, it proved that the policy of the White Paper, carried out with unbelievable blindness by the Attlee-Bevin government, could not be imposed on the Jewish people of Palestine. This policy lay in ruins just like the walls of Acre. Having failed to grasp the fact that a Jewish Palestine, solidly allied with Britain, as Balfour had conceived it, could have been the surest guarantee of British interests in the Middle East, and having failed to dissipate Lawrence's mirage of the "Arab world," the Cabinet in London had blundered into an impasse that it could escape only by abandoning all its positions. The year 1947 would not end before the consequences became plain of British persistence in an error almost unexampled in history.

FOOTNOTES FOR CHAPTER 7

1. This and many other facts in this chapter come from the "Symposium," published by the Tel Aviv daily, *Ma'ariv*, April 4–29, 1966. This "round table," organized by Gueoula Cohen, a former announcer on the Stern group's clandestine radio, consisted of Menachem Beigin, the former Irgun commander in chief; Chaim Landau and Shmuel Katz, former members of the Irgun command; Nathan Yellin-Moor and Yitshak Shamir of the central committee of the Stern group; Moshe Sneh, former chief of the Haganah; Eliezer Livni, editor of the magazine *Eshnab*, the official organ of the Haganah; Yaakov Riftin, former member of the "X" Commission; and Shimon Peres, former undersecretary of national defense. The accounts of these four conversations will henceforth be referred to as "Symposium."

2. Conversation of David Ben Gurion with the author, 1967.

3. Vera Weizmann, *op. cit.*, p. 193.

4. Palestine Royal Commission. Minutes of evidence heard at public sessions, London, H.M.'s Stationery Office, 1937. p. 289.

5. Vera Weizmann, *op. cit.*, p. 193.

6. Cf. Gueoula Cohen. *Souvenirs d'une jeune fille violente.*

7. Beigin. *op. cit.*, p. 70.

8. Beigin. *La Révolte d'Israël.* p. 97.

9. Information from Eitan Livni in a conversation with the author.

10. Symposium.

11. Symposium.

12. The Stern group made a number of unsuccessful attempts on the life of Sir Harold MacMichael, the high commissioner of Palestine, although MacMichael was lightly wounded during the last of them, on the road to Jaffa.

13. Gerold Frank. *The Deed.* p. 260–63.

14. Testimony of Eli Tavin, Zeev Schiff, and others, sent to the author.

15. Statement made by Dr. Yehuda Slutsky, chief of the Haganah Historical Service, to the author.

16. Winston Churchill told Mrs. Weizmann in 1953 that "It was all Bevin—an anti-Semite." "Why should a socialist be an anti-Semite?" she asked. "All the Foreign Office is," replied Churchill. Vera Weizmann. *op. cit.*, p. 256.

17. Cf. Crossman. *Palestine Mission.* London, 1947; Bartley C. Crum. *Behind the Silken Curtain.* New York, 1947.

18. According to Crossman, *op. cit.*, p. 129, when Weizmann appeared before the committee he condemned all violence. Ben Gurion would say only that it was "futile" under present conditions to try to repress terrorism.

19. Francis Williams. *Ernest Bevin: Portrait of a Great Englishman.* p. 260.

20. Crossman. *op. cit.*, p. 191.

21. In a typical gesture of British "fair play," High Commissioner Cunningham congratulated Weizmann on the success of the operation.

22. Symposium.

23. These papers proved that the Jewish Agency was in agreement with the terrorists. They consisted mainly of a speech Moshe Sharett made behind closed doors to the Vaad Leumi after the bridge operation, of which he heartily approved.

24. Statement to the author by one of the persons present.

25. Vera Weizmann, *op. cit.*, p. 213.

26. "If you . . . wish to secure your redemption," he cried, "through means . . . which do not accord with Jewish morale and Jewish ethics or Jewish history, I say to you that you are worshiping false gods. . . . Go and reread Isaiah, Jeremiah, Ezekiel . . . 'Zion will

be saved through righteousness'—and not by other means." George Kirk. *Survey of International Affairs. The Middle East,* 1945–50. p. 232.

27. Chaim Weizmann. *Trial and Error.* pp. 543–44.

28. Beigin. *Rebelión.* p. 371.

29. Bracha Habas. *op. cit.,* p. 338.

30. *Op. cit.,* pp. 77–81.

31. Crossmann. *op. cit.,* p. 113.

32. Jon and David Kimche, *op. cit.,* p. 134. The Jewish Agency urged Arazi to accept this proposition "to avoid increasing the tension with the British."

33. Kimche. *op. cit.,* p. 149. This book of course reflects the viewpoint of official Zionism.

34. Figures were furnished the author by Mr. Shaul Avigour.

35. Symposium.

36. Henri Marcus. *Les Camps d'Internement Britanniques.* The manuscript was kindly put at the author's disposal.

37. *Ibid.*

38. For example, the officer who shouted at Yaakov Meridor, "A shame Hitler did not kill all the Jews! That would have saved us some work." Meridor. *Long is the Road to Freedom,* p. 245.

39. *Op. cit.*

40. G. Cohen. *Souvenirs d'une jeune fille violente.*

41. Jan Gitlin. *The Conquest of Acre Fortress.* Tel Aviv, Hadar Publishing House, 1962.

42. Arthur Koestler. *Promise and Fulfillment.* p. 147.

43. The Irgun emblem is composed of a map of historical Palestine on both sides of the Jordan on which is superimposed a hand holding a rifle, with two Hebrew words, "*Rak Kah,*"—"Only Thus."

8
THE
STATE
OF
ISRAEL

Palestine at the end of the Second World War was like a man healthy in body but sick at heart. The *yishuv* mourned for the victims of the great massacre and rebelled with growing bitterness against the Mandatory power that had closed the gates of salvation to the refugees. The Arab leaders, still shaken by the defeat of the Axis, hardened their opposition to Zionism. Palestine was a land of despair, violence, and hatred; and yet its prosperity and material success were increasing.

It was far from the dried-up, hungry land that had welcomed General Allenby, the British army, and the Jewish Legion when the Turkish Empire was breathing its last. More than two decades of hard work had turned the national home into a reality, in spite of insecurity and restrictions on colonization and immigration, even in spite of the war.

Between 1922 and 1944 the Jewish population had grown from 84,000 to 554,000. Most important, it had increased more rapidly in the country (811 per cent) than in the cities (505 per cent). Tel Aviv and Haifa had grown, of course, but it was in the agricultural colonies, whether collective or co-operative, that the Jewish people had most firmly taken root.[1]

The agricultural growth of the country did not stem entirely, or even principally, from official Zionist colonization of lands belonging to the *Keren Kayemet*. Of course the kibbutz and, from 1920, the co-operative village, or *moshav*, had spearheaded the land reclamation effort. A nationwide network of co-operatives for selling and distributing products, *Tnouva*, and supplying goods to the villages, *Hamashbir Hamerkazi*, contributed to an economic development that was furthered by numerous organizations supplying credit, argricultural insurance, instruction, and technical information. But in 1942, private colonization still accounted for 64 per cent of the total. More heavily populated than the collectives and co-operatives, the private colonies numbered 88 out of a total of 148. Later, by 1946, the *Keren Kayemet* had succeeded in establishing 250 colonies on the 195,000 acres it owned. Not surprisingly, Jewish farmers' production had increased considerably.

From 1938 to 1943 potato production increased 514 per cent, fruit 508 per cent, milk 63 per cent, meat 45 per cent, and fish 1,200 per cent (from fish ponds). During the war years Palestine could even victual the armies stationed in Palestine and the rest of the Middle East.

Had these gains been made at the expense of the Arab population? Numbering about 1,200,000, the Arabs made up two thirds of the total population. In twenty-two years, their birth rate had gone from 23.27 to 30.71 per 1,000 as marshes were cleared, hygiene improved, and infant mortality reduced — all this largely owing to the Zionist presence.[2] It is interesting to note that the evolution of Arab settlement was the reverse of that of the Jews: while in 1922 only 7.4 per cent of the Arabs lived in the cities, by 1944 11.8 per cent of them did. Even more remarkable is that the Moslem population had increased between 1922 and 1944 by 142 per cent in the coastal zone, that is to say the Plain of Sharon and the port cities where Jewish economic activity was greatest.

Moreover, the inflated prices that the Zionist immigrants paid for fallow land, sandy dunes, and marshes largely went to the Arabs. A good deal of this money undoubtedly went to the *effendi*, or absentee landlords, who spent it in Damascus, Cairo, Beirut, and Europe. But the rest was put to good use in reclaiming the usually superior lands that the Arabs had kept for themselves. This explains why the Arab citrus plantations rose from 7,200 acres in 1922 to about 34,000 in 1944, an area equal to the Zionist *pardessim*. In 1944–45, the Arabs were still producing eleven times more cereals, three times more vegetables, and three times more fruit (not including citrus) than the Jews, and were selling the Jews £500,000 worth of agricultural produce every year. In spite of the rapid growth of the Arab population, the per capita value of farm production had doubled.

Moreover, the prosperity created by Zionist perseverance had attracted thousands of Syrian, Transjordanian, and Egyptian Arabs to Palestine. In 1934–35, twenty-five thousand Syrian *fellahin*, discouraged by the dryness and the taxes exacted by the Bedouins of the Hauran, had emigrated to Palestine, particularly attracted by the high salaries paid at Haifa and Tel Aviv.[3] At least one hundred thousand from the neighboring countries had settled along the coast,[4] and it must be noted that the Mandatory administration had put no obstacle in the way of this immigration at the same time that it had severely restricted the immigration of Jews.

The British administration, alarmed by repeated complaints that the Jews were dispossessing Arab peasants when they bought up land, made a thorough investigation, and found that in twenty years 664 Arab families had been displaced, of which 347 had been provided with new land and the rest had found employment in the cities. It is known too that the Jews paid 70 per cent of the taxes exacted by the Mandatory. Besides that, the *yishuv*, through the Jewish Agency, itself provided for the expenses of development, irrigation, general and technical training, and scientific research[5] and that it allocated important sums to general expenses.[6]

Jewish and Arab interests were clearly complementary, not opposed, and if the former did not depend on the latter, the reverse was not true. The economic and social progress of the Arabs of Palestine rested on the development of the national home, which was building prosperity in a land so long abandoned to neglect and poverty.

This was exactly what the *effendi* feared most. Their spokesman and leader, the former grand mufti, had returned to the Middle East (though he had been declared a war criminal because of his close association with Hitler, Himmler, and Eichmann) to try to stir up anti-Semitic hatred. An Arab population with a higher standard of living obviously might escape the domination of the great feudal families. This explained the eagerness of the powerful Arabs to oppose the Jewish presence, small though it was—occupying 1 per cent of Palestine and 1 per cent of Arab territory in the Middle East.

The Zionists had always believed that developing the resources of both communities for equal progress would lead to peaceful coexistence. Although it was no longer even a talking point, Weizmann clung to this hope after the war. Worthy and justified on humanitarian and rational grounds, the concept was doomed by the ambitions of the so-called Arab nationalists and by British policy.

Even before the war had ended, the grand alliance between the United States, England, and the Soviet Union showed signs of internal tensions in the eastern Mediterranean and the Balkans.[7] The alliance quickly became the cold war. The key to British political strategy lay in the Arab League, conceived as a line of Arab and Moslem states tied to England by treaties and good will arising from numerous political and economic favors, subsidies, and so forth granted by Great Britain.

This idea was eagerly adopted by the same Arab leaders who during the war had put all hopes on an Axis victory and now saw a chance to extort from the British what they had been unable to get out of the Germans. The League furnished a new base for the pro-Arab specialists of the foreign office and the colonial office that intended, now that France was out of Syria and Lebanon, to maintain English influence throughout the Levant. These heirs of Lawrence and Saint-John Philby, such as Sir Miles Lampson (Lord Killearn), General Clayton, General Spears, and last but not least, the tenacious Harold Beeley,[8] were interested in Palestine only because it was next door to the Suez Canal and because Haifa would make a first-class naval base. The Jews had no place in such a geopolitical vision: Palestine as an Arab state, a member of the Arab League, and a satellite of England like Transjordan. A Jewish minority could be tolerated there on the express condition that it continued to be a minority "protected" by England, a *Schutz-judentum* as Jabotinsky had said; but there was to be no Jewish state.

In face of the dangers of Russian expansionism, the men behind this British policy said they lacked confidence in a Jewish Palestine. After all, had not a strong proportion of Zionist immigrants come from Russia? And the kibbutzim and the economic policies of the Mapai and the Histadrut—were these not Soviet ideas? As for the Arabs, the policy makers sometimes asserted that Islam was incompatible with Communism (a highly debatable statement in view of its community-mindedness), and sometimes asserted that if the Arabs grew angry over concessions made to the Jews they would throw themselves into the arms of the Soviet Union. Hence the Arabs must be supported and appeased at any price, either because they were a rampart against Communism, or because they were the reverse.

To these considerations were joined an almost fantastic overestimation of Arab military capabilities. It was taken as axiomatic that in any war between Arabs and Jews, the Jews would be immediately and decisively crushed. This belief was shared by all the British "experts" on the Middle East, particularly Beeley, and even by such American leaders as Forrestal, General Marshall, and most of the State Department.[9]

In 1945, Prime Minister Attlee seemed to have no definite ideas on the subject. The colonial secretary, Arthur Creech-Jones, was reputed personally to favor Zionism (the Labour party having stated its pro-Zionist position over and over), but found his authority usurped by Foreign Minister Bevin. Bevin was completely at the mercy of his advisers' ideas, especially Beeley's, and he devoted all the energy of his fiery temperament to seeing that they triumphed. No one in the higher echelons of the British government seems ever to have thought of basing policy on the solid pier of a Jewish Palestine, economically prosperous and militarily strong. The dogma of Arab supremacy blinded Whitehall. Only General J. C. D'Arcy, who commanded British forces in Palestine at the time of the visit of the Anglo-American Committee, understood the truth, no doubt because he had been in contact with a few realities. He stated flatly that if English troops withdrew, the Haganah would take over the whole country the next day and could hold it against the entire Arab world.[10] But such heresies could not shake the assurance of those who breathed the rarified air of London.

Why then did the British government suddenly decide in 1947 to put the Palestinian question before the United Nations? Did this mean that they had decided to give up Palestine, which had been until then one of the keys to its Eastern policy? Since this action resulted in the United Nations partition of Palestine in 1947 and the proclamation of the Jewish state in 1948, it would be tempting to conclude that Ernest Bevin was resolved or resigned to "disengage" his government from a country that had caused him such trouble. But that is probably an illusion, for the final outcome was probably not the one Bevin and his advisers had hoped for. David Horowitz of the Jewish Agency reported on a conversation he had with Harold Beeley that puts this apparently surprising decision in crude relief.[11] Beeley pointed out that in order to get the necessary two-thirds majority in the United Nations, the United States and the Communist bloc would have to vote together. And then he exclaimed, "that has never happened, it cannot happen and it will never happen!" And so the tactic of the foreign office was to ask for a United Nations decision; then to demonstrate that the organization could never reach a solution; and finally to return without obstacle to the White Paper. An ingenious plan, but the actual course of events proved that like the sorcerer's apprentice, the Labour government had let itself in for more than it bargained for: the thing that would "never happen" did indeed happen. The momentary conjunction of American and Russian policies brought about the partition of Palestine and with it the rebirth of the Jewish state in Eretz Israel.

A precise term like "American policy" hardly describes the incoherent mass of contradictory tendencies that shaped American diplomatic actions in the Middle East between 1940 and 1947. From the start of the war until 1943, American leaders looked upon the Mediterranean, North Africa, and the Arab countries as being in the British sphere of interest and responsibility. Indeed, England bore the brunt of the war in Libya and the defense of the Suez Canal. But in 1942, after the Allies had landed in North Africa and crushed Rommel in Tunisia, and when Eisenhower was supreme commander in Algiers, the western Mediterranean became an American responsibility. Roosevelt met the sultan of Morocco in Casablanca in January, 1943, and discovered the charms of the world of Islam. Henceforth he often expressed in private his opinion that the war should result in the liquidation of the empires, the French empire, of course, and the British as well.[12]

The principle of anticolonialism coincided with the interests of a powerful economic pressure group—the large oil companies. These companies first came into the Middle East in co-operation with Iraq Petroleum and the Anglo-Iranian oil companies, which were predominantly British. But in 1933 they got their own concessions in Kuwait, Bahrein, and Saudi Arabia. Standard Oil of California and Texas Oil formed a company in 1936, and in 1944 they called their joint Saudi Arabian operation the Arabian American Oil Company, or Aramco. Represented in Washington by a very active lobby, the oil trust spread the idea in political circles that the United States must at all cost remain on friendly terms with the Arabs, particularly ibn-Saud, in order not to lose access to the oil fields of the Middle East—which would have been a veritable economic and military disaster. "To keep the Arabs sweet and the oil flowing"[13] became the cornerstone of American policy, at least as the State Department and the military conceived it. Anticolonialism was satisfied by the policy of supporting independence for the states, kingdoms, and emirates of Arabia. The oil interests derived more substantial rewards from the situation.

In this light, Zionism, the Zionists, and the national home were only inconvenient nuisances and a permanent source of irritation and uneasiness for all those Arabs who had to be kept "sweet." This policy inevitably led to the sacrifice of a Jewish Palestine, supposedly to the claims of the Arabs, but in fact to the oil interests.

At the same time powerful forces in the United States were pulling in the opposite direction. American public opinion, deeply sympathetic toward the persecuted Jews, was reinforced by the propaganda activities of Zionist organizations, particularly the Revisionists. A survey conducted in December, 1945, by the public opinion institute at Princeton showed that 76 per cent of non-Jewish Americans who were informed about Palestine favored establishing the Jews there.[14] In 1941 an American Committee for Palestine had been formed under the leadership of Senator Robert Wagner. Among its seven hundred members were sixty-seven senators and one hundred forty-three congressmen (both Republicans and Democrats), twenty-two governors, ministers of many faiths, professors, writers, and others. By 1945, the committee had increased to fifteen thousand members. Legislatures of thirty-nine states, representing 85 per cent of the American population, had passed pro-Zionist resolutions. Public figures, such as senators Robert Taft and Robert Wagner, and congressmen Wright and Compton, introduced resolutions in Congress favoring massive Jewish immigration to Palestine in order to establish a free and democratic "Commonwealth." But this legislation ran against the stubborn opposition of Secretary of State Cordell Hull and Henry L. Stimson, the Secretary of War. They both maintained that if Congress approved the Taft-Wagner resolution, the United States would lose the good will of the Arab countries. They undoubtedly acted with the consent of President Roosevelt. Only in December, 1945, after two years of delaying tactics, and after Harry Truman was in the White House, did the two houses of Congress finally pass a slightly altered version of the Taft-Wagner resolution.

The two major parties, and consequently all elected officials including the President, of course could not fail to take account of the Jewish vote. There were then about four and a half million Jews in the United States, concentrated largely in New York, Illinois, Pennsylvania, and Ohio. Mostly pro-Zionist, they naturally watched quite closely the position taken by their candidates and the major parties on the Palestine problem. In 1944, an election year, the Democratic and Republican platforms both included plans favoring the establishment of a democratic Jewish state in Palestine. Some American leaders, particularly Defense Secretary James Forrestal, would have preferred to omit all reference to Palestine in the platforms, but they were not successful. In a country where the varied ethnic origins of the people still played an important role in their political choices, no presidential candidate could afford to offend Jewish voters, any more than Italian, Irish, or Scandinavian voters. However, it is only fair to say that, with the exception of the four states mentioned above, the Jewish population of America was nowhere higher than 5 per cent of the total, and it fell below 1 per cent in twenty-four states out of forty-eight. In New Mexico, for example, there were a total of 1,178 Jews, including minors below the voting age. Thus it was hardly from political expediency that Senator Chavez of that state was one of the most vigorous supporters of the pro-Zionist resolutions. Nor was he the only such example.

Thus, while making allowances for the perfectly legitimate activity of American citizens of the Jewish faith in support of their coreligionaries in Palestine, American politicians constantly found that public opinion was deeply and spontaneously favorable to Zionist objectives. This did not prevent certain government bureaus, especially the State and War departments, from opposing them. This state of affairs will have a familiar ring to anyone who has studied Washington's policies toward wartime France: public opinion was overwhelmingly on the side of the Free French, in spite of the stubborn hostility of Cordell Hull and Roosevelt.

Roosevelt seems to have had a great faith in the king of Arabia, ibn-Saud. In 1943 a series of confused deals involving Saint-John Philby and Roosevelt's man Colonel Hoskins came to absolutely nothing. Roosevelt had thought he might persuade ibn-Saud to take part in a Jewish-Arab conference. In exchange for recognizing the rights of the Jews in Palestine, the Arab king would theoretically have enjoyed American support for extending his rule over the Arab world. Ibn-Saud angrily refused this proposition, playing to the hilt the role of the great monarch outraged by the offer of a vulgar "baksheesh."[15]

After the Yalta Conference, Roosevelt, weak and ill, met ibn-Saud in Egypt. During their long conversation the President tried again and again to get a favorable response from the king, if not toward Zionism, at least toward the settlement of European Jewish refugees in Palestine. The king brutally and intractably refused. Ibn-Saud did not even discuss the subject; instead, he lapsed into a monologue on the theme that the Arabs would never stand for the settlement of the Jews in Palestine and that they cared nothing for the economic and social gains that the President waved under his nose. He even expressed the fear that too close a contact between his people and Europeans (meaning Americans, as well as Westernized Jews) would have disastrous consequences.[16]

The conversation was totally futile. Worse than that, Roosevelt, no doubt because of his exhaustion, seems to have given in on all points to the violent attack of the Arab king. "I learned more about . . . the Jewish problem," he said, "by talking with ibn-Saud for five minutes than I could have learned in an exchange of two or three dozen letters."[17] The Arab monarch did not hesitate to exploit this success. On March 23, 1945, he threatened Roosevelt with war in the Middle East if the United States took a pro-Zionist position. In his answer, dated April 5, 1945, Roosevelt reminded his "great and good friend" that he had been glad to "obtain so vivid an impression of His Majesty's sentiments on the question of Palestine," and he added, "Your Majesty will doubtless recall that during our recent conversation I assured you that I would take no action in my capacity as Chief of the Executive branch of the government that might prove hostile to the Arab people."

This astonishing message gave the Arabs veto power over American policies in the Middle East. Since it went without saying that any action favoring Zionism was bound to appear hostile in the eyes of Arab leaders, particularly ibn-Saud, the President was actually promising to abandon Palestine altogether. This did not keep him from saying a few appeasing words to the Zionist leaders. But the fact remains that after his talk with ibn-Saud, Roosevelt left his Middle Eastern policies in the hands of the pro-Arab elements of his administration.

Harry S. Truman, who took his oath of office on April 12, 1945, was reputed to be inexperienced in international affairs. At the time he indeed seems to have had rather vague ideas about the problems of the Middle East and the Mediterranean. Under his leadership, however, the United States became deeply involved in Eastern Europe, replaced Great Britain in Greece (through the Truman Doctrine), and brought its support to the creation of the Hebrew state in Palestine. Only five days after his swearing-in, Truman received a memorandum on Palestine from the State Department in which the Secretary of State, Edward Stettinius, urged him to adopt the greatest prudence toward this area "vital to the United States."[18] But this former Missouri haberdasher had a healthy mistrust for what he called the "striped pants boys" of traditional diplomacy, and he had the gift of making decisions. From the start of his administration he was under strong pressure from the State Department, and then from Azzam Pasha, who was secretary general of the Arab League, and from many Arab governments, but he did not hesitate to move away from the position that the ailing Roosevelt had adopted. This is not to say that he invariably took a perfectly clear stand. We shall see that he often vacillated, maneuvered, took two steps forward and one back. But it is impossible to overlook his good faith and his humanity.[19] Unlike many other statesmen he never lost sight of the agonizing problem of the fate of the Jews in D.P. camps if they were not admitted to Palestine.

On June 22, 1945, Truman asked Earl G. Harrison, dean of the law school at the University of Pennsylvania, to investigate the situation of the displaced persons, especially the Jews detained against their will in Germany and Austria. Harrison was highly qualified for this assignment; as an expert on naturalization and immigration, he had represented the United States on the International Refugee Committee. His report, presented in August, was overwhelming: "Three months after V-E Day . . . many Jewish displaced persons . . . are living under guard behind barbed wire fences, in camps . . . (built by the Germans for slave-laborers and Jews) . . . amid crowded, frequently unsanitary and generally grim conditions, in complete idleness, with no opportunity, except surreptitiously, to communicate with the outside world." He added, "They want to be evacuated to Palestine. . . . It is morally wrong and politically indefensible to impose obstacles to the immediate entry into Palestine now of any Jews who desire to go there," and he recommended the immediate evacuation of one hundred thousand Jews from Germany and Austria. He underlined the "inhuman" character of a policy that forced these poor people to stay in the camps.

This is what Truman himself emphatically said to Clement Attlee when he sent him the Harrison report on August 31. He did this clearly and generously but—unfortunately, for this omission irritated Attlee and Bevin—without saying anything about how the United States might share in the costs of the evacuation (a secondary consideration, actually, since the Zionist organizations were as ready to pay for legal immigration as they had been for illegal immigration), nor what it would do to keep order in the Middle East if Arab threats materialized. Great Britain was in the midst of a serious financial and economic crisis brought on by the war effort. The Cabinet answered bitterly that it would take Truman's proposal under serious consideration at such time as the United States showed itself willing to bear a share of the attendant obligations.

Thus brought up short, the President preferred not to "see a political structure imposed on the Near East that would result in conflict,"[20] and he sent the whole problem back to the United Nations: an utterly unrealistic position since, as the founders of Zionism had known, the key to the whole Jewish question was inescapably political and, moreover, the United Nations had no way of solving the problem if the United States would not help.

In answer to Truman's appeal, and as a result of the Harrison report, Bevin proposed the creation of the Anglo-American Committee. Months passed. Only in April, 1946, were the committee's recommendations submitted to the two governments and rejected by the British Cabinet. Truman was plunged into an ocean of difficulties: Zionist organizations in the United States pressured him about the one hundred thousand immigration certificates that the committee had called for, and simultaneously the Arab League, in a memorandum to Washington, threatened reprisals against American holdings in the Middle East. The Joint Chiefs of Staff told the President that if Jewish immigration led to war, the United States did not have sufficient troops to intervene, and that moreover they ran the risk of losing the Arab countries' oil. Truman's diplomatic advisers whistled up the specter of Communism, for according to them, the Arabs were on the verge of joining the Soviet camp.

Meanwhile, the Russian leaders themselves were evolving not in the direction of a rapprochement with the Arabs but rather toward a change in their traditional position on Zionism. They had a long road to travel, for the post-Revolutionary regime had fought Zionism just as vigorously as the czarists, if not more so. According to official doctrine, the desire to establish a Jewish state in Palestine was a bourgeois deviation. Worse than that, Zionism was an arm of British imperialism. On the strength of similar grievances, Menachem Beigin, for example, was arrested and sent to a concentration camp in 1940.

By adopting this attitude, the Soviets were certainly giving in to the old temptation of anti-Semitism, the demon that is still not exorcised in Russia and that is always ready to reappear as circumstances require. Simultaneously, as coldly realistic politicians, the Soviets were taking aim at the adversary that they had to eliminate from the Middle East, that region of the first importance for Russian expansionism. They were aware that the relationship between the powers in that part of the world was changing. Zionism was no longer the ally or client of England, but more and more its adversary. British imperialism in the Levant was being gravely undermined by the armed resistance to the Mandatory that was being led principally by the Irgun under the command of the same Beigin whom the Soviets had once imprisoned as a Zionist. For this reason, Zionism, and particularly militant Zionism, which was struggling to throw off the British yoke, was becoming worthy of attention and support. Yesterday's retrogression was today's progress.

The Irgun leaders soon became aware of these changes in Russian attitude. Certain contacts assured them that it had changed, particularly that made by Yaakov Meridor with the Russian ambassador in Addis Ababa. He clearly expressed his government's professed sympathy for the fight that was so deeply undermining the British position in the Levant. Amusingly enough, the Palestine Communists and left-wing socialists of the *Hashomer Hatzair* were totally ignorant of this change. Their newspapers, including the official Communist party organ *Kol Ha-am*, and the left-wing *Hamishmar*, calmly continued to oppose the idea of a Jewish state until the day when Andrei Gromyko, in a speech before the United Nations, revealed the new "party line" like a thunderclap out of a sunny sky. They of course made haste to adopt it.

In July, 1946, the Anglo-American Expert Committee met in London. This title was woefully inappropriate, at least for the American members: their chairman, Ambassador Henry F. Grady, knew nothing at all about Palestine. The committee was an attempt by President Truman to save whatever he could from the wreckage of the Anglo-American Committee. He had decided in spite of the State Department to reopen negotiations with the British on the one hundred thousand immigration certificates that he had requested more than a year before. To smooth the path, he even promised that the United States would assume the "technical and financial" responsibility for transporting the immigrants.[21]

The Grady-Morrison plan that emerged from the discussions was devoid of novelty. According to the Labourite deputy, Richard Crossman, it was a rehash of an old project "prepared in the Colonial Office before the Labour government came to power."[22] The Anglo-American Committee had studied and rejected it as a "typical piece of Constitution making that solved none of the underlying problems and reserved the keys of power in British hands."[23] Known as the "plan for provincial autonomy," it proposed to cut Palestine into five pieces:[24] one of these, which included a narrow strip east of Galilee, the Valley of Jezreel plain, and the coastal zone to Tel Aviv, would be the Jewish province. The Arabs would have all of central and western Galilee and the rest of Palestine including Beersheba. The British administration would keep Jerusalem and the Negev. Jaffa, although inside the Jewish zone, would remain Arab. Each of these provinces would enjoy a certain degree of internal autonomy, but a British central government under the high commissioner would have the supreme control over defense, foreign relations, customs, postal services, communications, radio, and police; it would retain a veto over the decisions of provincial legislatures, and it would choose the members of local governments.

The Grady-Morrison plan provided for the admission of one hundred thousand European Jews to Palestine the year after this new administrative system was set up, but since the establishment of the system itself depended on the agreement of all concerned parties — and thus on the consent of the Arabs — it was certain that the Jews still detained in concentration camps a year after their "liberation" would wait a long time before the gates were opened.

Actually the only people who saw any merit in this plan were those who proposed it; it met with universal disapproval. In the House of Commons on August 1, part of the majority party joined the opposition in criticizing it. Winston Churchill for the first time formulated an idea that was to point the way: Great Britain, he said, must surrender its Mandate to the United Nations and promise to get out of Palestine by a pre-arranged date.

Both Jews and Arabs rejected the plan, the Arabs, because they wanted independence and all of Palestine, including Tel Aviv; the Jews, because the plan solved nothing — not even the immigration problem — and left them with a tiny territory, simply a ghetto.

President Truman, restricted by the position Ambassador Grady had taken and by the support offered the plan by Secretary of State Byrnes and Undersecretary Acheson, at first tried hard to see some merit in the idea. He angrily refused to listen to the opposing views of several congressmen and one of the members of the Anglo-American Committee, James G. McDonald.[25] But later, after he had "studied the proposed plan with care," and realized that "nothing could come out of it except new unrest," and that "the admission of the 100,000 was conditional on its being accepted by the Arabs, so no relief was offered,"[26] he decided definitely to reject the plan. James F. Byrnes and James Forrestal received this news bitterly. Byrnes told Forrestal that he would henceforth disassociate himself from the President's policies and that he "washed his hands" of the whole Palestinian question.[27]

Now there was no plan for Palestine at all. In August, 1946, the Jewish Agency began to try to formulate a new one. Nahum Goldmann, one of the American members of the executive committee of the Agency, after attending a meeting of the executive committee in Paris with David Ben Gurion, went to Washington in order to submit a plan to the United States government that for the first time proposed a partition of Palestine in the name of the Zionist organization.

To understand how shocking this was to many Zionists, one must recall that in 1942 the Biltmore Program had stated that the movement's aim was to establish a Jewish state in all Palestine; that this conception of Palestine west of the Jordan represented but a fraction, less than a fourth, of historical Palestine mandated to England and arbitrarily divided by England in 1922 for the benefit of the Hashemite dynasty; that a considerable part of the Zionist movement was faithful to Jabotinsky's teaching and held firmly to the motto "Palestine on both banks of the Jordan." It was a serious step to give up the Biltmore Program, for that plan was itself a retreat from the original program of Herzl and Jabotinsky.

Through its spokesman and president, Dr. Abba Hillel Silver, the American Zionist Organization reacted vigorously against Nahum Goldmann's proposals. The rights of the Jewish people, the organization declared in a resolution, "apply to all of Mandated Palestine, undivided." Moreover, Dr. Silver pointed out, by announcing that it would discuss the establishment of a "viable Jewish state in an adequate zone," the Jewish Agency had made a grave tactical error, for it had abandoned the precision of the Biltmore Program for a vague formula open to all sorts of interpretations.

The Jewish Agency's idea was proposed simultaneously in Washington and London. It envisioned the creation of two states: the Jewish state would comprise Galilee, the coastal plain, and the Negev; the Arab state would be the rest of the territory, including Lydda and Ramle in the suburbs of Tel Aviv, and a corridor joining the territory to Jaffa. Jerusalem would remain under British control. Dr. Weizmann offered this plan as a "basis for discussion" to the British colonial secretary. The Arab League responded by presenting its own plan: a united, independent Palestine with a Parliament elected in proportion to the population by Arabs and Jews, with the provision that in no case could Jewish representation exceed a third of the total. Palestinian citizenship would be reserved for those born in the country under the Ottoman regime or during the Mandate, or those naturalized before 1939. The Jewish community would be authorized to operate its own schools, under regulations tending to forbid all "subversive teaching," provided that Arabic be a required course. The restrictions of the White Paper of 1939 concerning the acquisition of land by the Jews would continue to be enforced, and Jewish immigration would be forbidden, except when the Arab majority in Parliament decided otherwise.[28] Could this extravagant plan, practically a caricature, have been taken seriously even by its authors? It might be construed as just another maneuver in the long series of debates, proposals, and counterproposals if it were not for the fact that two years later the prime minister of Egypt, Nokrashi Pasha, expressed his views and those of the Arab League in almost identical terms to Count Folke Bernadotte, the United Nations mediator. Nokrashi proposed a unified Palestinian state, without a Jewish state, and with the presence of Jews in Palestine being regarded as "fundamentally abnormal."[29] That such ideas could have been entertained in May, 1948, when the State of Israel already existed, had been recognized as a nation by a number of great powers, and had routed invading Arab armies, gives some idea of the kind of irresponsibility and unreality that pervades Arab policies regarding Palestine.

In October, 1946, President Truman published a statement supporting a partition of Palestine, implying the creation of a Jewish state, and urging the immediate immigration of one hundred thousand displaced persons. Ibn-Saud protested violently. The President responded firmly that the United States government had supported the idea of a national home since 1918. Most Middle Eastern countries, he added, had gained their independence, but the national home had yet to come into being. Truman thus clarified his position as favoring the fundamental ideas of Zionism, but his administration hardly made haste to join him. The chief of the Middle East desk at the State Department, Loy Henderson, was among those who favored an appeasement policy toward the Arabs as a necessary part of combatting Russian expansion,[30] and he informed Moshe Sharett that the Jewish Agency should not hope for positive intervention by the American government.

By the end of 1946 the Palestinian problem seemed hopelessly bogged down. No political solution was in sight, and the situation on the spot was becoming more and more chaotic. Early in February, 1947, Bevin felt impelled to propose a new compromise, which in many respects was just like the ones that had already been rejected: Britain would stay put for five years but in the fourth year an elected constituent assembly would be invited to set up an independent state if the majority of its Jewish and Arab members could agree. If not, the United Nations would be consulted about the next step. Some one hundred thousand Jews could immigrate at the rate of four thousand a month during the first two years, after which time the British high commissioner would set immigration quotas. Relatively autonomous local governments would take charge of Jewish and Arab zones.

Such a confused compromise between partition and unified state, between a continuation of the Mandate and the creation of independent governments, of course, pleased nobody. Jews and Arabs both rejected it immediately.

On February 14, Bevin announced that the British government had decided to submit the problem to the United Nations without any specific recommendations for a solution.[31]

As has already been indicated, Britain was counting on the inability of the United Nations to find a solution. "There is no likelihood," said Harold Beeley to Abba Eban, "of mobilizing a two-thirds majority for an anti-British solution, owing to the split between the big powers, and any such motion is doomed to failure."[32] Bevin and his associates hoped that the General Assembly would demonstrate its impotence in such a way that Great Britain would by default find itself reconfirmed as the power charged with administering Palestine. America would be forced to take account of the new situation. The Zionists, thus isolated and without the support of world opinion, would have to listen to reason.

Creech-Jones, the colonial secretary, specified that England was not surrendering the Mandate to the United Nations, but rather was asking for a decision on how to administer it. Thus, although it was not a question of Great Britain leaving Palestine, the idea of a full withdrawal took shape as the days went by. In the House of Commons Winston Churchill strenuously criticized Bevin's policies. He demanded that the Palestinian question be brought before a special session of the United Nations, rather than be held over for the regular autumn meeting, and that England get out of that "squalid war" that was ruining its good name and draining its treasury and the pockets of its citizens.

The British economy was in desperate need of labor and investments. More than one hundred thousand men were nailed down in Palestine in increasingly bitter warfare, using up resources that Britain could scarcely spare. Bevin had originally abandoned the pro-Zionist preachings of his own party on the pretext that Britain had to send a division to Palestine to combat the Arab revolt. Now, paradoxically, each day he found himself throwing more men and money into the Palestinian abyss to combat the Jewish revolt.

The Irgun had again seized the offensive, or rather had never relinquished it, in spite of the Haganah's retreat and the dissolution of the Tenuat Hameri. The Lehi had also fought on. In January, 1947, the British high command decided to organize "Operation Polly," (which was dubbed ironically "Operation Folly") to evacuate the families of the military and civil servants, as well as all unnecessary personnel, and to consolidate British offices, police stations, and army headquarters inside special compounds that would be heavily guarded and fortified. More than two thousand Jews and eighty Arabs were driven out of their homes in Jerusalem to make room for the British enclave. The British soon found themselves behind barbed wire in Jerusalem, Tel Aviv, and Haifa, in self-imposed concentration camps that the public irreverently called Bevingrads. Naturally, these fortresses made perfect targets.

On March 1, the Irgun attacked the "Goldschmidt House" in Jerusalem, and in spite of its heavy guard, blew the building up. The British suffered eighty dead and wounded. The same Saturday (up until this time the Irgun had suspended operations on the Sabbath) they made more or less co-ordinated strikes on military bases at Haifa, Beit Lid, Pardess Hanna, and Rehovot, and on army communications lines at Tulkarm, Petach Tikvah, Kfar Sirkin, and others. The results in London were disastrous. The *Sunday Express* took up the cry of a growing segment of the English people: "Govern or get out."

In one last attempt to gain control of events, the British high command declared martial law at Tel Aviv, Ramat Gan, Petach Tikvah, and in the Jewish quarter of Jerusalem. This operation, called "Elephant" at Tel Aviv and "Hippopotamus" at Jerusalem, included the suspension of all public services, the closing of banks, and the interruption of commerce (food distribution was to be carried out by the army). People and vehicles were stopped and papers verified; civil laws were suspended, and military courts were set up. Many terrorists, or so-called terrorists, were arrested. Economic activity ceased, with a resulting loss of £200,000 to the Jewish community.[33]

Simultaneously in London, Churchill cried out, "We are getting ourselves hated and mocked by the world."[34] Some of the Zionist leaders in Palestine, frightened by the growing violence, wondered whether the answer was not to come to an agreement with the Mandatory. This tendency, which could be traced back to Weizmann, was expressed in the newspaper *Ha-Aretz*. In a series of editorials, the first published on March 11, the daily chided the Jewish Agency for clinging to the Biltmore Program and thus encouraging the "terrorists," whose prestige was on the increase. It called for the formation of a new executive committee under Weizmann, whose mission would be "to make one more attempt to find a basis for negotiation with the British government before the matter is taken to the United Nations."[35]

But Weizmann did not feel able to take action. The director of *Ha-Aretz*, Gershom Schocken, visited him at Rehovot. "Our only hope," said the aging leader, "is that Great Britain becomes strong again. Then she can support Zionism without taking account of the resistance." When Schocken expressed skepticism about a reinforcing of British power in the Middle East (he thought it was sure to weaken even more), Weizmann cried, "Then there's nothing to be done. We are lost anyway."[36]

On the eleventh day of martial law, an Irgun commando unit led by Yehoshua Goldschmid infiltrated and blew up the Schneller building in Jerusalem, which housed British headquarters and a strong garrison. Martial law was lifted on March 17. Not only had it failed but it had caused the majority of the *yishuv* to take a harder line. After much debate, the executive committee and the Vaad Leumi declared their unanimity. Ben Gurion had made a surprisingly tough speech against the British administration and against all British policy in the East. "Its intention," he declared, "was to liquidate the Jews as a people and to recognize only the existence of individual Jews who could serve as objects either of pogroms or of pity."[37]

The armed resistance redoubled in violence. The Irgun resolved that when its men were taken prisoner it would no longer tolerate their subjection to inhuman treatment or the death penalty. On one occasion when a young soldier of the Irgun was given eighteen lashes, a number of English officers were kidnapped and similarly punished. On July 29, three Irgun boys who were captured during the assault on the fortress at Acre (Avshalom Haviv, Meir Nakar, and Yaakov Weiss) were hanged inside the fortress. Two British sergeants subsequently vanished. They were found the next day hanged near Natanya. It was a desperate, atrocious struggle: the Irgun had sworn to break up the gallows. There were no more hangings in Palestine after that date.[38]

On April 2, 1947, the British delegation to the United Nations asked the secretary general to put the Palestine question on the agenda for the fall session of the General Assembly. They also asked for a special session of the General Assembly as soon as possible, so that it could appoint and direct a special committee.

The special session opened on April 28. It took twenty-five hours of emotional and acrimonious debate before the Assembly drew up its agenda. The Arab countries demanded that it include a statement on the "end of the British Mandate and the proclamation of Palestine's independence." This would have decided the question in favor of the Arabs before an investigation had taken place. Another procedural battle raged over Jewish representation in the United Nations. While many Arab member-countries were inundating the Assembly with propaganda, the Jews had no spokesman. At last it was decided that the Jewish Agency could be heard by the first commission but not the General Assembly. But the British delegation saw to it that members of the Arab Higher Committee were also admitted — and it was still under the chairmanship of the Axis agent and war criminal Haj Amin el Husseini![39]

The Assembly appointed a special committee, UNSCOP — the United Nations Special Committee on Palestine — and gave it vast powers of inquiry. It was made up of delegates from eleven nations: Austria, Canada, Guatemala, India, Iran, the Netherlands, Peru, Sweden, Czechoslovakia, Uruguay, and Yugoslavia. This committee was to report to Trygve Lie, the secretary general, no later than September 1. It held its first meeting at Lake Success on May 26, and its last at Geneva on August 31.

Soviet delegate Gromyko astonished the Assembly, especially the British and Arab delegations, in his speech at the last meeting of the special session. He first stated that the Mandate had failed, then said that if a unified, independent Palestine was impossible, he would look favorably upon the partition of Palestine between the Jews and the Arabs. Ernest Bevin's entire strategy, based on the perennial disagreement of Russia and the United States, was in danger of collapsing, for Truman had already come out for the partition plan presented by the Jewish Agency. The two great powers were effecting an unforeseen rapprochement.

UNSCOP, whose chairman was the Swedish judge Emil Sandström, arrived in Palestine to find that the country was on the verge of anarchy. Attacks, reprisals, and counterreprisals followed on each other with dazzling rapidity. The committee members immediately found themselves in an atmosphere of civil war, in which troublemakers acted with complete freedom. Thus, for example, a sixteen-year-old Jewish boy, Alexander Rubowitz of the Lehi, was kidnapped by a commando unit of anti-Semitic British policemen, known as the British League. He was never seen again. The League distributed tracts of a sadly well-known sort, full of allusions to the *Protocols of the Elders of*

Zion, and to the "dirty Jews' " wish to run the world — unlike the "chivalrous children of Arabia" — and promised to "finish Hitler's job." This racist and fascist organization was responsible for two bombings of Jewish civilians, first at the *Palestine Post,* next in the business district on Ben Yehuda Street in Jerusalem, where more than one hundred fifty people were killed or wounded.[40]

The United Nations committee was in Palestine when the passengers aboard *Exodus-1947* reached Haifa, only to be forcibly transferred to prison ships amid indescribable scenes of violence. The committee conducted its deliberations in the "shadow of the gallows" because at the same instant young Irgunists were being sentenced to death by hanging.

There is no doubt that most of the members of UNSCOP were deeply impressed by what they saw and heard. This torn and bleeding Palestine, rocked by explosions, stinking of cordite and gelignite, was the scene of a tragedy whose human dimension the calm offices at Lake Success could hardly grasp. The committee members learned above all else that there existed an armed Jewish resistance, unconquerable and determined never to give up.

The Haganah presented UNSCOP with a memoradum that explained, not without a few sideswipes at the Irgun, why the *yishuv* could never accept immigration restrictions, and stated that the Jews would not hesitate to use force to defend Zionist gains.[41]

But the committee's relations with the Irgun Zvai Leumi perhaps decided the issue. Associated Press correspondent Carter Davidson was acquainted with Shmuel Katz, the information chief of the Irgun, and arranged an interview (surrounded by all kinds of security measures) between Sandström of Sweden, Hoo of China, and the American Ralph Bunche, on one side, and Menachem Beigin, Chaim Landau, and Shmuel Katz on the other. They talked for more than three hours. Bunche took detailed notes.[42] They mentioned every important aspect of the Palestine problem. Sandström asked cold, precise questions and got unequivocal answers. For example, "Would the Irgun disband if the English got out and a Jewish state were founded?" Beigin's answer was *yes.*

It was agreed that this interview would be kept secret. But one of the three United Nations members took a newspaperman into his confidence, and the news was soon made public, to the great detriment of Carter Davidson, who had kept the secret. Sandström published a denial, which of course nobody believed. Two of the Latin-American members of UNSCOP, Jorge García-Granados of Guatemala and Dr. Fabregat of Uruguay, demanded a second interview so that they, too, could meet the chief of the Irgun. At this meeting the conversation was not just technical and precise but enlivened by a deep sympathy. García-Granados did not hide his admiration for the Irgun's struggle. He and Dr. Fabregat had both known secrecy and exile while fighting for their own countries.

Henceforth the committee leaned toward partition. Beigin upheld the traditional thesis of Jabotinsky: the Hebrew state in all of Palestine. But the Guatemalan, in spite of his sympathy for the Zionist cause, knew that the majority of the committee leaned toward partition as a kind of concession to the Arabs. And besides, he added, was not the Jewish Agency in favor of partition? Could non-Jewish friends of Zionism ask more than the Zionist leaders asked for themselves?

On one point, at any rate, the United Nations delegates were quick to reach agreement. The British Mandate must be ended at once; its failure was glaringly obvious. But what would replace it? A Judeo-Arab federated state, or two sovereign states? In case of partition, which state would get what land? Would an Arab state be economically viable without the support of the Jewish economy? The committee discussed these questions for a month at Geneva.

A three-member minority favored the idea of a binational state. The Yugoslav delegate thought that the federal system of his own country could be used in Palestine; the Indian, a Moslem, wanted the state that, with some federal trappings, would actually have been under Arab control with a Jewish minority; the Iranian sided with his Indian colleague. Eight out of eleven delegates favored partition, but which partition? How could they divide a small country, no larger than the state of Maryland, between two peoples who in many cases were inextricably mixed?

It was evident that the toughest problems were Galilee, Jaffa (an Arab city on the edge of the larger Jewish city of Tel Aviv), Beersheba, the Negev, and of course, Jerusalem. Bending over maps and population figures, the delegates carved, carved again, and restitched. Moshe Sharett, Horowitz, Abba Eban, Moshe Tov, and Weizmann multiplied their interviews, efforts, conversations. Sometimes the extent of the future Jewish state shrank, sometimes it grew, corridors opened and closed, and the ancient land of the Prophets was carved up in mosaics. Only a series of compromises enabled the committee to finish and sign its report at 12:05 A.M. on September 1.

To solve the unsolvable, they had cut Palestine in half lengthwise and superimposed on it a triple horizontal section, as well as creating international enclaves at Jerusalem and Bethlehem. This complicated geometry created a three-part Jewish state: eastern Galilee, including Safed and Tiberias, the coastal plain with Haifa and Tel Aviv, and part of the Negev extending to the Gulf of Aqaba. The Arab state also got three sections comprising western Galilee with Acre, Central Palestine with Lydda, Ramle, Tulkarm, Kalkilya, and even Beersheba, and finally, south of Tel Aviv, a long coastal band including part of the Negev. This weird configuration left the two states to communicate through two "kissing points," one in the Valley of Jezreel, the other south of Tel Aviv. The Jewish state was not militarily viable; the Arab state was not economically viable. No provision was made for overcoming the strategic malformation of the former; but an "economic union" was supposed to help the latter survive through the productiveness of the Zionist zone.

The Australian delegate having refused at the last minute to ratify either of the two reports, the majority text was signed by seven members of UNSCOP. Besides the territorial dispositions just described, it authorized one hundred fifty thousand Jewish immigrants to enter Palestine in the first two years. At the end of this period, each of the two states would become sovereign and fully independent.

Faced with this lame compromise, what would be the attitude of the concerned parties? The Arabs' reaction was swift and clear. They absolutely rejected the plan put forth by the committee. In an interview at London with Abba Eban and Horowitz,[43] the secretary general of the Arab League, Azzam Pasha, stated: "The Arab world is not in the mood to compromise. We shall fight. You will gain nothing by peaceful means and compromises. Or perhaps you will gain something, but it will have to be by force of arms. It is too late to speak of peaceful solutions." And when Eban urged him to "make an effort to reach an accord," he answered, "No accord is possible except on our terms!"

The Zionist organizations were more cautious. They hailed all that was positive in the UNSCOP recommendations, particularly the idea of creating a Jewish state with the least possible delay. But they also measured the extent of the sacrifice the Jews would have to make, condemned as they would be to occupy only a small fraction of their country, and they realized that there were many bridges to cross before the United Nations General Assembly — the only agent qualified to make a partition — would reach a decision.

The British government quickly let it be known that it would not support the recommendations of the committee, since both the Arabs and the Jews did not consent to them. "The United Kingdom government was not prepared to undertake the task of imposing a policy in Palestine by force of arms," declared Colonial Secretary Creech-Jones. . . . "In the absence of a settlement, it had to plan for an early withdrawal of British forces and of the British administration from Palestine."[44]

In the United States, while public opinion regardless of party boundaries overwhelmingly favored the partition plan (Eleanor Roosevelt, Governor Thomas Dewey, and Senator Taft publicly supported the idea), the government itself took no official position. To take sides against the British was naturally distasteful. And besides, the oil interests, under Arab pressure, were bringing all their influence to bear in Washington. Secretary of State Marshall went so far as to assure the Arab members of the United Nations that the United States would keep "an open mind," and would not yet endorse the committee's recommendations.

The regular Assembly session opened on September 16. An *ad hoc* committee was appointed to study the Palestine question in the light of the recommendations of UNSCOP. It was a long, slow process. But on October 11, Ambassador Herschel V. Johnson, head of the American delegation, announced that his country would support partition, and Semyon K. Tsarapkin made a similar statement two days later in the name of the Soviet Union. The two great powers, of course, had reservations on certain points, notably about the territorial limitations suggested by UNSCOP; but they agreed on the principle — much to the surprise of all, and to the fury of the Arabs. The British adopted an attitude of nonco-operation in the hope that a two-thirds majority would still be impossible in a General Assembly vote. Sir Alexander Cadogan announced that Great Britain "would undertake no action that might oblige it to apply the partition, create a militia, or organize the new regime. . . . The British will take no part in applying any decisions [resulting from partition]." He added that England would pull its army out of Palestine on August 1, 1948, but until that date would still govern the zones where its army was stationed.[45] It would retain "undivided control" right up to the time of evacuation. In other words, the Attlee-Bevin government rejected an American-originated plan for a progressive British withdrawal that would coincide with a transfer of power to a provisional United Nations commission. Chaos would be the only possible result, and the Arabs hoped to benefit from it. As the debate went on at Lake Success, Arab violence began to get underway in Palestine.

May 1, 1948, was set as the end of the Mandatory regime, after the Soviet Union had proposed January 1, and the United States July 1. July 1 was to be the date when the two new states would be proclaimed.

The borders continued to be bitterly debated. The Jewish Agency, wanting to take possession of an immigration port as soon as possible, offered to give up Beersheba and about eight hundred square miles of the Negev if the British would evacuate one port before February 1. But the British delegation would only "take note" of the proposal and promised nothing, and the Arab delegation did not soften its line.

Washington's instructions to the American delegation often seemed unusually restrictive. Even after the representatives of the Jewish Agency (Moshe Sharett, Abba Eban, Walter Eytan, Eliahu Epstein, Moshe Tov, David Horowitz, and others) had won Herschel Johnson to their cause, the State Department did not change its directives, which were that Jaffa should not be part of the Jewish state; that the Jews should not extend their territory in Galilee, and that their land in the Negev should be severely cut back. Hoping to appease the Arabs, Washington suggested giving them most of the Negev and especially the Gulf of Aqaba, which was Israel's sole access to the Red Sea. Alerted to the danger, Zionist organizations stepped up their appeals to President Truman and Robert A. Lovett, Acting Secretary of State. The American delegation supported a new compromise: Beersheba and a Negev zone bordering Egypt would belong to the Arabs, and the rest of the Negev and the Gulf of Aqaba would belong to the Jews.

On November 26, the *ad hoc* committee approved a plan for partition, but lacked one vote of having a two-thirds majority. There were many abstentions, among them France. The same day, a feverish debate opened in the General Assembly on the partition plan, and no one could predict if the necessary majority would be obtained. Some of the abstainers seemed to lean toward *yes*, others toward *no*. France was uncertain. A *coup d'état* in Thailand left that nation with no delegate (Thailand had voted against the resolution in committee). The scramble for voters was on. The Thanksgiving Day holiday prolonged the suspense and the French delegate, Alexandre Parodi, asked for one more day to try to reach a compromise. On November 29, the voting began in an atmosphere of unusual tension, under the chairmanship of Oswald Aranha of Brazil, with Trygve Lie at his side.

As is the custom at the United Nations, a roll-call vote was taken. The head of each delegation simply answered "yes," "no," or "abstention." The procedure was carried on in tense silence that was interrupted just once by an ovation when the French delegate said *"oui."* By thirty-three votes to thirteen, with ten abstentions, the General Assembly approved the partition of Palestine.[46]

The United Nations resolution seemed to make the future clear: the gradual retreat of the British civil and military forces, the establishment of an Arab and a Jewish council in each of the two corresponding zones, installation of the United Nations Commission, and finally an end to the Mandate and the proclamation of the new states.

The vote on November 29 aroused a wave of optimism and enthusiasm among Jews of the whole world, particularly in Palestine. Their feelings were quite justifiable on the occasion of this historic decision that restored the Hebrew state after two millenia. But they tended to underestimate two less positive aspects. First, Palestine was divided by borders that were totally absurd. Of course there was a Hebrew state there, but confined to an area less than one sixth of Palestine, painfully pieced together from little bits and pieces and resembling nothing so much as an Indian reservation. In the second place, it was unrealistic to think that the transition from Mandate to statehood would occur smoothly.

Gueoula Cohen describes in her memoirs the contrast between the optimistic crowds dancing in the streets and shouting "Long live the Jewish state!" and the confusion of the militants, whose struggle had resulted in a state "lacking Jerusalem, Bethlehem, and Hebron and cut off from the mountains of Gilead and Bashan." These men and women who had risked everything now felt the "terrible agony of seeing their dream stamped out, the agony of standing by while something indivisible was nevertheless being sliced up – the land of Israel."[47]

The Jewish Agency was officially optimistic. But Ben Gurion had been busy since 1946 collecting money and buying armaments for the Haganah in case of war.[48]

At the risk of being a kill-joy, the Irgun thought it ought to put the *yishuv* on guard. On October 1, in a broadcast on its "Voice of Fighting Zion," an Irgun spokesman presented an analysis of the situation that events were to bear out. He said that only an international force could maintain order in Palestine at the end of the Mandate, but that such an army would never exist because Russia or other Communist countries would insist upon being part of it and the United States would never permit that.

In its broadcast of November 16, the Irgun leaders denounced "three illusions": that partition would be effected peacefully; that in case of war the United Nations Commission at Jerusalem would re-establish peace; and that if the Commission failed, the Security Council would end the hostilities. Two days later, Irgun radio said, "The blood shed in the days to come to impose partition will not be less than what we should have to pay for liberating the homeland in its entirety."

After the Assembly had voted, the Irgun proclaimed: "The parti-tion of the homeland is illegal. We shall never recognize it. . . . Jerusalem was and will ever be our capital. . . . Partition will not ensure peace. . . . [It means] a war for our very existence and for our future."

In an appeal entitled "We Warn," the Irgun command stated at the beginning of December, 1947: "The people must know the truth, for only this knowledge can avert catastrophe. The blockade at sea will continue for five months. . . ." After outlining what was likely to happen — violence, collapse of the economy, chaos — the document spoke of the mortal peril Jewish populations were facing. As soon as the British left, Arab bands would cross the new frontiers. Thus, said the Irgun, we must be prepared, and "above all, take up the offensive." And they appealed for unity against the common danger.[49]

Even before the United Nations had voted, there had been spo-radic acts of violence by the Arab Higher Committee under the former grand mufti. The latter had set himself up at Damascus and had once more taken charge of the anti-Zionist movement. His terrorists were in all the cities and in many of the villages of Palestine.[50]

A wave of anti-Semitism swept the Arab world; the ulemas of the University El-Azhar in Cairo proclaimed a holy war; pogroms claimed many victims among the Jewish communites in Syria, Lebanon, and Aden.[51] And on November 29, the day of the vote in the United Nations, a surge of anti-Jewish violence broke out in Palestine. Its first victims were struck down while sitting peacefully in a wayside café, The Garden of Hawaii, between Tel Aviv and Jaffa. A number of Jews were killed at Haifa. Roads were ambushed, automobiles sprayed with machine-gun fire. Snipers clinging to the minarets of the mosques in Jaffa harassed passers-by in the crowded streets of Tel Aviv. It was like a return to the worst days of 1936–39.

From Damascus the former mufti called for a three-day general strike beginning December 2. In Jerusalem, Arab agitators set fire to

Jewish shops. Although British security forces were responsible for maintaining order, and according to London, the only ones responsible until evacuation, they took an attitude that was described as "apathetic" even by the English president of the city commission of Jerusalem. But at the same time the Mandatory administration did not intend to permit the Haganah to defend the Jewish population.[52]

Interestingly enough, the Palestinian Arabs themselves played only a minor role in the violence. The dregs of the big cities were of course always willing to take part in pogroms and pillage, but most Palestinian Arabs looked hopefully to the future. In the growing anarchy, armed bands more and more frequently infiltrated Palestine from the outside, led by Syrian officers, such as Adib Shishakli and Akram Haurani, and the infamous Fawzi El Kaukji, who had secretly returned to the Middle East after spending the war years in Germany. The least that can be said about the British is that they scarcely bothered to guard the land borders of Palestine, while continuing to enforce their rigid coastal blockade against illegal Jewish immigration. An uninterrupted stream of men and arms flowed across the northern and eastern borders of Palestine. The Arab Legion of Transjordan was trained, commanded, armed, and financed by the English. It sent Arab "irregulars" across the Jordan bridges in trucks.[53]

By December, guerrilla warfare raged everywhere. The Irgun was the first to mount a counteroffensive. Its tactic was to locate and attack terrorist bases in the mountains or villages. From December 11–13, Irgun units made strikes at Haifa, Jerusalem, Jaffa, Tireh, and Yazur. They went into Yehudia, a village near Lydda where several armed Arab bands were entrenched, and inflicted severe losses. The moderate Zionist newspaper Ha-Aretz, hardly famous for its excessive sympathy toward the Irgun, said that this counterattack caused "a fundamental change in the situation."

It was obvious that the transfer of power would not occur peacefully but amid disorder and bloodshed. The fight had to be co-ordinated as in the time of the Tenuat Hameri. The Jewish Agency and the Irgun began to talk in the middle of December. Menachem Beigin, Chaim Landau, and Shmuel Katz represented the Irgun; David Remez, Rabbi Fishman, Yitzak Gurenbaum, and Moshe Shapiro, the Agency. The representatives of official Zionism still thought that England would open a free port before February 1, 1948, through which both immigrants and armaments could be brought into the country. They only realized that this would not take place when a delegation from the

Jewish Agency led by Professor Brodetsky met Creech-Jones in London and heard him give a response so evasive as to be a refusal.

The Irgun and the Jewish Agency continued to negotiate fitfully until January, 1948. There was almost another "open season": the Haganah kidnapped several Irgunists. One of them, Yedidiah Segal, "Gabriel," was abducted and released by the Haganah but was found dead in mysterious circumstances in the Arab village of Tireh near Haifa. Such troubles did not make it any easier to unify the fighting forces. Indeed, during the dark winter months of 1947–48, the Irgun (aided frequently by the Lehi) and the Haganah each conducted its own fight against incoming guerrillas. The Irgun came out of hiding, in spite of the presence of English troops, recruited members by the thousands, organized regular fighting units, and trained them in barely camouflaged camps in the orange groves of Ramat Gan and Petach Tikvah.

The Haganah, involuntarily re-enacting the King David affair on a smaller scale, blew up the Hotel Semiramis at Jerusalem, which was Arab general headquarters. Many civilians, including a Spanish diplomat, lost their lives.

In January, thirty-five young men of the Haganah sent from Jerusalem to guard religious farm colonies near Hebron were massacred by the Arabs.[54] British forces at this time often resorted to the practice of disarming Jewish combatants and leaving them unprotected near Arab guerrilla zones. Four Haganah soldiers met death in this way near Meah Shearim in Jerusalem, eight others near Tel Aviv.

At Lake Success, the five-member commission (Bolivia, Denmark, Panama, the Philippines, Czechoslovakia) that was to oversee partition, met for the first time on January 9, 1948. Before it were reports of the deeply troubled situation in a land where the struggle grew bloodier every day. The British delegation let the commission know that its members would find themselves in serious danger if they went to Palestine: the Mandatory authorities could not guarantee their safety. London, moreover, was not disposed to hand over even part of its power to the commission. Despite a United Nations resolution to that effect, it also refused to open a free port in the Jewish zone, "since the arrival of large number of immigrants, and possibly of arms, would undoubtedly further inflame the internal conflict."[55] Next, England raised objections against the "provisional councils" that the plan had called for. Nothing, in short, could be accomplished until the end of the Mandate.

A strange situation it was. Great Britain would allow no authority but its own in Palestine until the moment when the Union Jack was lowered, but it was also withdrawing its police, its army, and its civil service, closing its eyes to the action of the terrorists from outside Palestine, and in general acting as if it deliberately meant to plunge the land into chaos. The impression that Britain was sabotaging the United Nations was heightened in February when the British government announced that it had decided to block Palestine's sterling reserves, and to separate the Palestinian pound from the English one. The United Nations Commission protested the more loudly as this decision was founded partly on the evaluation of expenses, as, for example, the £2,000,000 destined for the "maintenance" of the illegal immigrants detained on Cyprus, and because it seemed at the very least inequitable to hamstring the finances of the future Jewish state. But the commission protested in vain.

As time passed and the situation in Palestine worsened, largely because of the negative attitude of the British government, the American leaders who had favored partition now began to doubt their own wisdom, and those who had accepted it only grudgingly saw a chance to reverse it. The State and Defense departments came to feel that the United Nations resolution of November 29, 1947, was not applicable. Besides, said the head of the Middle East desk, Loy Henderson, should the resolution not be regarded as a simple "recommendation," resting on the condition that it would prove "just and workable?" Forrestal, who wanted to be convinced, adopted this idea. Since the resolution appeared to be inapplicable, the problem had to be "re-examined."[56] The rumor spread at Lake Success that the United States was going to modify its stand. "American leaders fear that the Arab chieftains will enforce reprisals against us and against the British," said The New York Times on March 3, 1948, "and will keep us from obtaining the oil in Saudi Arabia and Iraq, which would be essential in case of war with the Soviet Union. Moreover, the United States is most reluctant to send troops to Palestine, not only because of the predictable loss of life but because that would give the U.S.S.R. an excuse to send troops as well." The cold war was worsening along with events in Palestine. The Soviet Union was opposed to the Marshall Plan, and the coup in Prague in February, 1948, had raised the specter of world war.

President Truman must have brought the full weight of his office to bear in November in order to persuade Defense Secretary Forrestal and Secretary of State Marshall to rise above their departments' objections to partition. Three months later, these departments were exerting the same kind of pressure on Truman. Just as had happened when the administration led him to approve the Grady-Morrison Plan, the President grew irritable with the pro-Zionist elements trying to reach him now. He refused on numerous occasions to see Weizmann. When he finally granted an audience to the elderly Zionist leader on March 18, he insisted that the meeting be kept secret. Yet the interview was cordial. The President "indicated a firm resolve to press forward with partition. I doubt, however," Weizmann added in his memoirs, "whether he was himself aware of the extent to which his own policy and purpose had been balked by subordinates in the State Department."[57]

And, indeed, the next morning Senator Austin, delegate to the United Nations, announced a complete reversal of American policy. He referred to the growing anarchy in Palestine, the bloodshed, the obvious impossibility of putting the November 29 resolution into effect. "There must be an immediate stop to the loss of life in the Holy Land." Consequently he proposed the establishement of a temporary trusteeship of the United Nations that, without taking any position "as to the rights, redress, or position of the parties involved, nor the character of the final political outcome" would try to re-establish peace and seek agreement among the Jews, the Arabs, and the Mandatory power. Obliquely he was suggesting that the November resolution be annulled. As to the search for an agreement, who could think seriously of such a thing after so many attempts to reach one had failed during the past years?

This speech provoked a sharp reaction. Truman, it appears, did not expect it to be interpreted as an about-face. He was surprised by the hostile reaction of the press and American public opinion. Tens of thousands of letters and telegrams flooded the State Department and the White House. Naturally, American and Palestinian Jews were deeply displeased, while the Arab delegations at Lake Success were delighted. Gromyko took advantage of this obvious opportunity to stigmatize the policy of the United States that, he said, had decided "to bury the partition idea because of its oil interests and its strategic position." The Canadian and Australian governments were critical of the plan for a temporary trusteeship. Even in Washington a number of well-known senators vigorously opposed the change of policy.

Truman's vague and embarrassed statement on March 25—"The trusteeship plan was not proposed as a substitute for partition but...

to establish the orderly conditions necessary to a peaceful solution"—
far from calming the tempest, only aroused a fresh wave of criticism
and protests.

On March 23, the Jewish Agency and the Vaad Leumi announced
that they felt it was already too late to back down on partition, and that
the Jewish people of Palestine would oppose all attempts to stall.
Already, in the midst of the fighting, an embryonic Jewish administration was taking shape in the zone allocated to the future state. This
process could not be stopped.

The British attitude was most equivocal. While Sir Alexander
Cadogan supported the temporary trusteeship at Lake Success, British
troops and administrators in Palestine imperturbably continued their
withdrawal. The American delegation, now under heavy criticism,
tried to come up with a coherent plan, but it could have done so only
by firmly committing American troops to Palestine, which was exactly
what everyone, from Truman on down, was unwilling to do.

After long weeks of argument and confusion, Creech-Jones made
a speech at Lake Success that finally killed the American proposal.
He suggested that trusteeship be abandoned in favor of a "neutral
authority" that would be called in to maintain a minimal administration in Palestine. But it was already May 3, and the Mandate expired
eleven days later at midnight.

On May 8, Moshe Sharett flew to Washington for a meeting with
General Marshall and Undersecretary of State Robert A. Lovett. The
two Americans were completely convinced that the Arabs would crush
the Hebrew state the moment it was created. Marshall warned Sharett
solemnly against the "military advisers" of the Jewish Agency. Of
course the Jews had succeeded here and there, but now they ran the
risk of succumbing before a general invasion. The United States, he
added, could not come to their aid.

During the last days of the Mandate, the debate at Lake Success
was rendered more and more unrealistic by the news from Palestine.
The plan for a temporary trusteeship had been abandoned for lack of
support in the Assembly, and on May 13, the American delegation
proposed that a "mediator" be designated to "promote a peaceful
solution." But everything was being swept away in the flood of events.

Meanwhile, in the Holy Land guerrilla action was giving way to
war. On March 8, the talks between the Jewish Agency and the Irgun
resulted in an agreement similar to the one that gave rise to the Tenuat
Hameri. Irgun forces were brought under Haganah command, but

Haganah orders were to be transmitted to the troops through Irgun officers. Menachem Beigin's general staff would submit its operational plans for Haganah approval and would see that operations ordered by the Haganah were carried out. But it was understood that Irgun soldiers would resist British attempts to disarm them, while Haganah men would not. It was also understood that the Jewish Agency would not finance the Irgun, which was therefore authorized to do its own fund raising (though not by confiscation). The Irgun was actually able to conduct a public campaign for the "Iron Fund," (Keren Habarzel) that brought them considerable sums for the purchase and manufacture of arms. Thus the militants emerged almost completely from the life of hiding they had lived for so many years. Often hotly condemned by official institutions, they now appeared in daylight, dedicated and disciplined, and the welcome accorded them by the Jewish masses at Tel Aviv and elsewhere proved how much their resistance had made them dear to those for whom they had long acted as the spearhead.

The agreement between the military forces became all the more important as the Arab offensive grew. At the beginning of April the governments of the neighboring Arab states publicly gave their blessings to the guerrilla bands called the Army of Arab Liberation, which could field seven to eight thousand well-armed men, mostly from Syria and Iraq but with an Egyptian contingent at Gaza. In the north the Arabs threatened to cut Jewish territory in half by attacking Mishmar Ha'emek, southeast of Haifa. In the east they stepped up their attacks and ambushes in the Old City of Jerusalem and on the Jerusalem-Tel Aviv road. If they could cut off this road, which was a veritable umbilical cord between the old capital and the coast, the invaders could hope to starve Jerusalem and capture it easily.

It is worth noting that nobody in the first months of 1948 had the slightest doubt that the Arabs were the aggressors. They themselves boasted of it publicly. Trygve Lie, the secretary general of the United Nations, stated that "the Arabs had continually maintained that they would oppose partition by force. They seemed determined to put their words into practice by attacking the Jewish community of Palestine."[58] The vice-president of the Arab Higher Committee, Djamal El-Husseini, did not hesitate to tell the United Nations Security Council that "we have never hidden the fact that it was we who started the hostilities."[59] Radio broadcasts from Cairo, Damascus, and Amman exalted the "Liberation Army" for months, and swore that the Jews would be massacred.

The Palestinian Arabs themselves remained pretty much in the background. In January, the British high commissioner reported to the United Nations that large numbers of relatively well-off Arab families were leaving the country, usually in automobiles, carrying with them quantities of furniture, clothing, and other possessions.[60] More than twenty thousand Arabs left Haifa in March, and fifteen to twenty thousand left Jaffa. In the countryside, Arab villages that had been occupied by Syrian or Iraqi "liberators" and counterattacked by the Jews, were losing their original inhabitants. Neither the urban *bourgeoisie* nor the *fellahin* wished to take part in the hostilities. Besides, the Arab leaders did not want to be encumbered by a population they would have to care for after their presumably successful operations. "We shall drive the criminal Zionist bands into the sea," declared the rector of El-Azhar University in Cairo in an appeal that was constantly rebroadcast by Radio Cairo from March 18–24. "Not one Jew will be left in Palestine. In order that our victorious armies may accomplish their holy mission without the risk of harming our Arab brothers, the latter must leave the country for a while, so that our fighting forces will have complete freedom to carry out their mission of extermination."

The evacuation of Palestine was the work of the Arabs themselves. In January, Arab leaders meeting at Haifa ordered the first departures.[61] An uninterrupted flood of radio propaganda was loosed on the Palestinian Arabs, urging them to leave the country without delay, in order to return shortly in the footsteps of the army of liberation. "The Palestine refugees were certain that their absence would be brief and that they would come back after a few days. . . . Their leaders had promised them that the Arab armies would easily crush the Zionist fighters and that there was no reason to panic or to fear a long exile."[62] M. Ghory, the secretary of the Arab Higher Committee asserted that "the fact that the refugees are there is the direct consequence of the action of the Arab states against partition and against the Jewish state. The Arab states unanimously established this policy."[63]

At the start of April a large Arab force made up of Syrians, Iraqis, Transjordanians, and a few Europeans (Germans from the agricultural colonies and British deserters) attacked the Jewish quarter at Mount Carmel and almost captured it. British troops had been pulled out of the city and concentrated near the port; they announced that they would not intervene and made preparations to embark.[64] On April 21, a violent counterattack by the Haganah and the Irgun dislodged the

Arabs from their positions; during the night the general staff of the "liberation force" fled and the abandoned army broke up. A delegation of the Arab Higher Committee at Haifa "proudly refused to sign a truce and demanded that the population be evacuated into neighboring Arab countries. . . . Jewish representatives expressed their deep regret over this decision. The Mayor [Jewish] of Haifa, Mr. Shabetai Levi . . . made an impassioned appeal to the Arab delegation to reconsider this decision."[65]

One witness wrote that "the Jewish authorities . . . urged all Arabs to remain in Haifa and guaranteed them protection and security. . . . However, of the 62,000 Arabs who formerly lived in Haifa not more than 5,000 or 6,000 remained . . . [chiefly as a result of] the announcements made over the air by the Arab Higher Executive urging all Arabs in Haifa to quit. . . . It was clearly intimated that those Arabs who remained in Haifa and accepted Jewish protection would be regarded as renegades."[66]

The same process was repeated at Acre. Now that the Zionists had defeated a numerically superior Arab force at Mishmar Ha'emek, commanded by Fawzi El Kaukji, there was no longer any danger that Galilee might be cut off from the rest of Palestine. At Tiberias, a truce established on English initiative was broken by Arab irregulars. The Arab population, which made up slightly less than half of the total, was evacuated by the British and the city was left in Jewish hands.

Furious fighting went on between Zionist and Arab units around Jerusalem. On April 9, the Haganah captured the fortified village of Kastel, a few miles from the ancient city. Abdelkader El-Husseini, head of the Arab sector of Jerusalem, lost his life in battle. Nearer the city, the Arab village of Dir Yassin commanded a key position, and the Haganah commander of the Jerusalem sector, Shaltiel, thought of building an airstrip there. In a letter to Raanan, the Irgun head at Jerusalem, he emphasized the strategic value of the locality, "the capture and holding of which constitutes one phase of our general plan." In the same letter, he authorized the Irgun to undertake this operation "provided that you are able to hold the village."

On April 9, Irgun combatants, with some Lehi reinforcements, surrounded the village. A loudspeaker truck was sent up to the entrance. Foregoing the advantages of a surprise attack, the Irgun warned the population that a general attack was about to begin and advised them to take to the hills. A number of women, children, and old men followed this advice and left the village. The fight was especially murderous. Met by heavy firing from the houses, the Jews suffered severe losses, among them the chief of the detachment. They had to take the village house by house, using grenades. Inevitably, there were many dead and wounded among the civilians who had not fled.[67] At the end of the battle some Palmach units arrived to support the Irgun and the captured village was put under Haganah control.

Arab propaganda used the battle of Dir Yassin as the theme of a violent and persistant propaganda campaign against "Jewish atrocities." It had a twofold result: first, to provoke a veritable panic among the Palestine Arabs, who stepped up their exodus in the belief that the Jews meant to exterminate them; and second, to give the official Zionist leaders a new pretext to condemn "terrorists" of the Irgun. A legend was fabricated about Dir Yassin that made it look like a deliberate massacre of civilians, rather than an act of war, bloody, no doubt, as were many others, but conducted with more caution than many other actions, and preceded by a gesture of humanity that could have compromised its success.

A few days later, a Jewish hospital convoy that was on its way from Jerusalem to the Hadassah Hospital on Mount Scopus, and was clearly identified by its red star of David (the Jewish equivalent of the Red Cross), was ambushed by the Arabs, who murdered seventy-seven doctors, nurses, and students.

Zionist forces also suffered a severe setback in April in the Etzion bloc, an enclave of four religious agricultural villages (Kfar Etzion, Revadim, Ein Tsurim, Massout Yitzhak) in the middle of a rural Arab zone between Jerusalem and the Hebrew holy city of Hebron. Many women and children had been evacuated, leaving 214 men, 101 women, and 230 Haganah troops, including medical personnel. The bloc had been nearly isolated since late March, when a large supply convoy from Kiryat Anavim, west of Jerusalem, had managed to reach Kfar Etzion, only to be ambushed on the return trip by a band of Arabs and British deserters.[68] Since then, the road that linked the four villages to Jerusalem had been cut off, and supplies could be delivered only by plane, thanks to an airstrip that had been built north of Kfar Etzion. However, the Haganah had only a few small planes of no real transport or military value.

The Arab Legion under General Glubb took control of this region at the beginning of April and his high command decided to liquidate the bloc. The first attack on May 4 was turned back and the Arab League, with guerrilla reinforcements, launched the final assault on

May 12. They had enormous numerical superiority and heavy armaments, including artillery and armored cars. On May 13, Kfar Etzion was taken in an assault led by a British colonel serving under the flag of Transjordan.

Of the eighty-eight men in the village, only nine survived. The three other colonies fell the next day. The dead numbered one hundred twenty-seven, of whom twenty-one were women. The survivors were taken to the Oum Djamal camp in Transjordan, where they remained until February, 1949. The population of the surrounding Arab villages sacked the four colonies and murdered the Moslem family of Ibrahim Hazbun, who had stayed with their Jewish neighbors and with whom they lived on good terms.[69]

Even in Jerusalem the Jewish quarter of the Old City was blockaded, and the New City, with its one hundred thousand inhabitants, drew fire from Arab snipers on the heights. On April 25, the Palmach succeeded in capturing the Arab quarter of Shaikh Djarrah, which dominated the city, but the British drove them out.[70] After the capture of Kastel and Dir Yassin, convoys of food began to reach the besieged city, but after a few days, Arab guns were in control of the defile at Bab el-Oued, twenty miles away, and the Iraqis had captured the installations that supplied water to Jewish Jerusalem. Until May 14, while a truce committee composed of the American, French, and Belgian consul generals tried to arrange a cease-fire, attacks and counterattacks were launched all along the vital Tel Aviv-Jerusalem road, and in the Old City. The contingent of several hundred Jewish soldiers (about two thirds of them Haganah and the rest Irgun and Lehi) had only a ridiculously small supply of arms that they had bought from the friendly Arabs at Abu Gosh and from Armenian merchants. However, at the end of April they occupied the Arab quarter at Katamon, from which some of the Jewish suburbs had been ceaselessly harassed, and at the beginning of May, a few days before the Mandate ended, the situation in the ancient capital seemed to be turning in favor of the Jews. But the Arab Legion, having crushed the Etzion bloc, was preparing to intervene in Jerusalem.

One of the most astonishing feats of this period was the conquest of Jaffa by the Irgun. As previously stated, Jaffa and the suburb of Manshiah had for months served as a base for sniping against Tel Aviv. More than a thousand people were killed or wounded by bullets from the Hassan-Bek mosque and by mortar fire directed toward Allenby Street.

The operation had been long in the making. First, armaments had to be obtained. On April 4, an Irgun unit commanded by Guiddi attacked British camp #80 near Pardess Hanna and seized a large number of rifles, Bren guns, and munitions. Two weeks later, the Irgun intercepted a munitions train whose contents — transferred to Irgun trucks by the British escort of the train — were hidden at Zikhron Yaakov in the famous wine cellars of this grape-growing village.

On April 25, a long convoy of trucks at last left Ramat Gan for Jaffa. Six hundred men under Beigin's personal command opened the attack on the Arab city. The battle lasted until May 1, for the Jews encountered fierce resistance, first from the Arabs and then from the British themselves. Indeed the latter not only used armored cars and mortars against the Zionists but also threatened to stage an R.A.F. bombardment on Tel Aviv.[71] The Haganah had sent Israel Galili and Yigael Yadin (later to become chief of staff and a distinguished archaeologist) to see Beigin on the second day of the battle. The Haganah was undoubtedly sympathetic to this Irgun operation and hoped to see it succeed. But certain political elements and part of the press came out against what they called a futile and irresponsible assault. Turning this hesitation to good use, the British obtained a temporary cease-fire. But Arab resistance at Jaffa was broken. Most of the inhabitants left by sea, and while the crowds in Tel Aviv celebrated the end of the sniping, Irgun and Haganah units together occupied the city.

Another two weeks were to pass before the Mandate came to an end and the British authorities departed. Would the Jewish Agency take the decisive step of proclaiming a provisional government of the Hebrew state? At the heart of the executive committee, headed by Ben Gurion, there were still some doubts. Some were still wondering if it would be better to accept temporarily the vague United Nations "trusteeship" that Washington had recommended.

The position of the Irgun was clear. Beigin and his friends refused to outstrip the official institutions by forming an insurrectional government, because "that would be the road to civil war."[72] But they were resolved to establish a government if the executive committee of the Jewish Agency ducked its responsibilities. If, on the contrary, the committee formed a government, the Irgun would unreservedly support it. This is what the Irgun said publicly, clearly, and repeatedly.

David Ben Gurion was well aware that the moral pressure thus exerted by Menachem Beigin was invaluable. He sent one of his close collaborators, Eliezer Liebenstein, to see Beigin. Would the chief of the Irgun emphasize in his public statement that the Hebrew government, if established, could count on the support of his organization? Begin responded by making the following announcement: "If the leadership [of official Zionism] establishes a government, we shall support it with all our might." He added that if they did not establish one, a Jewish government would inevitably arise "from the depths of clandestinity to lead the people in the war for liberty and victory."

On May 12, the Zionist executive committee voted 6 to 4 (Ben Gurion voted *for*) to proclaim the state. Until the very last moment the pessimism of Marshall and Lovett, as reported by Moshe Sharett, served as an excuse for those who wanted to temporize. In responding to their hesitations, Ben Gurion made good use of the Irgun declarations. The executive could not hold back, it must plunge ahead, for otherwise there would be a revolution.

The provisional national administration that was to act as a government as soon as the English departed was made up of thirteen members chosen by the executive and the Vaad Leumi. Ben Gurion was elected president, with Moshe Sharett heading foreign relations, Eliezer Kaplan finances and the economy. But this was scarcely a joyful distribution of honors. War was raging throughout the land, Arab attacks on villages and kibbutzim were increasing, supply convoys had to try to make their way through ambushes with considerable loss of life. The situation in besieged Jerusalem remained extremely critical. No assistance could be expected from the United Nations. It looked almost as though the newly born Jewish state was to be annihilated — crushed by an immense pogrom. Forty million Arabs were coming from every direction to attack six hundred thousand Jews.

Precisely because this desperate battle offered no alternative to victory but total annihilation, the Jewish community was galvanized by its awareness of the tragic alternative and fought back with all its might. The nationwide motto became *"Ein B'reira,"* — "no other solution." Their backs were to the wall.

On May 14, at midnight, Sir Alan Cunningham, the last British high commissioner, folded up the Union Jack and left for Haifa. At the same moment, the Vaad Leumi and the executive committee met at the Municipal Museum in Tel Aviv, in a room whose only ornaments were the white and blue flag with the Star of David and a portrait of Theodor Herzl. After summing up the age-old tragedy of the Jewish people, the past fifty years of Zionist action, the holocaust in Europe, and the

United Nations' decision, David Ben Gurion read the declaration of independence. "We ... hereby declare the establishment of a Jewish State in Eretz-Israel, to be known as the State of Israel." The new state, the text continued, offered complete equality to the Arab inhabitants of Palestine and peace and friendship to neighboring lands. "With trust in Almighty God, we set our hand to this Declaration ... in the city of Tel Aviv, on this Sabbath Eve, the fifth day of Iyar, 5708, the fourteenth day of May, 1948." Eighteen centuries after the destruction of Jerusalem, and only a half-century after Herzl's prophecy, the Hebrew state was restored in Palestine.

FOOTNOTES FOR CHAPTER 8

1. Figures in this section of Chapter VIII are taken from an excellent study by a specialist in Mediterranean agriculture: George Reutt. *L'Expérience Sioniste.* Algiers, 1948.

2. S. Ilany. *Les problèmes de la paix israélo-arabe.* Paris, 1967.

3. Ilany. *op. cit.,* p. 4.

4. Reutt. *op. cit.,* p. 47.

5. For example, the Rehevot research station for agronomy, created in 1932 and financed by the *Keren Ha'Yessod,* was given a £23,000 subsidy by the Jewish Agency in 1941 compared with £5,000 from the Mandatory government. Reutt. *op. cit.,* pp. 175-77.

6. In 1934-35, medical expenses were paid in the following way: £166,000 by the British administration, £350,000 by the Jewish Agency and nothing by the Arab organizations. Ilany. *op. cit.,* p. 4.

7. Harold MacMillan. *The Blast of War.* London, 1967.

8. David Horowitz. *State in the Making.* pp. 13-20.

9. J. Schechtman. *The U.S. and the Jewish State Movement.* New York, 1966.

10. Horowitz. *op. cit.,* pp. 81-82. Testimony of Bartley Crum, member of the commission.

11. Horowitz. *op. cit.,* p. 143.

12. Elliot Roosevelt. *As He Saw It.* New York, 1945.

13. Drew Middleton in *The New York Times.* July 16, 1961.

14. *Public Opinion, 1935-1946.* Princeton, 1951, p. 386. Seven per cent were opposed to a Jewish Palestine and 13 per cent had no opinion or other opinions.

15. Weizmann. *Trial and Error,* pp. 531-32: Schechtman. *op. cit.,* p. 100 ff. One wonders whether Saint-John Philby did not deliberately confuse the issue in order to keep the Palestine question open and undermine American influence in Arabia.

16. William A. Eddy. *F.D.R. Meets Ibn-Saud.* New York, American Friends of the Middle East, 1954.

17. This statement provoked varying reactions in the United States. Senator Edwin Johnson (Democrat, Colorado) commented, "The choice of the desert king as an expert on the Jewish problem is nothing short of amazing. I imagine that Fala would be more of an expert."

18. Schechtman. *op. cit.,* p. 120.

19. Truman had an emotional spontaneity rare in political men. David Ben Gurion related that when he met Truman many years after the formation of the State of Israel, he said to him, "Your name will live in the history of the Jewish people." To his great surprise, the former President's eyes filled with tears. (Conversation of Ben Gurion with the author.)

20. Harry S. Truman. *Memoirs*. Vol. II. Garden City, N.Y., 1955, p. 140.

21. Statement made July 2, 1946 by Truman to the American members of the Zionist executive committee. Bulletin of the *Jewish Telegraphic Agency*, July 3, 1946.

22. Crossman. *op. cit.*, p. 196.

23. *Ibid.*

24. Map in Kirk. *Survey*, pp. 22–24.

25. "The President was so angry with my protests against the Grady-Morrison Plan that he refused to let me read a one-page memorandum of my views." James McDonald. *My Mission in Israel*. London, 1951, p. 11.

26. Truman. *Memoirs*. Vol. II., p. 152.

27. Schechtman. *op. cit.*, p. 171.

28. The analysis of this Arab plan is in Kirk. *Survey*, p. 228.

29. Folke Bernadotte. *To Jerusalem*. London, 1951, pp. 23-27.

30. This is what he told Bartley C. Crum, who was a member of the Anglo-American Committee. Crum. *Behind the Silken Curtain*. New York, 1947, p. 7.

31. Kirk. *Survey*, p. 237.

32. Horowitz. *op. cit.*, p. 190.

33. Kirk. *Survey*, p. 238.

34. During a debate on March 3 in the House of Commons, Churchill, "shouting in irritation," according to Reuters, demanded that the government hasten to lay the problem before the United Nations.

35. Kirk. *op. cit.*, p. 239.

36. Article by Schocken in *Ha-Aretz*, December 16, 1962.

37. Kirk. *op. cit.*, p. 239.

38. A total of eight Irgunists were hanged: Shlomo Ben Yossef, aged twenty-five, in 1938; Dov Grüner, aged thirty-five, in 1947; Yehid Drezner, aged twenty-five, in 1947; Eliezer Kashani, aged twenty-four, in 1947; Mordehai Alkahi, aged twenty-two, in 1947; Avshalom Haviv, aged twenty-one, in 1947; Meir Nakar, aged twenty-one, in 1947; and Yaakov Weiss, aged twenty-three, in 1947. Two of them were born in Poland, one in Hungary, one in Czechoslovakia, four in Palestine.

39. The three delegates of the Arab Higher Committee were Ghuri, Kamal, and Khalidi. They had all been active German agents during the war. One of them, Khalidi, was refused a visa to the United States because of his activities in Nazi Germany during the war.

40. Kirk. *Survey*, pp. 242–43.

41. "Memorandum submitted to the U.N. Committee on Palestine by the Jewish Resistance movement, somewhere in Palestine, July 11, 1947." Nine mimeographed pages. From the author's personal files.

42. Published in Beigin. *Rebelión*, p. 442 ff.

43. Horowitz. *op. cit.*, pp. 232–35.

44. Kirk. *op. cit.*, p. 247.

45. Horowitz. *op. cit.*, p. 293.

46. FOR: Australia, Belgium, Bolivia, Brazil, Byelorussia, Canada, Costa Rica, Czechoslovakia, Denmark, the Dominican Republic, Ecuador, France, Guatemala, Haiti, Iceland, Liberia, Luxembourg, the Netherlands, New Zealand, Nicaragua, Norway, Panama, Paraguay, Peru, the Philippines, Poland, Sweden, the Ukraine, the Union of Soviet Socialist Republics, the United States, Uruguay, Venezuela, and South Africa.

AGAINST: Afghanistan, Cuba, Egypt, Greece, India, Iran, Iraq, Lebanon, Pakistan, Saudi Arabia, Syria, Turkey, and Yemen.

ABSTENTIONS: Argentina, Chile, China, Colombia, El Salvador, Ethiopia, Honduras, Mexico, the United Kingdom, Yugoslavia. Thailand did not vote.

The required two-thirds majority was obtained in spite of the abstentions.

47. G. Cohen. *op. cit.*, pp. 337–38.

48. Statement of Ben Gurion to the author.

49. Beigin. *Rebelión*, pp. 489–95.

50. Kirk. *Survey*, p. 253.

51. Three hundred Jewish houses and eleven synagogues were burned at Aleppo; sixty-six Jews killed at Aden. American diplomatic missions were attacked at Damascus, Beirut, and Baghdad. At Damascus demonstrators also attacked the Soviet mission.

52. Kirk. *Survey*, p. 252.

53. These facts came from the official (and anti-Zionist) *Survey* by George Kirk, p. 253, notes 4 and 6. The head of the Arab Legion was a well-known British officer, Glubb "Pasha." The Arab Legion was wholly financed by the Exchequer because of an Anglo-Transjordan Treaty of 1946 that was renewed in 1948.

54. Knohl. "Siege in the Hills of Hebron," *The battle in the Etzion Bloc.* New York, 1958, p. 99 ff.

55. Kirk. *op. cit.*, p. 255.

56. Schechtman. *op. cit.*, p. 258.

57. Weizmann. *Trial and Error*, p. 472.

58. Trygve Lie. *In the Cause of Peace.* New York, Macmillan, 1954, p. 163.

59. Statement of Djamal El-Husseini in the Official Minutes of the Security Council, Third Year, No. 62, 287th Meeting, April 23, 1948, p. 14.

60. U.N. Palestine Commission. First Special Report to the Security Council. Document A/AC. 21/9 on February 16, 1948.

61. Mohammed Nimr Al-Khatab. *Results of the Catastrophe* (in Arabic), Damascus, 1951. Quoted by Philip Hochstein. *The Arab Refugees*, Washington, 1963, p. 4.

62. Mgr. Hakim, Greek Orthodox Archbishop of Galilee, August 16, 1948. Statement to the Lebanese daily *Sada Al-Djanub*.

63. Interview published in *Le Télégraphe*, Beirut, September 6, 1948.

64. Kirk. *op. cit.*, p. 262.

65. Memorandum of the Arab Committee of Haifa to the governments of the Arab League. April 27, 1948.

66. *The Economist.* London, October 2, 1948.

67. Beigin. *Rebelión*, pp. 260–62.

68. The accounts of this period often mention these "deserters." One wonders whether they were indeed deserters or rather officers and noncoms "lent" to the Arab units with the avowed or tacit approval of the British command.

69. Dov Knohl. *op. cit.* (A collection of documents, memoirs, and accounts of this period, with an introduction by Abba Eban and epilogues by Yigael Yadin and Yigael Allon.)

70. Kirk. *Survey*, p. 264.

71. Kirk. *Survey*, p. 263. See also Beigin's account of the capture of Jaffa, *Rebelión*, p. 512 ff.

72. Beigin. *op. cit.*, p. 510.

9
THE
WAR
FOR
INDEPENDENCE

The rebirth of the Hebrew state had scarcely been proclaimed before the first Egyptian bombs fell on Tel Aviv and its suburbs. Air raids multiplied during the days that followed; the city and the airbase near Sde Dov were attacked daily. On May 18, forty-two civilians were killed in the bombardment of the central bus station at Tel Aviv. Simultaneously, four armies invaded Israeli territory, adding their regulars, their organization, and their armaments to the guerrilla units that already existed. In the north, the Syrian army and a weak Lebanese contingent tried to get a foothold in Galilee, alongside the guerrillas of Fawzi El Kaukji; the Iraqis took the offensive all along the Jordan to the outskirts of Jerusalem; the Arab Legion of Transjordan, commanded by Glubb Pasha and some forty English officers had just wiped out the four villages of the Etzion bloc and were moving toward Jerusalem. In the south, the Egyptians were trying to push toward Tel Aviv along the coast, reinforced by a few Saudi Arabian elements and units of the Moslem Brotherhood.

These armies not only were numerically superior to the forces the new state could throw against them, they also were much better equipped: modern arms, medium and heavy artillery, tanks, planes, all of British origin (or French origin occasionally, in the case of Syria and Lebanon), in great abundance and in excellent condition. The secretary general of the Arab League, Azzam Pasha, had announced that there would be "a momentous massacre which will be spoken of like the Mongolian massacre and the Crusades." The aggressors were convinced that the war would turn into a military parade and that the Arab armies converging on Tel Aviv would meet there within a week. A gigantic pogrom, with the usual raping and looting, would then put an end to the existence of Israel before it had had a chance to take root. Arab Palestine would be founded upon the bodies of the Jews and on the ruins of their work.

But what would this Arab Palestine be like? On this point the beautiful unanimity of the armies contrasted with the plans and motives of their governments. Behind the united façade of the Arab League, each capital was nurturing contradictory projects. The Syrians wanted to annex the Lake Huleh zone in Galilee on the pretext that the boundaries France and England had established after the First World War had deprived Syria of land that was rightfully its. The Iraqis and the Egyptians supported the former mufti Haj Amin el Husseini, the perennial candidate for the presidency of an Arab state of Palestine. King Abdullah of Transjordan, whose army was the best organized and the most powerful, coveted Jerusalem above all else and the whole of Palestine if possible. He dreamed of finding himself at the head of a kingdom that would embrace all the territory of the British Mandate as it had been set up by the League of Nations, from the Bedouin desert to the coastal plain, including Tel Aviv and Haifa.

The plans of the clever sovereign in Amman were of long standing. This Hashemite had not forgotten that his father, Sherif Hussein, had derived great prestige from his domination of the two Arab holy cities Mecca and Medina before ibn-Saud had thrown him out. Jerusalem, the third holy city of Islam, would have been a brilliant compensation for the loss. On a more practical level, the king knew that if he could unite Transjordan with Arab Palestine west of the Jordan, and especially the Jewish plain and the coastland transformed by half a century of labor by the *yishuv*, he would no longer be king of a little underdeveloped Bedouin state but one of the most powerful Eastern monarchs.

Politically very sharp, Abdullah had long refrained from a frontal attack on Zionism. He would have much preferred to calm the fears of the Jews with honeyed words and promises in order to persuade them to recognize his suzerainty. In November, 1947, he secretly met Golda Myerson (later Golda Meir), then secretary general of the Histadrut, at the home of Pinhas Rutenberg, the founder and director of the great Palestine Electric Works on the Jordan. The interview took place near the Naharayim generating station. Abdullah told Golda Meir that he would not be a party to any aggression against the Jews and that if Palestine was partitioned, he would annex the Arab section of the country. Besides, he added, did not he and the Jews have a common enemy in the former mufti?[1]

During the winter and spring of 1948, Abdullah kept in touch with the Jewish Agency, which was growing uneasy over rumors that the king was preparing to make common cause with the other Arab states. In his messages, Abdullah used all the finesse of a noble Moslem to reassure them. He told Golda Meir that he had only one word of honor to give, and it had a triple bond—he gave it as a Bedouin, as a king, and as a man, since he had made his promise to a woman.

Nevertheless, on May 10, 1948, with Ben Gurion's approval, Golda Meir embarked on a dangerous and romantic mission to uncover the real intentions of the Hashemite king. Escorted by Zera Dannin, an Eastern Jew who spoke perfect Arabic, and disguised as a Moslem woman, she crossed the Jordan at Naharayim and traveled to Amman over roads that the Arab Legion patrolled night and day. At Amman, Abdullah came to talk with her in a private home, and there he unmasked himself. Things had changed, he said. He was no longer free to act on his own, as much because of the British attitude as because of his alliance with the other Arab states. He could no longer refuse to intervene on the Palestine front. And his ambitions had grown. Arab Palestine would no longer be enough—he wanted to extend his authority over the whole country. He offered the Jews citizenship in his kingdom and equal representation in his parliament. "Not ten Jews in Palestine would accept such a thing," Golda Meir answered.[2]

Always the great nobleman, Abdullah deplored the fact that they were on the verge of war, and took his leave courteously. The die was cast. But the fact remains that the war aims of the Arab "allies" were not all the same. Mistrust and often hatred divided these governments.

In the expectation of a "brisk and joyous" war, the Arab forces invaded the tiny territory given to Israel by the United Nations from all sides. To oppose them, the Hebrew state had small means and they were scattered and weakly organized. Barely having emerged from secrecy, the Haganah depended chiefly on the two thousand men and women of the Palmach, the well-trained elite units that were divided into four battalions. Three of them were mobilized and ready in the Jezreel Valley, Galilee, and on the Jordan. Backing them up were fighting units called the *Hish*, composed of young men under twenty-five who by March, 1948, numbered twenty thousand; finally there were the garrison forces, called the *Him*, of about thirty thousand men from the kibbutzim, all over twenty-five, who were entrusted with defensive missions.[3]

The Irgun had also just come out in the open from an even more profoundly secret existence than the Haganah. Its membership was over ten thousand in 1947,[4] plus several thousand sympathizing auxiliaries. Trained for daring actions like the assault on the fortress at Acre, the men of the Irgun had yet to adapt themselves to fight a regular army. The Lehi, for its part, contributed several hundred men.

The effective fighting force drawn from the Jewish population of Palestine was joined by a relatively small but technically important group of foreign volunteers, some of them Jewish, some not, known as the *Mahal*. They numbered about five thousand, of which nearly two thousand were Americans and South Africans.[5] They were qualified personnel, such as pilots, officers, and veterans of the Second World War, who wanted to serve the cause of Zionism. Using them created some problems, for most of them spoke neither Hebrew nor Yiddish. Their previous combat experience nevertheless allowed them to play an important role. The most illustrious of them was the American Colonel David Marcus (with the battle name of Mickey Stone), who was a West Point graduate and had served on Eisenhower's general staff in Europe. He came to Palestine to volunteer at the beginning of the war and took command of Israeli defenses in the Jerusalem region. He was killed at dawn on June 11, 1948, at Abu Gosh.

On the Arab side, the "irregulars" consisted of the so-called Liberation Army of Fawzi El Kaukji with about three thousand men, plus thirty to forty thousand men from the nationalist organizations Al-Futuwa and An-Najjada, supported by the former mufti,[6] and two battalions recruited in Egypt by the fanatical Moslem Brotherhood. These great masses were undisciplined and ill-equipped, and they leaned on the well-equipped European-style armies that immediately fielded four Arab Legion battalions, a Syrian brigade comprising three infantry and one armored battalion, one tank company, and one artillery regiment, besides the Egyptian Expeditionary Corps with four infantry and two armored battalions and two artillery regiments.[7]

The Arab armies were equipped with British tanks and cannons. The Syrian air force had a squadron of light Harvard bombers piloted by Germans, Italians, and a few Syrians. The Iraqi air force, based in Transjordan, was equipped with English fighter planes. Egypt had about forty Spitfires, two squadrons of bombers, and various other aircraft. Before and during the war, R.A.F. bases in Egypt supplied munitions and replacement parts. Israel at this time had only three squadrons of small reconnaissance planes, some Piper Cubs generally known as "Primus" (their engines sounded like the rumbling of the gasoline stove of that name), not one fighter, two transport planes (against the Arabs' thirty), and three light bombers, improvised for the situation, against more than thirty Arab bombers.

The Israeli "fleet" comprised an ancient British ice-breaker hastily repaired at Haifa that was equipped with old field guns and christened the *Eilat*, a few launches and escort vessels, and a small immigration ship, the *Hannah Senesch*. The Egyptian navy had forty-five ships, including armed troop transports, mine sweepers, landing craft, and fast coast guard cutters. All these ships carried naval cannons and their crews had been trained by the British.

The arming of Israeli troops had long been one of the most important jobs of the Haganah and the Irgun. They were able to do it only illegally, and even after the United Nations voted for partition, the embargo against arms shipments to the Middle East decreed by the United States worked exclusively against the Israelis. The frontiers of the Arab countries were not under surveillance, and the British gave them all the arms they wanted.

The Jewish Agency had organized a secret service—the *Rehesh*—for the purchase of arms. It worked in Palestine itself and in Europe. In Palestine, the Arabs had no compunctions about selling arms to the Jews, and several officers of the Arab Legion were "perfectly willing to do business with the Jews, who paid well and asked no questions."[8] As the end of the Mandate drew near and British troops began leaving the country, some officers and noncoms were not above handing over arms to the Rehesh, sometimes in truckloads, some out of sympathy for the Zionist cause, others for money. At the end of April, 1948, the Rehesh even managed to seize three Cromwell tanks at Haifa with the help of British soldiers.[9]

Italy was the first European country in which the Haganah procured arms. A boatload of cannons and munitions bought there by Yehuda Arazi reached Tel Aviv on May 15. In France, arms depots left by the *maquis* were sent to help the young Israeli army. But it was in Czechoslovakia, beginning in March, 1948, that the Israelis found their most substantial source of matériel. (Czechoslovakia also sold arms to the Arabs.)[10] On March 31 the first shipment of mortars, rifles, and munitions was loaded aboard a Dakota rented from a private American company; it landed near Beer Tuvia in Palestine just as its fuel was giving out. This was the start of what was called Operation Balak,[11] a sort of aerial bridge to which was added land and sea shipments via Hungary, Yugoslavia, and the Mediterranean. A large cargo of Czech arms destined for the Syrian army fell into Israeli hands when the ship that carried it, the *Lino*, was sunk at Bari by Zionist commandos. Afterward what could be salvaged was sent to Palestine on another ship.

In addition, a secret organization for the manufacture of arms—*Ta'as*—had been created during the time of the Mandate. It supplied light arms, grenades, mines, and a sort of mortar called the Davidka that, they say, made a noise that did more damage among Arab ranks than its rudimentary shell. At Safed especially, these improvised arms caused a veritable panic. Lacking armored cars and tanks, the Israelis reinforced their trucks with sheets of thick iron. These "sandwiches," as they were jokingly called, constituted the primary mechanized force of Israel.

Despite all these ingenious efforts, when hostilities broke out, the Haganah's equipment was scattered, scanty, variable in quality, and limited mostly to light weapons. The defenders of Galilee had only a few 20-mm. cannons to mount against the powerful Syrian artillery. A little later, on the southern front, they got hold of some old French "75's" that were nicknamed Napoleonchiks, and whose reputation far outstripped their effectiveness.

The Irgun had also set up a secret service for making explosives, mines, grenades, and all sorts of weapons improvised under the inventive direction of the chief of operations, Guiddi. The Irgun bought arms and munitions out of its meager resources, but its favorite method of acquisition was "recuperation" from stockpiles in depots, military encampments, and British police stations. Prior to the conquest of Jaffa, Irgunists seized large quantities of rifles, automatic rifles, machine guns, antitank guns, mortars, and shells in an attack on a camp and military train.[12] The "artillery" of the Irgun at the battle of Jaffa consisted in its entirety of two three-inch British mortars.

The Irgun naturally had to try to buy arms in Europe. The establishment of its general headquarters in Europe was delayed, as we have seen, by the wanderings and adventures of Meridor, Ben Eliezer, and Lankin after their escape from East Africa. But in March, 1948, an Irgun delegate at Paris, called Ariel, opened unofficial but far-reaching conversations with the foreign minister. Ariel proposed that they draw upon the displaced persons camps in Germany to organize a brigade in France that would go to Palestine in May. He also asked for authorization for the Irgun to purchase enough French arms to equip two brigades. Ariel's ideas were well received at the Quai d'Orsay and the interior department, and in the higher reaches of Georges Bidault's government.

In May, Ben Eliezer arrived, having been given passage along with Shamir on the aircraft carrier *Dixmude* at Jibuti. Meridor, Lankin, Shmuel Katz, and Eli Tavin soon appeared. They took up residence on Avenue de Messine. On May 19, Georges Bidault informed Ariel that the French government had decided to furnish the arms itself. The necessary transport ship—a war surplus landing craft—was bought in the United States by the Hebrew Committee for National Liberation, a Revisionist organization. They called her the *Altalena*, which had been one of the pen names of Vladimir Jabotinsky. An American Jew, Monroe Fein, was her captain.[13]

When the ship anchored at Port-de-Bouc, the Israeli-Arab war was already well under way in Palestine. Despite feverish preparations, the *Altalena* was not ready to sail until June 11; she carried 900 men, 5,000 rifles, 300 machine guns, 150 Spandaus, 4,000,000 rounds of ammunition, and several thousand grenades.[14] The equipment was brought to the port by the army under police protection.[15] Lankin took command of the shipboard army. London radio announced the departure of the ship with its cargo of armaments and "terrorists," and it was over the BBC that Beigin heard the news. It was extremely important news, for these desperately needed reinforcements had left Europe just as a truce had been proclaimed under the aegis of the United Nations.

We shall return later to the *Altalena* and its tragic fate. The first phase of the Palestine war lasted from May 15 to June 11. It can be summed up in two words: invasion repulsed. But it must also be added, not without reverses, not without suffering, not without heavy losses.

In the north on May 15, the Syrian army attacked Ein Gev, an isolated kibbutz on the eastern shore of the Sea of Galilee; then it attacked the agricultural colonies of Degania. During the next few days, the Syrian offensive spread to the Jordan valley. The ill-armed pioneers and a few Palmach fighters defended every foot of ground, attacking Syrian tanks with Molotov cocktails. One of these tanks broke down in the middle of the kibbutz at Degania Aleph, where it can be seen to this day. Taking the offensive in their turn, the Israelis made a daring and successful raid on a Syrian base east of the Jordan and then drove back a Lebanese contingent and captured the village of Malkya in Lebanon itself. It is interesting to note that the Arabs of the Heibi tribe, in the Jordan valley, rallied to the Jewish forces and formed a Bedouin unit commanded by a Palmach officer. Likewise, after some hesitation, the Druses of Galilee joined the Israelis.

But although the Israelis pushed back the Syrians and routed the Lebanese and the irregulars of El Kaukji, they suffered grave reverses a little farther south in the Jordan valley. The Daughters of Jacob bridge—a position of paramount strategic importance—was guarded by the agricultural colony of Mishmar Ha-Yarden ("the sentinel of Jordan"), an outpost of Zionist colonization linked by a single road to Rosh Pinah and the interior of Galilee. The Syrian plan of attack included crossing the bridge in force and taking Mishmar Ha-Yarden in order to invade Galilee and, by pressing on to the coast, cut the region off from the rest of Palestine.

The village was defended only by a group of former Beitari, the Wedgwood group, and a small Irgun detachment. At the end of April, an Irgun unit on its way to reinforce them was intercepted by the Haganah and disarmed.[16] After that, the defenders' increasingly urgent demands for help from the Zionist high command were ignored. After many days of fierce aerial and artillery bombardment, the Syrians attacked on June 5 and were driven back. The next day, however, they cut off the road to Rosh Pinah and isolated the colony. On June 7, a Haganah detachment finally reached the besieged village, only to be called back two days later, leaving Mishmar Ha-Yarden in the hands of thirty surviving Irgun men. The Syrians took the village on June 10, thus opening the way to the interior of Galilee. But they could not turn this to advantage because the truce went into effect on June 11, and they contented themselves with fortifying the village and digging into their bridgehead on the west bank of the Jordan.

The sector situated farther south along the Jordan, and extending to the northern approaches of Jerusalem, was also the scene of alternating successes and failures. The Arabs destroyed the electrical plant at Naharayim, seized the pumping station at Rosh Haayin (which furnished water to Jerusalem), and successfully drove back numerous Haganah assaults on Latrun, but they were beaten at the old crusader citadel at Belvoir (Ramat Kochba), and lost Megiddo on the age-old road from the Mediterranean to Syria, where the armies of the Pharaohs, the Assyrians, the Turks, and the English had fought during all the wars of the Middle East. The "triangle zone" (Jenin, Tulkarm, Nablus) was the scene of furious fighting that left the Iraqis and the Arab Legion largely in control.

On May 14, Glubb Pasha's army, having wiped out the Jewish villages between Hebron and Jerusalem, crossed the Jordan by the Allenby Bridge, intending to surround Jerusalem. The farm colonies of Atarot and Neve Yaakov, to the north of the city, were evacuated by the Israelis on May 14–15; on May 17, Transjordanian troops relieved Fawzi El Kaukji's undisciplined bands at Latrun and Dir Ayub. Lacking food and water, the one hundred thousand inhabitants of the Jewish city were subjected to ceaseless bombardment and harassment by snipers starting on May 15. More than twelve hundred were killed and wounded in two weeks. Their situation, and that of almost two thousand Jews in the Old City, became more critical with each passing day, particularly since their defenders (two hundred Haganah men and one hundred or so Irgunists) had no hope of getting reinforcements or arms. It looked as though the armored cars of the Arab Legion would take Jerusalem without difficulty. However, when they attacked the Damascus Gate on May 23, they met organized resistance at the Monastery of Notre Dame. From May 21–25, Egyptian forces (the Moslem Brotherhood) supported by tanks attacked the Ramat Rahel position. Thanks to the heroism of Irgun fighters it was fiercely defended. But on May 28, the handful of men who still held the Old City had to give up. Prisoners of the Arab Legion, they were sent to a camp in Transjordan, where they remained for nine months.

By June 1, through superhuman efforts, the Israelis succeeded in converting some foot paths into a replacement road, their own Burma road, south of the highway that had been cut off by the Arab Legion. The blockade of Jerusalem was thus partially lifted. They tried to recapture Latrun from Glubb Pasha, but a new attack failed on June 10. When the truce went into effect the next day, Jerusalem was cut in half by the cease-fire line and was still fairly isolated from the coastal zone, for communications lines were in danger.

On the southern front, the Egyptians began rolling toward Tel Aviv even before the Mandate had ended. On May 10, a battalion of the Moslem Brotherhood attacked the village of Kfar Darom and were driven back with severe losses. On May 13, the departing British turned over to the Arab irregulars the small fort at Irak-Sudan, an important position that gave them a lasting advantage throughout the campaign. On May 14 the Egyptian army, with great quantities of supplies, began to move over land and sea; after capturing several positions, they entered Ashdod, the ancient city of the Phillistines, scarcely fifty miles from Tel Aviv. On June 2 the Haganah and the Irgun counterattacked. They could not liberate the city but they did pin down an Egyptian column of five hundred vehicles that had progressed that far. During this time, the chief of the Moslem Brotherhood, Abdelaziz, led a battalion to Hebron and Bethlehem. There he was received coldly by the Transjordanians and the Arab Legion who had little desire to see the former mufti's Egyptian partisans gain a foothold in territory that Abdullah coveted.

Meanwhile, the few planes of the *Sherut Aviri* (the Israeli Air Force) attacked the Arabs on all fronts, day and night, with such primitive means as it had—machine-gun fire, bombs thrown out of the airplane doors. Four Messerschmitts purchased in Europe went into action on May 29. On June 3, an Egyptian aerial attack on Tel Aviv ended in disaster for the Egyptians. Taking the offensive, the Sherut Aviri pilots threw bombs on Amman and Damascus. They did not inflict serious damage, but the psychological effect of the raids was important. On the sea, three Egyptian vessels, among them the troop transport *Amira Faouzia*, were put to flight by the old ice-breaker *Eilat* just off Tel Aviv.

When the truce was declared on June 11, the Israelis held almost all of Galilee and even a few positions in Lebanon, such as Malkya. They had lost Mishmar Ha-Yarden on the Jordan, and had only a tenuous toe-hold in Jerusalem. The Negev remained in the hands of the invaders, and the advance guard of the Egyptian army was in Ashdod. On the Dead Sea, Beth Haarava and the potash works had been abandoned to the Arab Legion and Sodom was cut off. Most of the territory relegated to the Hebrew state by the United Nations had been held, with the important exception of the Negev, which had potential for colonization and was the opening to the Red Sea. In spite of its overwhelming material superiority, the Arab invasion had been everywhere checked.

The State of Israel began its independent existence at midnight on May 14, at Tel Aviv, or six o'clock in the evening Washington time. One hour earlier, the representative of the provisional government of Israel, Eliahu Epstein (Elath), had presented a letter to President Truman in which he stated that the new nation would become independent "beginning at 6:01 this evening, Washington time," and expressed "the hope that your government will want to recognize Israel and welcome her into the community of nations."

The problem of recognizing Israel had been debated since May 12 by the President, his advisers Clark Clifford and David Niles, Secretary of State Marshall and Undersecretary Lovett. The State Department was against immediate recognition, arguing the necessity of first consulting England and France. But Truman overruled the objections of his administration and decided to recognize the new state immediately. What was the good of denying the plain fact that this state existed? And besides, were not the Russians planning to recognize it without delay? A few minutes past six o'clock, a brief communiqué made it known that "the United States recognized the provisional government [in Tel Aviv] as the *de facto* authority of the new State of Israel." This announcement exploded like a bombshell in the United Nations. The American delegates had not been forewarned, and had tirelessly continued to weave their tapestry of a "provisional trusteeship" for Palestine. Other delegations were stupefied, angry, or satisfied. The next day some pro-Arab Americans registered angry protests,[17] and the Arab press expressed surprise and resentment. Public opinion in the United States, however, was overwhelmingly behind Truman's decision.

The State of Israel was recognized on May 15 by Guatemala; May 17 by the Soviet Union; May 18 by Poland, Uruguay, and Nicaragua; May 19 by Czechoslovakia and Yugoslavia; May 24 by South Africa; June 1 by Hungary; June 11 by Finland; and June 12 by Rumania. Great Britain insisted that the Jewish state had no legal existence. Consequently, no one could accuse the Arabs of aggression against a state that did not exist.

Thus, thirty-one years after the Balfour Declaration, the two new superpowers sponsored the entry of Israel into the community of nations, while England, the former protector of the Jewish national home, refused to recognize the Hebrew state. As for France, it decided to wait and see.

American policy did not continue to be so clear and resolute as Truman's decision to recognize Israel. The President and the State Department were pulling in opposite directions, for the latter did not want to aggravate Arab hostility or break with Great Britain. Thus the embargo on arms and men of military age, which theoretically applied to the whole of the Middle East but actually affected only Israel, was maintained despite growing opposition by United States public opinion; and the one hundred million dollar loan that Chaim Weizmann[18] asked Truman for on May 25 was granted only in January, 1949.

The news from Palestine reaching Lake Success depicted a country torn apart by war. Everyone at the United Nations wanted a cessation of hostilities, a truce. But there was a difference of opinion between the United States, which asked that the Arab states be declared aggressors under Article 39 of the United Nations Charter, and Great Britain, which denied that there had been aggression and opposed all sanctions against the invaders.[19] On May 22 the Security Council voted down the American resolution. The only possible answer was therefore a simple cease-fire; but the Arab states, with England's support, still tried to obtain a delay.[20] The cease-fire was to have gone into effect on May 26, but the Arab representatives at the United Nations rejected the proposal on the pretext that Israel would use a truce to import arms and immigrants. On May 29, a British resolution calling for a month-long cease-fire was adopted. It set up an embargo on war matériel destined for any of the belligerents (as we have seen, this measure affected only Israel). Men of military age would be permitted to enter Israel, but Jewish authorities were forbidden to mobilize and instruct them.

It was the responsibility of the United Nations mediator to put these rules into effect with the agreement of all parties involved. The office of mediator was created on May 14, and accepted on May 20, by Count Folke Bernadotte.

Count Bernadotte, a member of the Swedish royal family and an active leader of the International Red Cross, devoted himself whole-heartedly to the task assigned him.[21] Unfortunately he was ill-prepared for it and knew nothing at all about the explosive problems he was going to have to solve. His pathetic good will could not accomplish everything. His memoirs reveal a curious paradox: he remarked time and again that the Arab leaders "will never accept the establishing of a Jewish state," that the secretary general of the Arab League, Azzam Pasha, "was quite capable of declaiming how peace-loving he was—and the next moment he would be ready to assert that the Arabs would fight to the last man," that the Arabs of Palestine "did not take an active part in the fighting but fled into the countryside," and "had totally given up." He stated that Arab complaints about "massacres" perpetrated by the Jews were false; he observed that the so-called Arab irregulars assassinated two French officers in his party, Lt. Col. Quéru and Captain Jeannel, before the eyes of Egyptian soldiers, and that other irregulars had blown up the pumping station that supplied water to Jerusalem. And yet, with all this proof of Arab belligerence and bad faith, it was the Jews that the Count reproached for what he called their "arrogance," and "hostility." He even wrote that the Arabs "gave us every possible help. . . . The Jews, on the other hand, constantly tried to put spokes in the wheel. . . ."[22]

James G. McDonald, the first United States emissary to the provisional government of Israel, judged the mediator severely. He wrote to Clark Clifford that "[he] is almost completely discredited, not only among the Jews but among the Arabs. His inability to enforce his 'decisions' and his wordy pronouncements have left him neither substantial moral authority nor dignity." Although he found the count "charming, public-spirited, wholly devoted, but not unusually able or perceptive," McDonald defined him as "in truth a tragic figure."[23]

Bernadotte's anti-Jewish bias may perhaps partly explain the attitudes of the Jewish and Arab leaders toward him. The Arabs were actually stubborn and intractable but they seemed compliant, and they knew how to treat their guest to every Oriental courtesy, to greet him as a prince of royal blood, and to offer him magnificent hospitality in the style of the Arabian Nights. The Jews, by contrast, appeared to him tiresomely rational, democratic in their manners and proposals, and implacably precise in their criticisms.

It is astonishing that having been appointed by the United Nations, Count Bernadotte decided from the start (and imprudently told his Arab interlocutors) that he was not "bound by the United Nations resolution of 29 November 1947," and that he had a "free hand for putting forward new proposals for the future of Palestine."[24]

He actually admitted his disapproval of what he called "the unfortunate decision of 29 November 1947."[25] The Arab leaders must hardly have been able to believe their ears. What incredible luck to have a United Nations mediator whose first act was to reject the decision of the United Nations!

There is no doubt that the British government encouraged Bernadotte to take this paradoxical position. In this connection he himself records a statement from Sir Alexander Cadogan: the mediator, according to the British delegate, was not appointed for the purpose of applying the resolution of November 29, but to try to find another solution now that partition was revealed to be inapplicable.[26] Evidently the aggressors could not help but be encouraged by this repudiation of the initial United Nations decision, which was the only legal basis for partition of Palestine and the creation of the Hebrew state.

Bernadotte's first duty was to organize a month-long truce beginning on June 11. Operations were supposed to cease on both sides. The mediator could authorize the immigration of men of military age, but they would be detained in camps under the surveillance of observers. Of course, eight thousand Jews of military age were still interned on Cyprus under British guard. The purchase and transportation of all arms were forbidden. But of the 131 United Nations observers under Bernadotte's authority (Swedish, French, Belgian, and American officers), 63 per cent were stationed in Israel and 8 per cent in Jerusalem but only 29 per cent in Arab countries.[27]

The propaganda of the aggressor states claimed that the intervention of the mediator had "saved" Israel, which had supposedly been on the point of surrendering. In reality, their own offensive had everywhere been turned back, and they urgently needed a respite, which they put to good use repairing equipment, obtaining and transporting new war matériel to the front, and reorganizing their armies. On the political level, their differences were growing. Abdullah, who had taken the empty title of "supreme commander," met in Cairo with King Farouk, and his eternal rival the former mufti, Haj Amin el Husseini. Then at Riad he talked with ibn-Saud, whom he had not seen in twenty-five years — not since the king of Arabia had run Abdullah's father, Hussein, out of Mecca and Medina. It is not known if these meetings resulted in any agreements. To judge by subsequent events, it appears that they probably did not.

Meanwhile, truce or no truce, the Iraqi government was sending into Transjordan and Palestine considerable quantities of arms and munitions, camouflaged in convoys of clothing and food, and Egypt was reinforcing its expeditionary force in Palestine with Sudanese and Saudi-Arabian units. Egyptian cannons and fighter planes were added to those already at the Ashdod front.

By May 28, the Haganah had become the Defense Force of Israel (*Zahal*), by Order #4 of the provisional government. On June 2, the Irgun high command, in accordance with the public promise made before the state was created, signed an agreement that the Irgun, "by its free decision, will cease to operate and to exist as a military entity in the State of Israel." This carefully worked-out formula meant that the Irgun would disband in all territory that had fallen to the new state, but would continue for the moment to exist as an independent force associated with the Haganah, outside this territory, especially in Jerusalem. The agreement specified that the Irgun would stop acquiring war matériel and would transfer its contacts to the Zahal for the benefit of the war effort.[28] General headquarters of the Irgun would be open for another month while this merger was completed.

Loyal to this agreement, Menachem Beigin decided to submit the problem of the *Altalena* to the provisional government. Its departure from Port-de-Bouc, as has been shown, had been announced on June 11. During an earlier meeting, the Irgun had informed Israel Galili, Levi Eshkol, and a Haganah representative of the preparations being made for the voyage.[29] The ship was supposed to have left in May, but unfortunately the cargo of war matériel was not then available. The arrival of these arms just as or just after the state was proclaimed, as Beigin remarked, could have changed the course of the war by enabling the Irgun to take the key position of Ramle.[30]

In any case, as soon as Beigin heard the BBC announce that the *Altalena* had sailed, he tried to fulfill his obligation to the state. First, hoping that the British broadcast might have been premature, he cabled Paris, "The ship must not sail. Await instructions." Shmuel Katz, who had remained in the French capital, cabled back that the *Altalena* had left port and was steaming toward Palestine. Beigin then tried to radio the ship. The first radiogram to the *Altalena* said "Keep away, await instructions."[31] Unfortunately the ship's radio equipment was so rudimentary that it could receive messages but could not transmit them. Monroe Fein and Eliahu Lankin were perplexed by the message. At the time they were getting contradictory broadcasts from the Middle East, for while the truce was being proclaimed, the Arab stations kept on announcing success after success, including the alleged capture of Natanya on the coast north of Tel Aviv. Fein and Lankin finally decided to keep going.

The Irgun position was clear. Its provisional headquarters, which was the official organ of command recognized by the agreement of June 2, turned to the ministry of defense. On the night of June 11, Beigin and his collaborators gave the ministry all the information they had about the *Altalena*: the number of men on board, a description of the arms, and the probable arrival date of the ship if Beigin's message to wait had not been received. "Now," said Beigin, "decide for yourselves whether you will permit the ship to come, whether you want it to return to France, or if it must be diverted to some other Mediterranean port."[32] The next day Israel Galili (then undersecretary of defense) told Beigin that the government had decided to let the *Altalena* proceed. Overjoyed, the directors of the Irgun sent another radiogram: "Proceed, full steam ahead." Fein and Lankin were even more pleased by the message, and the little ship made for Israel at top speed. Breaking the truce was serious business and a grave political decision. This was the reason that the Irgun, about to go into voluntary dissolution, insisted that the government take full responsibility. On June 13, there was no doubt on that score. The state had weighed the risks and, knowing that the embargo was in practice not affecting the Arabs, had resolved to get these desperately needed arms. The *Altalena* was sailing for Palestine under orders from Ben Gurion's government.

Moreover, it was this government that gave the instructions for docking and unloading the ship. The first plan worked out by the Irgun had called for the ship to dock on the waterfront of Tel Aviv, at the end of Frishman Street. The defense ministry thought that the ship would more easily escape the attention of United Nations observers if it docked north of Tel Aviv near Kfar Vitkin. The Irgun agreed. Another message was radioed to the ship: "Change directions. Do not come to Tel Aviv. Anchor at Kfar Vitkin."

When the message was decoded by Eliahu Lankin, he concluded at once[33] that the Irgun and the government had come to terms, for Kfar Vitkin was a village known to be wholly on the side of the Mapai party, that is to say, Ben Gurion's party. It would have been unthinkable to dock there if the differences between the Irgun and the official authority had not been settled.

The *Altalena* was due at Kfar Vitkin on June 20. In the course of many long discussions with Israel Galili, Menachem Beigin asked the government to reserve 20 per cent of the cargo for Irgun units in besieged Jerusalem. This request was only natural, since according to the June 2 agreement, the Irgun was not to be dissolved in the Jerusalem zone that was not controlled by the regular authorities of the Hebrew state. These units, which had fought gloriously in the defense of the Old City and in the hard battle that had stopped the offensive of the Arab Legion and the Egyptians, were tragically ill-armed. At the moment they had only one Lewis automatic rifle, a few rifles, some Sten guns and Molotov cocktails.[34] They were begging for equipment.

After much hesitation, Israel Galili telephoned Beigin to say that the ministry of defense had approved the request. But two days later, in an abrupt about-face, he told Beigin that the army would take no part in unloading the arms.[35] The government was not opposed to unloading them; it would not order the ship to turn back; it would simply limit itself to declaring that it would provide no help unloading. This decision, which was odd and disquieting in itself, foreboded at least serious technical difficulties. How were the Irgun to undertake such an operation on a remote beach, without small craft, pontoons, cranes, or machinery?

Count Bernadotte revealed in his memoirs[36] that he had been informed (he does not say by whom) of the departure of the *Altalena* and that a United Nations reconnaissance plane spotted it as it was approaching Palestine. The mediator regarded the men of the Irgun as "terrorists," even "gangsters." He appears to have known nothing about the agreement between the Irgun and the government. Reading his book leads one to believe that the delegates whom the Israeli government had sent him (he was at the time in Rhodes), and even Moshe Sharett, did nothing to enlighten him on this point. Sharett wrote to him inveighing against the Irgun's violation of the truce (a violation that the government had decided on and for which it took responsibility) and assuring him that the authorities had decided to disarm and dissolve the "illegal" organization—which was now a convenient scapegoat.

The *Altalena* reached Kfar Vitkin, but not seeing the red light that was to mark the landing point, she steamed for several hours between Tel Aviv and Natanya before at last finding herself by the beach at dawn. Unloading in broad daylight would have been too dangerous, so the Irgun command decided to send the ship out to sea again until dark, and duly informed the liaison officer from the ministry of defense of this decision. The latter said that he approved the decision, that he would tell Israel Galili, and that he might send a few trucks to help transport the arms.

At dusk, the *Altalena* dropped anchor before the beach of Kfar Vitkin. Beigin was there to greet his friends. The nine hundred passengers disembarked first, and the long slow unloading operation began. It took all night to transfer a third of the cargo to shore. At dawn, a United Nations observer's plane circled the ship. Soon a number of Haganah units surrounded the beach and sent Beigin a ten-minute ultimatum. Beigin replied that such things could not be settled in ten minutes, and sent Yaakov Meridor to negotiate at Kfar Vitkin and Natanya. Hours went by.

Two United Nations observers (an American and a Frenchman) presented themselves in the afternoon and were courteously refused entry. The circle around the ship tightened. In the evening, without any warning, the government forces opened fire with automatic weapons and mortars. Simultaneously, three small Israeli launches converged on the *Altalena*. It took all Monroe Fein's nerve and skill to evade them and set his course, with Menachem Beigin aboard, for Tel Aviv.

A little past midnight, the *Altalena*, followed by the launches, dropped anchor at the foot of Frishman Street in Tel Aviv. The waterfront was heavily guarded by Palmach units, which opened fire on the ship. The bullets whistled around Beigin's head; by some miracle he was not killed, but one volunteer was killed instantly and Abraham Stavsky, a veteran of the illegal immigration, was mortally wounded and died the next day. Still, the Irgun leaders announced that they would not return fire. A cease-fire was arranged by radio with the Palmach commander. But about 4 P.M., as they were waiting for a boat to take off the wounded, several cannon shots were fired. A shell set the ship on fire, and she sank with her precious cargo on board. In the ranks of the Irgun, many were wounded and sixteen died.[37]

The ship's captain, Monroe Fein, spent several days in prison. Eliahu Lankin was not accused of any crime but was kept in jail two months. When he was released he joined the regular army as an artillery officer, and later, at the front, he came across the officer who had given the order to open fire on the *Altalena*. It was a German Jew named Blücher.

As for Menachem Beigin, his greatest worry had been to avoid civil war at all costs. He used the full strength of his authority to oppose the reprisals his men wanted to inflict. Because of him, and despite this bloody episode, the accord with the government became a reality, and the Irgun subsequently took part in every battle, from Jerusalem to Beersheba, from Galilee to the Negev. "There was no fratricidal war in Israel to destroy the Jewish state before it was properly born."[38]

The official version of the story—that the Irgun was going to use the *Altalena*'s arms to stage a coup—does not stand up under examination. If such had been the intention of Beigin and his companions (and the idea was diametrically opposed to their thinking and their actions of many years standing), would they not have been insane to notify the government as they did, to give it all the details of their plans, and to follow its orders to unload the cargo at Kfar Vitkin, one of the strongholds of Ben Gurion's party? Why did the nine hundred trained men come off the ship unarmed? How can their conduct be interpreted, particularly their determined refusal to return fire even when fired upon? They demonstrated their good faith, and extraordinary self-discipline. A civil war at this moment would have sealed Israel's fate, and the great Zionist dream would have evaporated. The Irgunists had the uncommon intelligence to understand this and the even more uncommon strength of character to sacrifice everything for their ideal.

The tragic picture of the burning *Altalena* has continued to haunt Israel's soul—at the edge of its consciousness—like a warning against the mortal peril of its internal divisions. Time has passed since that dark day. Less than twenty years later, when Israel's very existence was once again threatened, it was Menachem Beigin who took the initiative in proposing a government of national union under the leadership of Ben Gurion.

On June 27, a few days after the *Altalena* sank, the United Nations mediator in Rhodes announced what came to be known as the Bernadotte Plan, which he himself more modestly entitled "Suggestions."[39] This plan differed in many respects from the United Nations resolution and in some respects contradicted it. It called not for two independent states west of the Jordan, one Arab and the other Jewish, but for a Palestinian union extending to all the territory that had been included in the British Mandate. Transjordan would be part of this Union, as well as Israel and all the Arab lands west of the Jordan. Governed by a central council, the Union would control economic development, customs, foreign policy, and defense. For two years immigration would be unlimited. Then the council would regulate it, and any dispute would be referred to the Economic and Social Council of the United Nations.

Bernadotte's territorial proposals were a marked departure from the United Nations plan. He wanted to give the Arabs "all or part" of the Negev, and the Jews "all or part" of western Galilee. Despite its overwhelmingly Jewish majority, Jerusalem would go to the Arabs, the holy places being put under a special law. Another special law was to be granted to Jaffa. Finally, there would be a free port at Haifa and a free airport at Lydda.

This unfortunate attempt to put Palestine back on the operating table pleased neither the Arabs, who would not accept even the idea of a Hebrew state, nor the Jews, who replied on July 6 that they regarded the lands assigned to their state by the United Nations as an "irreducible minimum." Besides, they continued, the United Nations had provided for the partition of Palestine west of the Jordan between two states, not for the absorption of the Arab parts of this territory by another state that already existed. Such a proposal would change everything. The Bernadotte Plan suited only the ambitions of King Abdullah, that "decidedly fascinating personality,"[40] whose expansionist aims would thereby be greatly advanced. In September, after Sir John Troutbeck, representing the foreign office in Cairo, and Robert McClintock from the State Department had visited Rhodes, Bernadotte announced his territorial intentions: this time the entire Negev would go to the Arabs.[41] In return, Israel would be made a United Nations Trusteeship.[42] After months of disagreement, London and Washington now presented a united front and agreed to support this modified plan in the United Nations.

Count Bernadotte's new plan was submitted to the United Nations Secretariat on September 16. The next day, while the mediator and a number of his observers were crossing Jerusalem, a jeep (not the model used by the Israeli Army) blocked his car. Two men got out of the jeep, shot Count Bernadotte and a French officer, Colonel Sérot, and then fled. The Frenchman died immediately, the count a few minutes later. The assassins were never caught. Investigations pointed to a faction of the Lehi, *Hazit Hamoledeth* (National Front), which had broken off from the Stern group shortly before. The Israeli police arrested hundreds of Sternists, among them Nathan Yellin-Moor.[43]

Such was the tragic fate of a man of good will who was crushed by forces whose magnitude he had improperly evaluated. He had gone blindfolded into a mine field, and succumbed, the victim of the violence he had believed himself capable of appeasing.[44]

The first truce had ended on July 8. A few days earlier the mediator had asked the belligerents to prolong it, but though the Israelis agreed, the Syrians and Egyptians refused, and the other Arab states followed suit. They "were in fact trapped by the lying propaganda with which they had fed public opinion during the May hostilities. Newspaper reports and official announcements had strayed so far from the truth that the public, particularly in Egypt, had been led to expect a rapid and total victory — 'Tel Aviv next week.' . . . Draconian censorship . . . had suppressed all news unfavorable to the Arabs in the local and foreign press and had stifled all criticism of the Arab leaders, to the point that a misled public opinion, believing in an imminent victory, clamored loudly for the battle to begin again."[45]

On the morning of July 8, the Egyptian expeditionary corps opened its offensive on the southern front. The Israelis evacuated Kfar Darom, since it could not be held, but on July 9–10, they captured Ibdis and repulsed an Egyptian counterattack. The heaviest fighting took place on July 12 at Negba, a strategically important spot north of Ashkelon. The one hundred fifty defenders, among them an Irgun contingent, fought back so furiously under the storm of artillery shells (4,000 shots were fired during the morning) that the Egyptians in their armored cars and tanks had to retire from the position. Three days later, the Egyptians failed again near Gaza at Be'erot Yitzchak, despite the superiority of their artillery and air support. After this double setback, there was no longer any question of the Egyptian forces marching north toward Tel Aviv.

In Galilee, the Israelis tried in vain to recapture Mishmar Ha-Yarden. The Syrians had put the truce to good use and had built solid fortifications that resisted all assaults. So they held this bridgehead but were not able to use it as a base for an offensive toward the interior. The

Israelis, reinforced by the Druses from villages in upper Galilee, began to liquidate El Kaukji's Army of Liberation, whose general headquarters was at Nazareth. On July 14, the Israeli command issued the following orders: "We now advance on a city . . . that is the cradle of Christianity held in reverence by many millions. The eyes of all the members of the Christian faith, wherever they be, turn toward that city, with its churches, monasteries, and many sacred places. Those who penetrate into this city will fight valiantly against invaders . . . at the same time they must meticulously . . . abstain from harming, despoiling, or pillaging holy places. They will not penetrate into churches, will not fight from them, or take up positions in them. . . . Our soldiers . . . act with respect for the religious feelings of others."[46]

They took the city on July 15. Kaukji fled into the mountains that evening. The Arab notables of Nazareth signed the surrender, and during the following days many Arab villages of the region surrendered without fighting.

In central Palestine, during a three-day operation (July 9–12) Lt. Col. Moshe Dayan made his audacious raid on Lydda that resulted in the capture of that city and of Ramle by the Israelis. This victory loosened the vise around Tel Aviv. The recapture of the pumping station at Rosh Haayin gave the Jews another key advantage. But the Arab Legion under Glubb Pasha stood fast at Latrun, blocking the road from Tel Aviv to Jerusalem. In Jerusalem, the Haganah, the Lehi, and the Irgun were cooperating closely despite the recent drama of the *Altalena*.[47] On July 9, they mounted an offensive but could not break the resistance of the Arab Legion entrenched in the Old City. On July 11, Egyptian airplanes bombed Jerusalem for the first time in its multimillennial history, and on the sixteenth Glubb Pasha's troops captured the Mandelbaum Building, which served for the next twenty years as the Israeli-Jordanian boundary in the divided city.

During this time Israel finally began receiving some of the modern armaments that had been bought in Europe, including three Flying Fortresses. One of these dropped a few bombs on Cairo on July 14. The decrepit old *Eilat*, with its companion the *Wedgwood*, steamed into Tyr and fired a few shells at the port.

On July 15, the United Nations Security Council adopted an American resolution calling for an indefinite truce to begin July 18, under penalty of sanctions, as outlined by Article #7 of the Charter. Great Britain supported the United States proposal as energetically as it had opposed the idea of sanctions against the Arabs the previous May.[48]

During this second phase of hostilities, the "Ten-Day War," the Israelis were unable to liberate the Negev or to take Jerusalem. However, they did have all of Galilee, the Ramle region, and Lydda. They had definitely driven back Egyptian aggression in the south. And Arab disunity was increasing: the retreat of the Arab Legion from Lydda and Ramle was looked upon in Cairo as a veritable act of treason to the Arab cause. In September, at Gaza, the former mufti grabbed the ball on the rebound and proclaimed a so-called Arab government for Palestine, under his presidency. It was recognized by all the Arab states except Transjordan. Abdullah himself convoked the National Palestine Congress that obediently asked him to take the Arab lands of Palestine under his protection and annex them to his kingdom. So, at the end of 1948, Arab Palestine found that it had two governments—the former mufti's in Gaza and Abdullah's in Amman.

The second truce was to have lasted, in principle, until the conclusion of an armistice and, if possible, peace treaties. Having learned from experience, the Israelis realized just how precarious United Nations protection could be. Thus they set about reorganizing and reinforcing their army. Conscription had brought the effective forces of the Zahal to ninety thousand men and women by October, 1948. New supplies of arms and munitions coming from Czechoslovakia had played an important role in the battles of May, June, and July. But in August, the government at Prague abruptly ended the airlift that the Israelis called Operation Balak. There were other resources: they bought field artillery and antiaircraft guns in Switzerland and Italy. Sherman tanks were purchased from United States Army war surpluses in Western Europe, and thirty of them reached Israel in September. A boatload of matériel, including fifty jeeps, left Antwerp for Palestine in October. Arms of various kinds and origins, as well as high octane gas, were purchased from Mexico.

Events soon proved these preparations necessary. The uneasy truce first began to deteriorate on the southern front. About twenty-five kibbutzim in the Negev had been isolated from the rest of Palestine since May. With the approval of the mediator[49] and the United Nations observers, they were to be supplied by truckloads of food passing north-south through the Egyptian lines. This the Egyptians accepted grudgingly.

An especially serious incident took place on October 15, for the Egyptians attacked a truck convoy. The Israelis retaliated by bombing

Gaza and El Arish and launching an assault on the key position of Beersheba, the Negev port. The city fell on October 21 after fierce fighting in which French volunteers — *maquis* veterans — distinguished themselves. At the same time the Israeli fleet — the *Eilat* and the *Wedgwood* — sank the Egyptian flagship the *Emir Farouk* just off Ashkelon.

The United Nations obtained a cease-fire on October 22. The Israeli advances had given them access to the Negev from the north and had taken them all the way to Beit Hanun, a few miles from Gaza, and toward Hebron as far as Beit Jibrin. An Egyptian brigade under the command of the Sudanese general Sayid Taha, was cut off at Al Faluja.

On the very day that the cease-fire went into effect on the south front, fighting broke out on the north front, initiated by Fawzi El Kaukji. After the fall of Nazareth, the chief of the Army of Liberation had retreated into Lebanon whence he departed on October 22 to attack Manara, close to the border. A counteroffensive known as Hiram, in memory of the Biblical king of Tyr who had been Solomon's friend, left Safed on the night of October 28, and drove back the Army of Liberation, taking 550 prisoners and leaving 400 dead. This was the end of the line for El Kaukji, the fanatic who had organized anti-Jewish guerrillas in 1936–39, the friend of the former mufti and the Nazi leaders. His troops deserted him before the thrust of the Israeli forces, which were strengthened by men from the Druse villages. The Arabs of Galilee decided they would simply stay put inside the State of Israel. The last few places in Galilee that remained in Arab hands were retaken, including the village of Peki'in, which had known uninterrupted Jewish occupation from biblical times until the present. Now all of Galilee belonged to the Hebrew state. The Israeli forces also occupied some fifteen villages a few miles from the border, which had asked for protection against guerrilla blackmail.

If the second truce was violated in the south by the Egyptians and in the north by Kaukji's bands, it never really was in effect at all in Jerusalem. With the Jews struggling against the Arab Legion and the Moslem Brotherhood, one incident after another broke out — rifle fire, artillery fire, ambushes. Abdelaziz, the commander of the Moslem Brotherhood, was killed while returning from one of these engagements by an Arab sentinel who fired on him in the confusion of battle. With the defeat of King Farouk's expeditionary corps in southern Palestine, Egyptians stationed in Jerusalem found themselves cut off from their bases. With no source of supply, they had to join Abdullah's army.

Meanwhile, the General Assembly of the United Nations was convening at the Palais de Chaillot in Paris to discuss the proposals formulated by Count Bernadotte on the eve of his death.[50] The American delegation was led by General George Marshall, the secretary of state, whose main concern seemed to be to settle Anglo-American differences over the Palestine problem. Without first consulting President Truman, he announced on September 21 that the United States considered the Bernadotte Plan "sound," and he urged the parties concerned and the General Assembly to accept it without changes. The next day, Ernest Bevin made almost the same speech in the House of Commons. The two great Anglo-Saxon powers apparently were in agreement that the plan should be imposed without delay, that is that Israel should be obliged to give up the Negev.

But the agenda of the Assembly was crowded, and a disparate majority made up of pro-Arab, pro-Israeli, and pro-Soviet elements rejected the Anglo-American motion to put the Palestine debate at the head of the agenda. Instead, debate was postponed from week to week. President Truman himself was facing a difficult campaign for re-election. Both the Democratic and Republican parties had announced their unequivocal support for Israel, its defense against Arab aggression, and its admission to the United Nations. Truman thought Marshall's speech inopportune. "The Bernadotte Plan was so different from the original partition plan that it could not be accepted without a change in policy."[51] On October 24, in answer to a pro-Israeli statement from Republican candidate Thomas E. Dewey, Truman reiterated his complete support for the platform of the Democratic party, and stated that he would not accept any modification of the partition plan approved by the United Nations the previous year, unless Israel agreed. On October 28, in a speech before fifteen thousand people at Madison Square Garden, he restated this position, without even mentioning the Bernadotte Plan. It was plain that the secretary of state and the President were far from seeing eye to eye.

The American delegation at Paris could do nothing more until after the election. Truman won his landslide victory on November 2, and on the fifteenth, the American delegation refused to support a British motion calling for the Israelis to retreat from Galilee as well as the south. Subsequent debate and voting were extremely confused. The Americans adopted for discussion a British proposal based on the Bernadotte Plan, but introduced one amendment after another, and the original text was watered down with each passing day.[52] Finally, on December 11, the Assembly passed a resolution that made no mention of the Bernadotte Plan and merely named a Conciliation Commission consisting of the United States, France, and Turkey, vaguely charged to "settle pending questions" between the Arab states and Israel. Truly, the mountain had labored and brought forth a mouse.

Israel's request for admission to the United Nations, sponsored in December by the American delegation, met the objections of the British and the hesitations of other countries, mainly France, Belgium, and Canada. It was voted down at a later session.

In Palestine, in spite of the truce, the Egyptians were making efforts to free their brigade isolated at Al-Faluja. A meeting between Taha, the brigade commander, and Yigael Allon, the Israeli commander of the sector, was fruitless; Taha refused to evacuate the position even with full military honors. Moreover, the Egyptian high command at El Arish rudely rejected a proposal from Glubb Pasha to evacuate the brigade in an operation code-named the Damascus Plan. Launching a blundering and inefficient campaign, the Egyptians massed reinforcements destined to aid the encircled garrison, raided Israeli villages, and kept up air raids on Haifa, Tel Aviv, and the Nazareth region.

Meanwhile, the political situation in Egypt was deteriorating. The Moslem Brotherhood, frustrated by their military failures, had been stirring up trouble, and one of their agents assassinated the prime minister, Nokrashi Pasha, on December 28.

The Israeli leaders accordingly decided to liquidate the Egyptian forces in southern Palestine and the Negev once and for all. Operation Horev, launched on December 22, led to the capture six days later of Hafir Al-Auja, an ancient Nabataean and Byzantine fortress. The Egyptians fought back ferociously, and for the first time in the war used flame throwers. But once they were dislodged from Hafir Al-Auja, they had to call a general retreat. In the days that followed, the Israelis captured Abu Agella and threatened El Arish.

On December 29, the United Nations Security Council ordered a cease-fire on this front. Egypt asked for help, but Iraq and Jordan refused to intervene. Great Britain decided then to invoke the Anglo-Egyptian treaty of 1936 (against which the Egyptian government had protested to the Security Council in July, 1947),[53] and announced a veritable ultimatum that the American government transmitted to Israel. The Jewish forces pulled out of Abu Agella and the El Arish zone on December 31.

Early in January, 1949, the Israelis launched a new offensive toward Rafa. Its object was to rid Israeli territory of Egyptian elements that were still north of the frontier. After desperate fighting in a wild sand storm, the Egyptians announced on January 6 that they were ready to negotiate, and a cease-fire was proclaimed the next day. Another cease-fire, on the Jerusalem front, had been concluded on December 1 following talks between Moshe Dayan and Col. Abdullah At-Tall of the Arab Legion.

One last stroke, as brutal as it was unforseen, finally brought about a normalization of Israeli-British relations. On January 7, Israeli fighter planes shot down five planes flying over the scene of the recent fighting. These planes turned out to be not Egyptian but British. Washington turned its back on London, and the British public reacted violently against Ernest Bevin and his disastrous policies. In a complete about-face, Bevin announced on January 18 that the British government had decided to release the Jewish immigrants still detained on Cyprus, and on January 29, Britain recognized Israel.

Negotiations between Israel and the Arab states began on January 13, at the Hotel of Roses in Rhodes, under the aegis of the acting mediator, Ralph Bunche. They dragged on until July. Egypt gave up Beersheba and the Negev; in March, two Israeli columns crossed the desert and planted the blue and white flag at Elath, as detachments of the Arab Legion withdrew without firing a shot.

In March, King Abdullah had met secretly in his winter palace at Shuna with two Israeli emissaries, Moshe Dayan and Reuven Shiloah. He agreed to pull back the Arab Legion about two miles all along the front from Kalkilya to Tulkarm to Jenin.[54] This agreement, made public in 1950 by Abdullah At-Tall and the Egyptians and denounced as an act of treason, was one of the reasons why Abdullah was assassinated the following year, on July 21, in Jerusalem. Israeli-Jordanian negotiations at Rhodes went on until April, 1949.

The armistice with Lebanon, which had taken a very small part in the war, was signed on March 23, at Rosh Hanikra, on the border. The Israelis pulled out of the few villages they had conquered in Lebanon.

Negotiations with Syria, which began April 5, in a no-man's-land near Lake Huleh, were the hardest of all. The Syrians still held Mishmar Ha-Yarden, which was a thorn in the side of Israel. The Syrians demanded adjustments of the border in their favor and claimed that Dardara and Ein Gev, Israeli villages east of Lake Huleh and the Sea of Galilee, were a threat to Syrian security. At last an agreement was reached on a compromise drawn up by Ralph Bunche: these areas would be declared a demilitarized zone until such time as a peace treaty established their status.

As for the Iraqis, they had not taken part directly in the armistice negotiations; they had let the Jordanians represent them.

The armistice with Syria was signed on July 20. Thus did the war for independence end — with an armistice, not with peace.

FOOTNOTES FOR CHAPTER 9

1. Marie Syrkin. *Golda Meir*, p. 183.
2. Syrkin. *op. cit.*, p. 185.
3. Netanel Lorch. *The Edge of the Sword.* pp. 45–46 and 77.
4. Kirk. *Survey.* p. 233.
5. Schechtman. *op. cit.*, p. 332. Lorch. *op. cit.*, p. 325.
6. Kirk. *Survey.* p. 247.
7. Figures from Lorch. *passim.*
8. Mardor. *op. cit.*, p. 113.
9. *Ibid.*, p. 198.
10. Mardor. *op. cit.*, p. 197.
11. Balak, son of Zipor—"bird" in Hebrew. Number 22.
12. Beigin. *Rebelión.* p. 514 ff.
13. Information about the *Altalena* affair derives mainly from the author's conversations with Menachem Beigin, Eliahu Lankin, Arieh Ben Eliezer, Shmuel Katz, Yaakov Meridor, and others.
14. Beigin. *Rebelión.* p. 249.
15. Statement to the author by Eliahu Lankin.
16. Beigin. *op. cit.*, pp. 282–89.
17. Especially Messrs. Badeau and Penrose, who were presidents of the American universities at Cairo and Beirut, respectively. Schechtman. *op. cit.*, p. 305.
18. Weizmann had been named president of the State of Israel on May 17, while he was in the United States.
19. Sir Alexander Cadogan, head of the British delegation, had been instructed to "go as far as possible in order to get a cease-fire but not to agree to the imposition of sanctions against the Arabs." Kirk. *Survey*, p. 273.
20. *Ibid.*
21. See his book *To Jerusalem.* London, 1951. The passages quoted here are from that work, pp. 81, 104, 111, 146, 217, 225, 226.
22. *Op. cit.*, p. 208.
23. J. G. McDonald. *My Mission in Israel.* pp. 51, 65, 67.
24. Conversation with Azzam Pasha. *To Jerusalem*, p. 33.
25. *Ibid.*, p. 131.
26. Bernadotte. *op. cit.*, p. 170.
27. Official figures of the United Nations cited by Kirk. *Survey*, p. 277, note 2. James G. McDonald (*op. cit.*, p. 41) says that later when the number of observers was raised to about three hundred, only fifty-five were assigned to Arab countries, of which fourteen were in Syria and six in Iraq.

28. Lorch. *op. cit.*, p. 239.

29. This meeting was attended by the following Irgun representatives: Beigin, Meridor, Chaim Landau, and Shmuel Katz. From Katz, *op. cit.*

30. Beigin. *Rebelión*, p. 249.

31. Beigin. *op. cit.*, p. 250.

32. *Ibid.*

33. Conversation of Lankin with the author.

34. The Irgun battles at Jerusalem were directed by three commanders: "Gideon," of Rumanian origin, was head of the Irgun in the Old City; "Amnon," a Tunisian, was responsible for arms, explosives, and the engineers; and "Nimrod," a Palestinian, was Irgun commander in Jerusalem. Nimrod repulsed the Arab assault on Ramat Rehel. Gideon was taken prisoner by the Arab Legion when the Old City fell. Some Sternist elements fought by the side of the Irgun in the Old City, at Notre Dame de France, and at the French Hospital. (From interviews of the author with the three commanders.)

35. Beigin. *op. cit.*, p. 292.

36. Bernadotte. *op. cit.*, pp. 115–16.

37. See the account of this episode by Arthur Koestler. *Promise and Fulfillment*, pp. 248–49.

38. Beigin. *Rebelión*. p. 301.

39. Bernadotte. *op. cit.*, p. 129 ff.

40. *Ibid.*, p. 42.

41. Schechtman. *op. cit.*, pp. 359–60.

42. Kirk. *Survey*, p. 289.

43. They were released in 1949 under a general amnesty. Yellin-Moor became a representative in the first Israeli parliament.

44. A description of the assassination by the Swedish General Aage Lundström will be found in the Appendix of Count Bernadotte's memoirs, *To Jerusalem*, p. 245 ff.

45. Kirk. *Survey*, pp. 279–80.

46. Lorch. *op. cit.*, p. 276.

47. *Ibid.*, p. 294.

48. Kirk. *op. cit.*, p. 282.

49. After the tragic death of Bernadotte, Dr. Ralph Bunche acted as mediator.

50. Kirk. *Survey*, p. 289 ff. Schechtman. *op. cit.*, p. 361 ff.

51. Truman. *Memoirs*, Vol. II., p. 166.

52. James G. McDonald. *op. cit.*, p. 104.

53. Kirk. *op. cit.*, p. 130.

54. *Ibid.*, pp. 297–98 and 310.

10
EPILOGUE

The proclamation of the State of Israel in May, 1948, and the armistices that ended the Jewish-Arab war were milestones in the history of Israel: the rebirth of a nation for the Jewish people after eighteen centuries. But the river of time flows on inexorably; people must live, survive. In the world as it is known, the survival of Israel for these twenty years is a miracle renewed each morning.

The cease-fire lines established by the armistices did not constitute true borders. In the north, the kibbutzim of eastern Galilee were still under fire from Syrian batteries. At Ein Gev and Gadot, innumerable "incidents" over the course of the years took a heavy toll among the pioneers. Farther south, between Natanya and Tel Aviv, Hebrew territory was squeezed between the sea and the Jordanian-occupied hills into a corridor barely ten miles wide—the obvious objective of any offensive aimed at cutting the country in half. The historic capital, Jerusalem, was truncated by barbed wire, barricades, and army posts. Access to the Wailing Wall was forbidden to the Jews. On top of that, Jerusalem was connected with Tel Aviv and the coast by only a thin corridor crossing Arab territory. Hebron, the holy city of the patriarchs, and Gaza, which had been part of Palestine since remote antiquity, were in alien hands.

The Israelis were, indeed, at home and masters of their destiny at last, but in a land without frontiers, without space, without any room to maneuver and regroup. Their parliament, their president, their cabinet ministers met within rifle range of the Arab Legion. Not one inch of the whole country was out of range of medium artillery. One glance at the map sufficed to reveal the germs of future conflicts and future battlefields.

These conditions weighed heavily on the development of the nation. In effect, Israel was obliged to devote an important segment of its resources to defense, to keep its men and women ready for intensive mobilization, and to sacrifice part of its economic growth to survival. Military readiness was all the more urgent because the enemy of 1948–49 did not disarm but eagerly aggravated all the problems that came up between itself and the Hebrew state.

In the first place there was the problem of the Palestine refugees. It is a fact that of all the Arabs, those who participated least in the war were the Palestinian Arabs. As pawns in the strategy mapped out in Damascus, Cairo, Amman, and Baghdad, they had been ordered by the Arab leaders to leave Palestine. Once the war was lost, these leaders thought only of using these refugees as tools in diplomacy and propaganda.

After the United Nations had created a special agency, UNRWA (United Nations Relief and Works Agency), to assist the four hundred fifty to five hundred thousand Palestinian refugees in Jordan, Lebanon, Syria, and Gaza, the Arab governments were content with the status quo, and in no hurry to integrate their "Palestinian brothers" into the economic and political life of their countries. Iraq, for example, has vast stretches of fallow but arable land. One can travel along the Euphrates for almost two hundred miles without meeting a living soul[1] in a region that once was a granary of the East. In 1955, the Arab League rejected a plan for sharing the waters of the Jordan among Israel, Jordan, Lebanon, and Syria, although this would have given resources and employment to a vast number of refugees. A two-hundred-million-dollar rehabilitation fund for Arab refugees was created by the United Nations on January 26, 1952, to finance irrigation and development projects in Arab countries that would benefit the refugees. Unfortunately, not one of the Arab governments involved (Jordan, Syria, Egypt, Libya) would consent to carry out these programs; in 1957, UNRWA had to abandon the idea, which would have gone a long way toward solving the problem.[2]

Although Jordan agreed to grant citizenship to the Palestinians, Egypt insisted on parking more than two hundred thousand refugees in a 150-square-mile section of the Gaza Strip, and setting up a military administration to keep them there.

Between 1950 and 1967, the total number of refugees (which is impossible to state precisely because UNRWA agreed not to take an exact census) had at least doubled. The natural population growth was swelled by an influx of fraudulent refugees who wanted the rations that were "given in bulk to distributory agencies, and parceled out not only among the refugees but also among indigents and other needy persons."[3] An official United Nations report estimated that the number of frauds in Jerusalem was 42 per cent.

While the Arab governments, press, and radio loudly proclaimed their solicitude for the fate of the refugees but did nothing at all about them, they took revenge by forcing five hundred thousand Jews to flee their ancient communities in the East and the Maghreb, where they were victims of discriminatory measures, confiscations, and pogroms. This was the case with the Yemeni communities (45,000 people) and those of Iraq (125,000). It should be kept in mind that beginning in 1948, there was a veritable population exchange between the Arab countries and Israel, consisting of 500,000 people from each side. But the Hebrew state integrated its refugees, plus about 500,000 Jews from Central and Eastern Europe. During the ten-year period following independence, more than 900,000 immigrants (of whom 700,000 arrived between 1948 and 1952) were absorbed into the country.

The law of return, passed by the parliament (Knesset) on July 5, 1950, permitted any Jew to come to Israel and enjoy all the rights of citizenship. Needless to say, the young country had to make an immense effort to absorb such a massive immigration. Nevertheless it did absorb it, thus proving the relativity of the famous notion of "absorptive capacity" that had caused so much debate during the Mandate era. Experience has shown that immigration could be not merely an obstacle to be overcome but a source of enrichment and a driving force in the economy. Of course, there were suddenly many more mouths to feed, but there were also many more arms to plow and build, and many more brains to think. The Israeli economy flourishes when immigration is high and stagnates when it diminishes. This was evident in 1966–67, at the time of the *mitun*, or recession in the rhythm of economic life that coincided with a low rate of immigration. One is forced to conclude that in the furious debates that went on between 1920 and 1940, it was the "visionaries," such as Jabotinsky, who were the true "realists."

In its twenty-one years of independence, Israel has reached a level of economic development superior to that of all other Middle Eastern countries and comparable to that of Europe. The socialist institutions of official Zionism—the kibbutzim, the Histadrut, the giant trusts like the *Solel Boneh*—have assuredly played an important role in this growth. However, it is possible that the inevitable evolution of these institutions tends in a certain sense to slow down the progress that they set in motion. In the industrial domain particularly, the preponderance of the enormous Histadrut enterprises tends to discourage private investment. Jabotinsky, again, was wise to call for an equilibrium between co-operatives and private enterprise—as Herzl had done—and to warn against organizations too powerful in too many domains.

In agriculture, the kibbutzim produce only about 12 per cent of the gross national product. Some of them have also founded and operated industries. In short, the Israeli economy is tending to become more liberal and diversified by simultaneously trying out different forms of administration and ownership. Like all heroic eras, the heroic era of the pioneers has given way to a new phase. Israel has come a long way from the dunam-by-dunam colonization of land just reclaimed from the desert and the marshes. It is no longer a "developing nation" of the Middle East but an extension of the modern West.

This is true in the political domain, too. Although the Hebrew state still has no written constitution (there are "constitutional laws," such as those defining the powers of the Knesset and the president), it is organized and it functions as a democratic nation founded on the representative system, with the chief executive responsible to the legislature. The Knesset is elected for four years by universal suffrage and proportional representation. It elects the president for a five-year term, and he in turn appoints a prime minister to form the government. The Knesset, by passing a censure motion, can overthrow the Cabinet.

Proportional representation in Israel as elsewhere accommodates diverse political parties. The Knesset of 120 representatives elected in November, 1965, embraced no less than twelve factions, whose strength ranged from 45 delegates (the Mapai-Ahdut Avoda coalition) to one (the New Force, or Communist party).[4] The government is necessarily composite. The traditional heat of Zionist controversies and the equally traditional taste for subtle discussions (*pilpul*) often lend a bitterly impassioned character to Israeli political life. But in a time of national danger the immense majority, sometimes everyone, joins together to save the country. Until now, Israel seems to have succeeded in resolving the eternal problem faced by democracies: how to reconcile human liberty with governmental effectiveness.

Following the cease-fire of 1948, and the armistice of 1949, it was reasonable to hope that negotiations might lead to peace treaties and a normalization of relations among the nations of that part of the world. This obviously was as much or more in the interest of the Arab countries as of Israel. Without effective economic co-operation between Israel and its neighbors, there was no chance for them to win the war against hunger, or revive agriculture, or set up large-scale irrigation systems, or industrialize the Middle East. The enormous sums of money thrown away on arms and military training would better have been used to rescue the *fellahin* from their age-old poverty.

The Arab League has continually rejected all co-operative programs for developing irrigation and agriculture. The Arab states preferred instead to try (futilely, as it turned out) to divert the waters of the Jordan away from Israel, snuff out the Israeli economy through boycotts, and close the Suez Canal and the Gulf of Aqaba to Israeli shipping. They have made a dogma out of the perpetual state of war between themselves and their Hebrew neighbors. Besides economic reprisals, they have sanctioned attacks by organized terrorists based in Gaza, Jordan, and Syria. These bands mine the roads, sabotage railroads, murder farmers, and set fire to crops. Reversing Clausewitz' dictum that war is a continuation of diplomacy by other means, the Arab states have used diplomacy as a continuation of war by other means.

One of these methods consists of persistent and artificial agitation over the refugee problem. "We must continue to prolong the refugee problem as a vital question," said the Jordanian legislator Abdullah Nawas in a speech on June 6, 1952. "The war in Palestine continues only because of the refugees. Their existence keeps the question open."

On December 11, 1948, the General Assembly of the United Nations passed a resolution (#194/III) of which Paragraph 11 states clearly that "refugees who so desire may return to their homes and live in peace with their neighbors, and may do so at once." The government at Jerusalem immediately agreed to reunite 50,000 refugees with their families in Israel, and took charge of 28,000 refugees under the care of UNRWA. Israel made other gestures of conciliation: Arab money still in Israeli bank accounts was unblocked, a sum of £2,783,000; Israel co-operated with the United Nations conciliation committee in taking inventory of Arab wealth that had been left behind in 1948; Ambassador Michael Comay (who appeared before the fifteenth session of the political commission of the United Nations on November 28, 1960), announced that Israel would "pay indemnities even before a final peace treaty is concluded and other pending questions are settled." There was no Arab counterpart to these efforts. Instead, the application of Paragraph 11 was rendered impossible as totalitarian propaganda of race hatred was intensified among the refugees, and as terrorist organizations were organized under adventurers, such as Ahmed Chukeiri. It was hard to see how refugees could decide to "live in peace with their neighbors" after years of listening to an obsessive campaign calling for genocide.

Arab propaganda soon stopped asking simply for the return of the refugees to their homes and concentrated on the slogan: Run the Jews into the sea, annihilate Israel. "The Israeli-Arab problem can be resolved only by war," said Nasser's valued adviser, Mohamed Hassanein

Heykal on May 12, 1961. "Israel knows that we shall settle for nothing less than her complete destruction."

Gamal Abdel Nasser, who rose to power by exploiting the frustrations of the Egyptian army after the defeat of 1948, surrounded himself with Germans—former officers of the Gestapo and the SS, specialists in the "final solution" to the Jewish question. Many of them converted to Islam and took Arab names before joining Nasser's political police or secret service. Nasser himself does not hesitate to use the neo-Nazi press to exalt the war against Israel.[5]

However, Nasser's accession to power in Egypt had at first raised hopes in Israel. Leaders in some circles imagined that the new Egyptian president and his colleagues, as successors to a discredited regime, would be strong enough and reasonable enough to turn over a new leaf. David Ben Gurion, the head of the Israeli government, twice tried to establish relations with Nasser and to arrange an interview with him, first through the intermediary of the Yugoslav government, then through the good offices of an American diplomat. Nasser turned down both these offers to talk.

The tension maintained in the Middle East by the permanent Arab campaign for revenge grew more dangerous as the cold war intensified, and the rivalry of the great powers was transferred more and more to the Middle East. On May 25, 1960, the United States, Great Britain, and France signed a "tripartite declaration" promising to act together to re-establish order and peace in the Middle East if the *status quo* there were upset. This promise was treated as a deadletter by the United States in 1956, and by France in 1967. In 1956, the United States and Moscow joined forces to save the Egyptian dictator from downfall. In 1967, repudiating its twenty-year-old policy of friendship for Israel, France moved to the side of the Arab states.

The Suez crisis was unleashed by Nasser on July 26, 1956. In a speech before a large crowd in Mohamed-Ali Square at Alexandria, he made the dramatic announcement that he had decided to nationalize the Suez Canal. "The Company has ceased to exist," he declared to loud applause; "We have seized it from the imperialistic profiteers. . . . Henceforth the Canal is Egyptian. It will stay Egyptian come what may!"

Nasser had recently returned from Brioni, where he had conferred with Tito and had met Nehru. During his stay in Yugoslavia he had learned that the American government, after much hesitation, had decided not to finance the Aswan Dam, which was a most important project for Nasser.[6] This refusal appeared to the Americans to be justified by the fact that Nasser had refused to forego other sources of capital, specifically Soviet sources, and that he was continuing to buy arms, heavy tanks, MIGs and Ilyushins from Russia, dangerously mortgaging the Egyptian economy.

For Israel, the nationalistic fervor unleashed in Egypt represented even more of a danger than the closing of the Canal to its shipping. War could probably have been avoided had the United States taken a firm and unequivocal stand in order to restore the international law that was violated by this act of brigandage. Nothing of the sort occurred. America was in the middle of an election. Eisenhower was campaigning on the slogan that he was a peacemaker. The oil lobby in Washington was as usual opposed to anything that might compromise the interests of the powerful oil companies. Dulles merely recommended an infeasible plan for forming an association of the countries that used the Canal. After several weeks of sterile talking, it became apparent that Nasser's unilateral decision would pay off for him.

However, anti-Israeli demonstrations were taking place in Egypt, Iraq, Syria, and Jordan. Nasser's action had heated popular emotion to the boiling point. The threat of war against Israel grew more serious from one day to the next. The Israeli government, now extremely uneasy, kept London and Paris informed of what was happening. Ben Gurion went secretly to Paris in early October to meet Guy Mollet.

Staff meetings throughout the summer resulted in the Zahal's lightning attack on the Sinai peninsula on October 29. Slow and unco-ordinated though it was, a Franco-British attack on Egypt captured Port Said. Egyptian resistance caved in all along the Canal. On November 6, when the Israeli army had occupied Sharm el Sheikh on the Strait of Tiran and the Gaza Strip, and the road to Cairo was open to the Franco-British expeditionary force, Nasser and his regime were saved by the combined intervention of Marshal Bulganin and President Eisenhower.

Sir Anthony Eden, violently opposed in Parliament and by his own party, threatened with a break in relations by India, and under terrific pressure from Washington, ordered a cease-fire, which obliged the French to stop fighting at a time when certain victory was only one or two days away.

Incredibly, the oil interests, the legalism of John Foster Dulles, and the election worries of Eisenhower coalesced with Soviet expansionism (at this moment the Russian army was drowning the Budapest revolt in blood) to the benefit of Nasser's Egypt and to the detriment of Israel.

Miraculously strengthened, Nasser was acclaimed the leader of the Arab and Moslem world. He could impose his will on the traditional monarchs of Jordan and Saudi Arabia. In North Africa, the rebellion of the Algerians against the French whom he had aided, financed, and armed since 1954, took a new lease on life.

During the lightning campaign that preceded the cease-fire, Israel made important gains against a rapidly crumbling Egyptian army. At the end it held Sharm el Sheikh and Gaza.

In February, 1957, General de Gaulle received Menachem Beigin, the leader of the Herut party, at rue Solférino in Paris. "Above all, don't give up Gaza," cried de Gaulle. He also expressed his regret that the triple offensive of October, 1956, had not been carried to Cairo.[7]

The Ben Gurion government, yielding to pressure from the United Nations, and especially from the United States, finally agreed to evacuate Sinai and Gaza. A cordon of United Nations troops was stationed at the Israeli-Egyptian frontier. Israel was given no real guarantees for the future. The Suez Canal remained closed to its shipping, the Gulf of Aqaba exposed to new aggression.

Ten years later, in May, 1967, Israel calmly celebrated the nineteenth anniversary of its rebirth, though the number of bloody incidents provoked by the terrorists of Ahmed Chukeiri was increasing. A modest military parade, without armored cars or airplanes, in respect for the armistice agreement, took place on May 15, at the university stadium in Jerusalem, in the presence of President Shazar and Prime Minister Levi Eshkol. On the evening of this *Yom Ha'atzmaut* (Independence Day), news agency and radio dispatches suddenly informed the world that Nasser was mobilizing and that a large and heavily equipped army had marched through Cairo, headed for the Sinai frontier.

The Israelis were not expecting any such initiative. In May, 1967, Syria seemed more likely than Egypt to be planning aggression against Israel: the Ba'athist regime, with strong Russian support, might be tempted to resort to an adventure outside its borders to distract attention from its internal troubles. Moreover, it was generally thought in Jerusalem that despite enormous Soviet arms shipments, Egypt would still need a year or two to prepare for war. Possibly Nasser, seeing his prestige brought low by the failure of his expeditionary corps in Yemen and cut to the quick by certain Syrian commentators,[8] believed it imperative to take action in order to consolidate his power.

Or perhaps in his own way Nasser was merely trying a bluff. On May 18 he demanded that the United Nations troops be removed. The next day, without consulting anyone, U Thant agreed to remove the international force that had been established ten years earlier as a sort of compensation to Israel for evacuating Gaza and Sinai.

Possibly Mr. Thant's retreat in the face of unilateral pressure led the Egyptian dictator to believe that he could risk everything without fear of external reaction. As to the Israeli army, he must have underestimated it, at least if he believed his own propaganda. A brochure entitled *The Truth: Comparison of Egypt and Israel*, published by the Egyptian general staff and distributed to the Sinai troops at the start of the war,[9] demonstrated that Egypt was capable of crushing Israel without the slightest delay, because Egypt had a population of 30,000,000 (against Israel's 2,600,000), and because Egypt produced 358,000 tons of steel to Israel's 12,000 and had nine rockets and missiles for every one of Israel's, 6.5 times more heavy artillery, 3.5 times as many tanks, six times as many submarines, and 3.5 times as many fighter planes. The brochure contained illustrations — drawings of pathetic little Jews weeping over toy airplanes, and a pin-up girl in shorts and a brassière who symbolized the feminine army of Israel. "We ourselves do not draft women!" the text proudly proclaimed.

The anti-Jewish frenzy was carried to its height by a propaganda campaign of unprecedented intensity. Cairo and Damascus Radio did not use euphemisms and circumlocutions. "The irrevocable will of the Arab peoples is to wipe Israel off the face of the earth," said Cairo on May 25. "The elimination of Israel is the imperative goal," said Damascus on May 28. Innumerable caricatures and drawings, on posters and in newspapers, obsessively repeated the theme: hooknosed, sickly Jews, trembling with fear, were driven into the sea by magnificent Arab soldiers with bayonets. These Jews, straight out of Streicher's obscene *Der Stürmer* magazine of the Nazi era, were depicted being crushed under a gigantic Arab fist, buried under an avalanche, hanged, guillotined, disemboweled, always sweating with terror — grotesque and harmless with their long beards and black hats.[10] Once again, as in 1947, racist fury gave rise to the illusion that the war would be "brisk and joyous," a military parade that would end in Tel Aviv with extermination, rape, and looting.

On May 22, Nasser, blockaded the Gulf of Aqaba. This, of course, meant war. On May 30, thinking it clever to play the winning card and participate in certain victory, King Hussein of Jordan (who until this time had been virulently denounced in Cairo and Damascus as the accomplice of Zionism) went to Cairo to make his obeisance to Nasser.

As proof of his submission, he left for Amman with Ahmed Chukeiri on board his plane — Chukeiri, who had been trying for so long to depose him.

At Jerusalem and Tel Aviv, however, there was some wavering in political circles. The deep rivalry of David Ben Gurion and Levi Eshkol seemed to place an insurmountable obstacle in the path of an imperative national unity. Menachem Beigin took the initiative by meeting his old adversary and broke the immobility of the government. Ben Gurion at last pulled out and the Herut and the National Religious party formed a cabinet, with General Moshe Dayan as defense minister and Beigin as secretary of state. With the exception of the Communists[11] and Uri Avneri, their one representative in the Knesset, every party, every nuance of Israeli opinion, was represented in the government.

This is not the place to describe in detail the Six-Day War. Between Monday, June 5, and Saturday, June 10, the Israeli defense forces, well organized and commanded, aided by a matchless intelligence service and an intense will to win (it was *Ein B'reira* again — "no other solution"), first demolished the Egyptian air force and then, having won mastery of the skies, drove Nasser's army back to the Suez Canal and the Strait of Tiran. The government at Jerusalem tried repeatedly to persuade King Hussein to take no hostile action. But when the Jordanian artillery at Kalkilya bombarded Tel Aviv, and Jordan-based Iraqi planes attacked Natanya, the Zahal struck toward the east, dislodging the Jordanians from the Old City, and reconquering the "triangle zone," Nablus, and Hebron. Finally, after fierce fighting and heavy losses, the Israelis captured the Syrian fortifications at Golan, which controlled Lake Huleh and the Jordan Valley.[12] And so Jerusalem was at last reunified and the Hebrew state extended its authority over all historic Palestine west of the Jordan.

This victory, brought about by organization, courage, and sacrifice, was joyously acclaimed by the people of all the democratic nations. In France, the president of the republic and his government defied popular opinion by accusing Israel of aggression and imposing an embargo on arms destined for Israel, particularly planes already ordered and two-thirds paid for.

This position was accentuated in November when the president made statements disagreeably anti-Semitic in tone. Later, in February, 1968, at his official government reception, Iraqi president Abdul Rahman Aref, speaking as an official guest of France, made a violently racist speech at the Hotel de Ville in Paris.

In the Jewish communities the world over, an extraordinary sense of solidarity manifested itself in enormous gifts of money and the dispatch of volunteers. In the tradition of the Mahal of 1948, numerous Christian volunteers came to Israel—but the war was over by the time most of them arrived.

The Arab states were stunned by this most unexpected defeat. Nasser pretended to resign and then returned to power. His general staff became the scapegoat. Marshal Amer was said to have "committed suicide" in prison. Ahmed Chukeiri was disowned by the Palestinians and faded from the scene. The few Jews still living in Egypt were arrested, imprisoned, and subjected to brutal and repugnant cruelties.[13] In Algeria, Col. Boumedienne took advantage of the occasion to stir up a violent anti-Jewish propaganda campaign. He and Marshal Aref visited Moscow in the role of spokesmen for the Arab world. Summit conferences and diplomatic meetings took place more and more frequently in Cairo and Khartoum. The war was hotly debated at the United Nations. But even with the support of France, the Soviet-Arab bloc did not win a real decision.

As for the Soviet Union, though undoubtedly disappointed by the defeat of its protégés in Cairo and Damascus, it rapidly began rearming them and replacing the war matériel the Israelis had destroyed or captured. In so doing it attained one of the time-honored objectives of Russian policy—a solid base in the Mediterranean. Its fleet could henceforth use Port Said and, in the western Mediterranean, it could hope to acquire the base at Mers el-Kebir that the French had abandoned.

Their experience in 1956 had taught the Israelis the high price of giving up concrete gains for vague promises. Above all else the Israelis want to negotiate a treaty or series of treaties that will guarantee their country the right to exist. If this is ever to be achieved, Israel's neighbors will obviously have to stop pretending that there is no Hebrew state. On them, and them alone, depends the establishment of a lasting peace founded on recognized boundaries and fruitful economic co-operation. This peace is possible if the statesmen responsible will check religious and racial passions even in the smallest degree. It would be assured if history had not so often proven that the folly of mankind prevails so easily over its wisdom.

The Hebrew state is the incarnation of a civilization of many millennia that for eighteen centuries remained without a territorial base or political machinery. When it consolidated to defend itself against the perils of the Diaspora, this civilization regained its homeland. Now a part of the modern world, animated by a powerful dynamism, and within the framework of a democratic state, this civilization is evolving at a faster pace than ever before, and this evolution will continue. Israel is unique because it is both the national state of the Jewish people gathered within its frontiers and the expression on Palestinian soil of world Judaism. This double vocation—to unite a certain population on a given soil, and to bear witness to a culture that over the course of centuries has bloomed in Alexandria as in Prague, in Granada as in Aix-en-Provence—means that Israel is not after all "a state like other states."

There are those who deplore this fact, in and out of Israel. The Canaanite movement in some Israeli circles would like to see Israel renounce this double vocation and content itself with living in the Middle East as a Levantine state among its neighbors. In the West there are voices exhorting Israel to separate itself from Zionism and settle down in its geographic region. The old yishuvism that has so frequently appealed to the Palestinian community is easily recognizable in all this.

Fifteen or so years from now, as Ben Gurion has pointed out,[14] the majority of Israelis will be of "Eastern" origin. From this arises a problem of primordial importance: how to pass on to the new generation the intellectual heritage of the Jews of Europe who played an essential role in the foundation of Zionism and the rebirth of the state. During the centuries of the Diaspora, Jewish culture in Europe absorbed many typically Western elements and attitudes, such as economic dynamism and democratic structures—whence the "Westernizing" character of Israel, which pan-Arab propaganda denounces as proof of collusion with imperialism, though it is actually a cultural trait, the result of a long historical process.

Without any doubt the Palestinian-born "sabra" is different from his father who came from Vitebsk or Vilno, and he will have sons who are different from him. Neither did the Zionist of 1900 resemble the Sephardim of the time of ibn Gabirol. The evolution of customs and beliefs in a world where communications are uniting all peoples proceeds more rapidly and deeply than it did one or two centuries ago. The Hebrew people of tomorrow will not be a copy of today's people. That is the law of life. But it does not necessarily follow—indeed far from it—that the Jewish state should cut the cords tying it to world Judaism, or that the Jewish people should try to put an end to itself as a recognizable entity.[15] Zionism has always been and still remains the synthesis of these two aspects of one civilization.

The mission of Zionism is not over. Events in 1967 showed to what extent the active solidarity of the Jewish communities of Europe and America were necessary to the young nation. No one can predict where or when political upheavals may endanger Jews in this or that country,[16] forcing them to seek refuge in Palestine. But, above all, in the immediate future and for an indeterminate time to come, Zionism must support the State of Israel from without, intellectually as well as materially. The work of Herzl and his successors has not been ended by its success. Doubtless assuming new forms, Zionism will remain consubstantial with Judaism—a human, cultural, and historic phenomenon whose political and territorial expression is Israel.

After a victorious campaign in Palestine, Pharaoh Merneptah, who ruled from 1225 to 1215 B.C., set down the following inscription: "Israel is devastated. Her seed is no more." More than three thousand years have passed. In spite of invasion, ruin, exile, persecution, massacre, and war, Israel has endured and has taken root in its own soil. Neither historian nor politician can contest this fact without making a serious mistake. Nor can any one refuse to see that the State of Israel, limited to a fraction of its original size, is proof of a transcendent reality and the bearer of a message with universal meaning, as its sages and prophets wished it to be.

The long march of Israel is not finished.

Israel, 1967—Switzerland, 1968

FOOTNOTES FOR CHAPTER 10

1. David Hacohen. Quoted by Claude Renglet. *Israel, an 20,* p. 280.

2. Documents of the United Nations, 1957. A/3686.

3. Report of a U.N. Mission of Economic Inquiry, December, 1949. This report estimated that there were 160,000 "false refugees."

4. The main parties outside the Mapai are the Gahal (coalition of the Herut, which arose out of the Irgun, and the Liberals), with 26 Knesset members; the National Religious party, with 11; the Rafi, 10; and the Mapam, 8.

5. Interview with Colonel Nasser in the neo-Nazi newspaper *Deutsche National und Soldaten Zeitung,* May 1, 1964. Concerning former Nazis in the employ of the Egyptian government, a study by Dr. Leon Boutbein (see *Today in France,* vol. 7, no. 7, New York, September, 1967) sets the number at several hundred. He mentions the following especially: SS Standartenführer Leopold Gleim, alias Lt. Col. Ali Al Nasher (Office of police and concentration camps); SS Obersturmbannführer Bender, alias Col. Ben Salem, Gleim's aide; SS Gruppenführer Heinrich Selliman, alias Col. Hamid Soleiman (police); SS Sturmführer Wilhelm Boeckler, alias Abdel Nah Krim, who was one of those responsible for the massacre of the Warsaw ghetto (anti-Israeli section of the intelligence service); SS Brigadeführer von Dirlewanger ("adviser" to the *fedayeen*); Dr. Willermann, former doctor at Dachau and perpetrator of "experiments" on inmates, is now a doctor at the concentration camp at Samarra; Louis Heiden, Hans Appler, and many more of Goebbels' former functionaries, all in charge of anti-Jewish propaganda; Hans Eisele, former Hauptsturmführer at Buchenwald; et cetera. To this list should be added the German technicians employed by Nasser in the manufacture of rockets and missiles. Cf. S. Landman. *German Scientists in Egypt.* London, Political and Economic Circle, 1964.

6. It might be noted that given the galloping rate of population increase in Egypt, the surplus agricultural production that will be made possible by the Aswan Dam is already insufficient.

7. Related to the author by Menachem Beigin. See also Mr. Beigin's statements in *l'Express,* December 4, 1967.

8. In April, six Syrian MIGs that had tried to fly over Galilee were driven back and shot down by the Mirages of the Sherut Aviri. Damascus reproached Nasser for doing nothing to help Syria. The Egyptian dictator retorted that his fighter planes could not fly to Syria without landing in Jordan, and that King Hussein, "that lackey of imperialism," refused to let Egyptian planes use his airports.

9. Reissued with an English and a French translation by the Information Offices of the Defense Forces of Israel, Tel Aviv, 1967.

10. Collection of caricatures published under the title *Israel Must Be Annihilated.* Tel Aviv, Zahal Information Office, 1967.

11. There are two branches of the Communist party in Israel. The one directed by Dr. Sneh (a convert to Communism in 1945) sided with resistance to aggression. The other, essentially Arab, lay low.

12. For further reading, see the works, listed in the bibliography, by Ben Dan, Ben-Elissar and Z. Schiff, Julien Besançon, Randolph and Winston S. Churchill, Eliahu Levi, Claude Renglet, Samuel Seguev, as well as the collection *Allo, Tel-Aviv? Allo, Le Caire?* and the brochures *Arab War Against Israel, David and Goliath,* and *Israel Must Be Annihilated.*

13. Cf. the report entitled "Les Juifs de Nasser," in *l'Express,* December 25, 1967.

14. David Ben Gurion. "A Nation of Working Intellectuals." *The Jerusalem Post,* September 28, 1962.

15. George Friedman. *Fin du Peuple juif?* Gallimard, 1965.

16. To quote two recent examples: the Jews of the Congo and of Cuba.

GLOSSARY

ALIYAH — Literally, "ascent," "going up." Designates immigration to Palestine. The immigrants are called *olim* (sing. *oleh*), and illegal or clandestine immigrants are *ma'apilim*. *Aliyah Bet* is illegal immigration.

ASHKENAZIM — The Jews of Central and Eastern Europe.

BAR MITZVAH — A Jewish boy attains his religious majority at age thirteen when he becomes a "son of the commandment" — bar mitzvah. This stage of life is marked by a ceremony at which the young man is called on to read publicly from the Torah.

BEITAR — Abbreviation of Brit Yosef Trumpeldor. A youth organization founded by Vladimir Jabotinsky to train future cadres for Revisionist Zionism and the Irgun by giving them an intensive civic and paramilitary education and instilling in them a chivalric ideal compounded of pride and self-denial. Beitar is also the name of one of three fortresses (the others being Yodefet and Massada) that fell to the Romans in the last phase of Jewish resistance. Hence the verses of the *Beitari* song, written in Hebrew by Jabotinsky:

> From the Abyss of Defeat,
> In blood and sweat,
> Our people shall rise again,
> Proud, chivalrous, invincible.
> Beitar that succumbed,
> Like Yodefet and Massada,
> Shall arise in their old nobility.

BILU — From the initials of Beit Ya'akov Lechu Venelcha — "O house of Jacob, come ye, and let us go" (Isaiah II, 5). A youth movement founded in Kharkov in 1882 to colonize Palestine.

BUND — In Yiddish, *Algemeiner Yiddische Arbeterbund in Rusland und Poiln*. Jewish Socialist party, founded in Vilna in 1897. It took part in founding the Russian Social Democratic party at the Congress of Minsk the following year, broke with it in 1903, was readmitted in 1906 as the Social Democratic Jewish organization, and in 1912 won approval for its cultural autonomy plan. Abolished in Russia by the Bolshevik Revolution, the Bund survived in Poland until it was abolished once and for all by the Nazi occupation and Soviet intervention. (See R. R. Abramovitch. *Jewish Socialist Movements in Russia*, Vol. II. Jewish Encyclopaedic Handbooks, New York, 1948.)

DUNAM — Palestinian land measure equal to .247 acres.

ERETZ ISRAEL — "The land of Israel," Palestine.

FONS VITAE — In Hebrew, *Mekor Hayyim*, "The Source or Fountain of Life." A work of neo-Platonic philosophy by Solomon ibn Gabirol, c. A.D. 1021–1158.

GALUT — Dispersion, Diaspora.

GEONIM — (Sing. *gaon*) "Eminences." Title given to the spiritual heads of Babylonian Jewry between the tenth and seventh centuries B.C. and by extension to other masters of religious thought, such as Eliser ben Salomon, who was called the Gaon of Vilna in the eighteenth century.

HAGANAH—"Defense." The armed organization founded in Israel by official Zionist institutions. Its origins go back to the *Ha-Shomer*, or guard of the agricultural colonies and to the Jewish Legion created by Jabotinsky during World War I.

HALUKAH—Pious Jewish communities in Palestine.

HALUTZIM—Agricultural pioneers.

HANUKKAH—Festival commemorating the dedication of the Temple in 164 B.C. after the victory of Judah Maccabee over the forces of Antiochus Epiphanes.

HASIDIM—"Pious men." Usually applied to the most orthodox of all Jews, and especially the followers of Hasidism, which was founded in the Ukraine by Israel ben Eliezer, known as the Besht (1700–60) and Dov Baer (1710–72).

HAVLAGAH—"Self-moderation." The doctrine of the Zionist institutions according to which the Haganah must limit itself to defensive actions against Arab aggression.

HIM—Garrison forces of the Haganah.

HISH—Fighting units of the Haganah.

HISTADRUT—General confederation of Israeli trade unions, closely allied with the workers' party, the Mapai. The Histadrut controls an important part of the nation's economic machinery.

HOK—The Irgun combat force.

HOVEVE ZION—"Lovers of Zion." The members of the first Zionist movement, founded in Warsaw in 1881 by Samuel Mohilever, then organized at Katowice in 1884 under Leon Pinsker.

IRGUN ZVAI LEUMI—"National Military Organization," born from a schism within the Haganah. Commanded by Menachem Beigin from 1943 onward, the Irgun played a key role in achieving Israel's independence.

KEREN HA-YESOD—Foundation created in 1920 to finance colonization and develop lands acquired by the Keren Kayemet.

KEREN KAYEMET LE-ISRAEL—"Perpetual fund for Israel," a national foundation created on Herzl's suggestion by the Fifth Zionist Congress in 1901 to buy land in Palestine that would become the inalienable property of the Jewish people.

KIBBUSH HA-AVODA—"Conquest through Work," the watchword of groups of young pioneers, mostly of Russian origin, who determined to work with their hands on the farms and agricultural colonies of Palestine.

KIBBUTZ—(Pl. *kibbutzim*). Farming village or settlement organized on collectivist lines.

LEHI—*Lohamei Herut Israel*, or "Fighters for Israel's Freedom," usually called the Stern group. A secret armed group created by Abraham Stern ("Yaïr") at the start of World War II and dissolved after Independence.

MAGEN DAVID—The six-pointed star, Israel's emblem.

MAHAL—Corps of foreign volunteers serving in Israel's army during the war for independence.

MASKILIM—Disciples of Moses Mendelssohn (1728–86), who was the leader in Germany of rationalism and the school of Enlightenment philosophy (*haskalah*) as applied to Judaism. From 1784 to 1811 they published a periodical in Hebrew yet at the same time tried to spread modern German-language culture among the Jews of Germany and Austria.

MISHNAH — Teaching of the laws by oral transmission, and systematization of the traditions, in contrast to the *midrash*, or commentary on biblical texts.

MIZRACHI — Religious Zionist party founded in 1901 within the World Zionist Organization. It merged in 1955 with the workers' religious party, *Hapoel Hamizrahi*, to form the National Religious party.

MOSHAV — Farming village of the co-operative type.

PALMACH — Haganah elite units.

PAYETANIM — Palestinian poets who from the seventh century onward specialized in poetry and religious songs to accompany festivals and ceremonies.

PHARISEES — From the second century B.C. on, an essentially religious party that held that the political policies of Israel should be dictated entirely by the Torah. The universalist tendency of the Pharisees contrasted with the nationalism of the Sadducees.

POALEI ZION — "Workers of Zion," the Zionist Socialist party. The first Poalei Zion group was created in New York in 1903. Meetings in Baltimore in 1905 and The Hague in 1907, which were attended by Palestinian delegates, set the party in operation. Subsequent divisions have given rise to four Israeli political parties: the Mapam (left-wing socialist), the Mapai (labor party), the Ahdut Avoda (workers' union), and finally the Rafi, founded in 1965 by Ben Gurion. The latter two fused with the Mapai in 1967.

PURIM — The yearly festival, celebrated on the fourteenth of *Adar* (February or March) to commemorate the day the Jews of Persia escaped, thanks to Esther, from the edict of destruction prepared by Haman, the first minister of Ahasuerus.

REHESH — Secret organization assigned to buy or capture arms for the Haganah.

SADDUCEES — National party of the second and first centuries B.C.

SEDER — Religious service on Passover Eve, conducted in every home by the head of the family to commemorate the deliverance of the Hebrews from Egypt.

SEFER YETZIRAH — "Book of Creation." Mystical work in Hebrew, attributed to Abraham himself, but probably composed in Babylonia in the seventh century B.C. It sets forth a cosmological doctrine based on the "thirty-two pathways of God," which are the twenty-two letters of the Hebrew alphabet and the ten *sefirot*.

SEFIROT — Spiritual entities comparable to Platonic "ideas," and regarded as the principles underlying all created things.

SEPHARDIM — Jews of Spain and the Mediterranean countries.

SHAVUOTH — Feast commemorating the wheat harvest and the gift of the Ten Commandments, celebrated seven weeks after Passover.

SUKKOTH — Feast of the Tabernacles, also called Feast of the Ingathering, celebrated the end of the grape harvest.

TA'AS—Secret organization for the manufacture of arms.

TALMUD—Codification of the Law, which exists in the Jerusalem and the Babylonian versions. The common base for both is the *mishnah*, which was set down in Galilee by the Sanhedrin directed by Judah the Prince (A.D. 125–217) and completed by the *gemara*, meaning the commentaries and additional treatises written in Palestine in the third and fourth centuries and in Babylonia at the beginning of the sixth century.

TENUAT HAMERI—"Resistance movement." The alliance of the three secret armed services: the Haganah, the Irgun, and the Lehi between November, 1945, and August, 1946.

TORAH—The Law, as contained in the Pentateuch, or first five books of the Old Testament.

TSOM—Irgun reserve forces.

VAAD LEUMI—"National Council." The representative and deliberative organ of the Jewish Agency.

YAM—*Yehidot Mahatz*, Irgun shock troops.

YESHIVOT—(Sing. *yeshiva*) Rabbinical schools, of which a large number were founded in the nineteenth century in Central and Eastern Europe, particularly in Lithuania.

YISHUV—The Jewish community of Palestine.

YOM KIPPUR—Day of Atonement, the holiest day of the Jewish year, ten days after the New Year (Rosh Hashanah). It is devoted to fasting and prayer. Each man seeks the forgiveness of God and his fellow man.

ZADDIKIM—"The just ones," mystical leaders of the Hasidic communities. Unlike sages, doctors, and rabbis, the *zaddik* is noted not for his erudition but for his virtue. He was often thought to possess supernatural gifts.

ZAHAL—"Defense Force of Israel," formed on May 28, 1948, by the merger of the Haganah and the Irgun Zvai Leumi.

ZOHAR—"Splendor." The fundamental book of Jewish mysticism, written in Hebrew and Aramaic, attributed to Shimon ben Yochai. (second century A.D.) but actually written by Moses de León in Granada (d. 1305).

BIBLIOGRAPHY

Allô, Tel-Aviv? Allô, Le Caire? Ici Europe n°1. Preface by Jean Gorini. Paris, Robert Laffont, 1967.

Antonius, George. *The Arab Awakening.* London, Hamish Hamilton, 1938.

Arab War Against Israel. (Statements and Documents). Jerusalem, Foreign Affairs Ministry, 1967.

Bar-Zohar, Michel. *Ben Gourion, le prophète armé.* Paris, Fayard, 1967.

Beigin, Menachem. *La révolte d'Israël.* Paris, Plon, 1953.

            La rebelión en Tierra Santa. Buenos Aires, Ed. Santiago Rueda, 1951.

            White Nights. The Story of a Prisoner in Russia. London, Macdonald, 1957.

Ben Dan (Ben Porat and Uri Dan). *Mirages contre MIG.* Paris, Laffont, 1967.

Ben-Elissar, Eliahu, and Zéev Schiff. *La guerre israélo-arabe.* Paris, Julliard, 1967.

Ben Gurion, David. *Regards sur le passé.* Monaco, Editions du Rocher, 1965.

Ben Zvi, Itzhak. *The Exiled and the Redeemed.* Philadelphia, 1957.

Ben Zvi, Rahel Yanait. *Coming Home.* Tel Aviv, Massadah-P.E.C. Press, 1963.

Bernadotte, Count Folke. *To Jerusalem.* London, Hodder and Stoughton, 1951.

Besançon, Julien. *Bazak: la guerre d'Israël.* Paris, Seuil, 1967.

Bracha, Habas. *The Gate Breakers.* New York, Yoseloff, 1963.

Broszat, Martin, Hans Adolf Jacobsen, Herlmut Krausnick, and Hans Bucheim. *Anatomie des SS-Staates.* Friburg-en-Breisgau, Walter Verlags, 1965.

Byrnes, James F. *Speaking Frankly.* New York, 1947.

Chouraqui, André. *Théodor Herzl, inventeur de l'Etat d'Israël.* Paris, Seuil, 1960.

Churchill, Winston S. *The Sinews of Peace.* London, 1948.

Churchill, Randolph S., and Winston Churchill. *The Six-Day War.* London, Heinemann, 1967.

Cohen, Gueoula. *Souvenirs d'une jeune fille violente.* Paris, Gallimard, 1964.

Cohen, Israel. *The Zionist Movement.* London, Muller, 1945.

Crossman, R. H. S. *Palestine Mission.* London, Hamish Hamilton, 1947.

Crum, Bartley C. *Behind the Silken Curtain.* New York, 1947.

David and Goliath, Egyptian Version. Exact reprint of "The Truth: A Comparison between Egypt and Israel," the brochure published by the Egyptian general staff and distributed to troops in the Sinai just before the Six-Day War. Tel Aviv, Zahal Information Offices. 1967.

Delpeyrou, Jacques. "Kurt Gerstein ou l'ambiguïté du bien." *Combat,* Paris, July 17, 1967.

Eddy, William A. *F. D. R. Meets Ibn-Saud.* New York, American Friends of the Middle East, 1954.

Eldad, Dr. Israel. *Israel, The Road of Full Redemption.* New York, Futuro Press, 1961.

Epstein, Isidore. *Le Judaïsme*. Paris, Payot, 1962.

L'Exode des Juifs des Pays arabes. Jerusalem, Foreign Ministry of Israel, 1961.

Extermination and Resistance. Historical records and source material published by Ghetto Fighters' House in memory of Yitzhak Katznelson. Kibbutz Lohamei Haghettaot. Israel, 1958.

Frank, Gerold. *The Deed*. New York, Simon and Schuster, 1963.

Garcia-Granados, José. *The Birth of Israel: The Drama as I Saw It*. New York, 1948.

Gellhorn, Martha. *Les réfugiés arabes de Palestine*. Paris, L'Arche, 1962.

Gitlin, Jan. *The Conquest of Acre Fortress*. Tel Aviv, Hadar Publishing House, 1962.

Gruber, Ruth. *Destination Palestine. The Story of the Haganah Ship "Exodus," 1947*. New York, A. A. Wyn, 1948.

Hecht, Ben. *Perfidy*. New York, J. Messner, 1961.

Herzl, Theodor. *Altneuland*. Haifa, Haifa Publishing Company, 1960.

    Der Judenstaat. Versuch einer modernen Lösung der Judenfrage. Leipzig-Vienna, 1896.

    The Diaries of Theodor Herzl. New York, M. Lowenthal, 1956.

Hochstein, Philip. *The Arab Refugees*. Washington, 1963.

Höhne, Heinz. "Die Geschichte der SS." Articles published in *Der Spiegel* from October 10, 1966, through March 6, 1967.

Horowitz, David. *State in the Making*. New York, Alfred A. Knopf, 1953.

Hull, Cordell. *Memoirs*. New York, 1948.

Hurewitz, J. C. *The Struggle for Palestine*. New York, Norton, 1950.

Ilany, S. *Les problèmes de la paix israélo-arabe*. Paris, Editions A.F.I., 1967.

Israel Must Be Annihilated. A selection of cartoons from the Arab press. Tel Aviv, Defense Ministry, 1967.

Jabotinsky, Vladimir. *Turkey and the War*. London, T. Fisher Unwin, 1917.

    Prelude to Delilah. New York, 1945. (Original in Russian, 1926.)

    The Story of the Jewish Legion, translated by Samuel Katz, with a foreword by Col. John Henry Patterson, D.S.O. New York, Bernard Ackerman, 1945.

    Verso lo Stato. Essays about Zionist politics selected and annotated by Leone Carpi. Florence, 1960.

    The War and the Jew. Philadelphia, 1942.

Kaplan, Chaim A. *Chronique d'une agonie*. Journal of the Warsaw ghetto discovered and edited by Abraham I. Katsh. Paris, Calmann-Lévy, 1966.

Katz, Doris. *The Lady Was a Terrorist*. New York, 1953.

Kimche, Jon and David. *Secret Roads*. London, Secker and Warburg, 1954.

Kirk, George. *Survey of International Affairs: The Middle-East, 1945–50*. Royal Institute of International Affairs, Oxford University Press, 1954.

Knohl, Dov. *Siege in the hills of Hebron. The Battle of the Etzion Bloc*. New York, Yoseloff, 1958.

Koestler, Arthur. *La Tour d'Ezra*. Paris, Livre de Poche, 1965.
         Promise and Fulfillment. Palestine 1917–1949. London, Macmillan, 1949.

Levi, Eliyahu S. *This Was Goliath*. Facts and figures on Arab military strength in the Six-Day War. Tel Aviv, 1967.

Levin, Harry. *Jerusalem Embattled*. London, Gollancz, 1950.

Lie, Trygve. *In the Cause of Peace*. New York, Macmillan, 1954.

Lorch, Netanel. *The Edge of the Sword: Israel's War of Independence*. New York, Putnam, 1961.

Macdonald, James G. *My Mission in Israel*. London, 1951.

Macmillan, Harold. *The Blast of War. 1939–1945*. London, Macmillan, 1967.

Mardor, Munya M. *Strictly Illegal*. Foreword by David Ben Gurion. London, Robert Hale, 1964.

Marlow, John. *Rebellion in Palestine*. London Cressett Press, 1946.

Meridor, Yaakov. *Long Is the Road to Freedom*. Tujunga, California, Barak Publications, 1961.

Monzie, Anatole de. *Destins hors série*. Paris, Editions de France, 1927.

Morton, Geoffrey J. *Just the Job*. London, Hodder and Stoughton, 1957.

Pearlman, Lt. Col. Moshe. *The Army of Israel*. New York, 1950.

Perkins, Frances. *The Roosevelt I Knew*. New York, 1946.

Renglet, Claude. *Israël, an 20*. Verviers, Belgium, Editions Gérard et Cie., collection Marabout-Université, 1967.

Reutt, Georges. *L'Experience sioniste*. Algiers, 1948.

Roosevelt, Elliott. *As He Saw It*. New York, 1945.

Roth, Cecil. *Histoire du peuple juif*. Paris, Editions de la Terre Retrouvée, 1957.

Samuel, Ludwig. *Jewish Agriculture in Palestine*. Jerusalem, 1946.

Schechtman, Joseph B. *The Jabotinsky Story*. Vol. I. *Rebel and Statesman (1880–1923)*. Vol. II. *Fighter and Prophet (1923–1940)*. New York, Yoseloff, 1962.
         The United States and the Jewish State Movement. The Crucial Decade, 1939–1949. New York, Yoseloff, 1966.
         The Jewish Legion. Fiftieth Anniversary of the Jewish Battalions, 1917–1967. Brochure (11 pages), 1967.

Seguev, Samuel. *La Guerre de Six Jours*. Paris, Calmann-Lévy, 1967.

Sidebotham, Herbert. *Great Britain and Palestine*. London, Macmillan, 1937.

Soustelle, Jacques. "Arabes et Juifs en Palestine." *Progrès*, Brussels, no. 12, December 1967, pp. 6–14.

Stein, Leonard. *The Balfour Declaration*. London, Valentine Mitchell, 1961.

Syrkin, Marie. *Golda Meir*. Paris, Gallimard, 1963.

Trevor, Daphne. *Under the White Paper*. Jerusalem, 1948.

Truman, Harry S. *Memoirs*. Garden City, New York, 1955.

Tsur, Jacob. *El Sionismo, movimiento de liberación nacional*. Jerusalem, Israel's Information Center for Latin America, 1965.
         Prière du matin. L'aube de l'Etat d'Israël. Paris, Plon, 1967.

Van Paassen, Pierre. *The Forgotten Ally*. New York, Dial Press, 1943.

Weizmann, Chaim. *Trial and Error*. London, Hamish Hamilton, 1950.

Weizmann, Vera. *The Impossible Takes Longer*. Memoirs by the wife of Israel's first President as told to David Tutaev. London, Hamish Hamilton, 1967.

Wiesenthal, Simon. *Grossmufti, Grossagent der Achse*. Salzburg-Vienna, Ried-Verlag, 1947.

Williams, Frances. *Ernest Bevin, Portrait of a Great Englishman*. London, Hutchinson, 1952.

Zineman, Jakob. *Histoire du Sionisme*. Paris, 1950.